Professional Social Work

Professional
Social Work

EDITED BY JONATHAN PARKER
AND MARK DOEL

Los Angeles | London | New Delhi
Singapore | Washington DC

Learning Matters
An imprint of SAGE Publications Ltd
1 Oliver's Yard
55 City Road
London EC1Y 1SP

SAGE Publications Inc.
2455 Teller Road
Thousand Oaks, California 91320

SAGE Publications India Pvt Ltd
B 1/I 1 Mohan Cooperative Industrial Area
Mathura Road
New Delhi 110 044

SAGE Publications Asia-Pacific Pte Ltd
3 Church Street
#10-04 Samsung Hub
Singapore 049483

Editor: Luke Block
Production controller: Chris Marke
Project management: Deer Park Productions, Tavistock, Devon
Marketing manager: Tamara Navaratnam
Cover design: Wendy Scott
Typeset by: C&M Digitals (P) Ltd, Chennai, India
Printed by Henry Ling Limited at The Dorset Press, Dorchester, DT1 1HD

Library of Congress Control Number: 2013947940

British Library Cataloguing in Publication Data

A catalogue record for this book is available from the British Library

MIX
Paper from responsible sources
FSC™ C013985

ISBN 978-1-4462-6013-5 (pbk)
ISBN 978-1-4462-6012-8

Contents

Acknowledgements

This book could not have been written without the commitment and support of the dedicated authors who have contributed chapters from their own areas of expertise. It has been a privilege for us to work with them. Our grateful thanks are also extended to Helen Fairlie and Luke Block at Sage for their expert help in smoothing the process of bringing this book to fruition. Also, we would like to acknowledge the many students we have taught over the years. It is often said, but nonetheless true, that we learn as much from our students as they do from us; it is a mutual process of exploration and growth. Those people with whom social workers practise also feature highly, having contributed greatly to our understandings of being or becoming a *professional social worker*, the subject of this book. And, last, but not at all least, we must thank our families who have accepted without complaint our constant 'reading of just another chapter', or rushing to the computer to write another paragraph or two before lunch. It is to our respective families that we dedicate this book.

Editors and contributors

Editors

Mark Doel is Professor Emeritus in the Centre for Health and Social Care Research at Sheffield Hallam University, England. He is a registered social worker and was in direct practice for almost 20 years. He continues to lead training workshops for practitioners, largely in the fields of practice education and group work in which he has an international reputation. He has published 17 books, the most recent being *Social Work: The Basics* (Routledge) which gets to the fundamentals of social work. Mark is founding co-editor of the journal, *Social Policy and Social Work in Transition.* He has extensive experience in eastern Europe, in particular helping to develop social work education in Georgia and he is an honorary professor at Tbilisi State University. (**www.shu.ac.uk/research/hsc/about-us/mark-doel**. Contact: doel@waitrose.com)

Jonathan Parker is Professor of Social Work and Social Policy, Deputy Dean for Research and Knowledge Exchange and Director of the Centre for Social Work, Sociology & Social Policy at Bournemouth University. Jonathan has been pivotal in developing the *Transforming Social Work Practice* series of textbooks and is author of the bestselling book, *Social Work Practice*. Jonathan's research interests include gender, conflict and violence, and social work education and methods. He has recently been conducting cross-cultural research on learning and practice with colleagues in Southeast Asia. (**www.bournemouth.ac.uk/csw/index.html**. Contact: parkerj@bournemouth.ac.uk)

Contributors

Marion Bogo is Professor at the Factor-Inwentash Faculty of Social Work, University of Toronto. Her research interests are social work education and supervision for clinical practice. She has published over 100 journal articles and book chapters, including her most recent book, *Achieving Competence in Social Work through Field Education* (2010). In 2013 she was the first Canadian to be awarded the Significant Lifetime Achievement Award by the Council of Social Work Education for these contributions and for innovations in assessing professional competence in students.

Stephen Cowden is currently course director for the MA in Social Work at Coventry University. Originally from Melbourne, Australia, Stephen has spent over half his life living in the United Kingdom. He worked as a social worker in London for over 10 years and while doing this completed his PhD in Australian Literature at the University of Kent. In 2001 he became a Senior Lecturer in Social Work at Coventry University. His teaching and research focus on social theory, critical pedagogy, philosophy and ethics in social work.

Professor Patricia Higham is an independent consultant who undertakes work for the Quality Assurance Agency and the Health and Care Professions Council. She is a graduate of Wellesley College, USA, and completed her postgraduate social work training at the University of Sheffield, and her PhD in Social Policy at the School of Management, Cranfield University. Her professional interests include continuing professional development, quality assurance and the integration of health and social care. Patricia was formerly Head of Department and Associate Dean at Nottingham Trent University, where she is Emeritus Professor of Social Work and Social Care. She is Vice Chair of the Mansfield and Ashfield NHS Clinical Commissioning Group. She is the professional adviser to the Northern Ireland Social Care Council Post Qualifying Committee. She chairs Nottinghamshire Relate, and is a Board member of Family Care (Nottinghamshire), the Child Migrant Trust and Accent Nene Housing Society.

Graham Ixer is Professor of Social Work and Social Policy at the University of Winchester. He has spent a life time in public service, in social work practice, academia and government policy and regulation. The past 15 years have been spent in social work regulation, where latterly he was Head of Social Work Education responsible for approving and inspecting education provision in higher education. He led the team that developed the first ever international standards for regulatory inspection, which other workforce regulators are now considering adopting. His key interest is not about more, less, right or even light-touch regulation, but effective regulation – that which works and achieves its aims. His research interests lie in the area of reflection and reflectivity.

Dr Ray Jones is a registered social worker and Professor of Social Work at Kingston University and St George's, University of London. From 1992 to 2006 he was Director of Social Services in Wiltshire. He is a former chief executive of the Social Care Institute for Excellence (SCIE) and was Deputy Chair and then Chair of the British Association of Social Workers (BASW). He has been the independent Chair of a local safeguarding children board, and of five safeguarding children improvement boards, and is a frequent media commentator and columnist. He has recently completed a book about 'The story of Baby P' and its impact.

Malcolm Payne is Emeritus Professor, Manchester Metropolitan University and holds honorary academic posts at Kingston University, London, Comenius University, Bratislava, Slovakia, and Helsinki University, Finland. He was Director of Psychosocial and Spiritual Care, St Christopher's Hospice, London. Among more than 360 publications, he is author of *Modern Social Work Theory* (4th edn, 2014, Palgrave Macmillan), *What is Professional Social Work?* (2nd edn, 2006, Policy Press), *Humanistic Social Work: Core Principles in Practice* (2011, Lyceum, Chicago, and Palgrave Macmillan), *Citizenship Social Work with Older People* (2012, Lyceum Chicago, and Policy Press), and (with Margaret Reith) *Social Work in End-of-Life and Palliative Care* (Lyceum, Chicago, and Policy Press).

Gillian Ruch is a Senior Lecturer in Social Work at the Tavistock Centre, London, and at the University of Southampton. She teaches and researches in the areas of childcare social work and relationship-based and reflective practice and is committed to enhancing the well-being of children, families and practitioners. In particular she is interested in promoting reflective forums that facilitate relationship-based practice and she has recently co-edited, with colleagues D. Turney and A. Ward, *Relationship-based Social Work: Getting to the Heart of Practice* (2010, London, Jessica Kingsley).

Steven M. Shardlow is Professor of Social Work at Keele University, which he joined in 2013; previously he held academic positions at the Universities of Salford (Professor) and Sheffield. He has held visiting professorial appointments, at Fudan University, Shanghai, the University of Nordland, Norway, and City University and Polytechnic University of Hong Kong – where he is currently Honorary Professor in Social Work. He is Editor-in-Chief of the *Journal of Social Work* (**www.sagepub.co.uk/jsw**). Previously he has been Chair of the Association of Teachers in Social Work Education (ATSWE) and a Member of the Board of the European Association of Schools of Social Work (EASSW). Professor Shardlow is a registered member of The College of Social Work (England) and has practised as a social worker with children and families, older people, mentally ill people and as a social work manager. His research interests include: programme evaluation; the human services workforce; professional ethics; and international and comparative social work. Professor Shardlow has published 16 books and over 70 articles and book chapters. **www.keele. ac.uk/pppp/staff/stevenmshardlow**

Gurnam Singh is a Principal Lecturer in Social Work at Coventry University where he has been since 1993. Prior to this he was involved in political activism and from 1983 worked as a professional social worker with Bradford Social Services. He completed his PhD at the University of Warwick in 2004 on anti-racist social work in the UK. His teaching and research interests centre on critical thinking, critical pedagogy and critical practice, specifically in relation to questions of social justice, human rights and anti-oppression. He has published widely on these and related issues. In 2009, in recognition of his contribution to Higher Education, he was awarded a National Teaching Fellowship from the UK Higher Education Academy.

Roger Smith is Professor of Social Work at Durham University, where he is Programme Director for the Masters in Social Work. As a practitioner and academic, his primary area of interest has been youth justice; he is also interested in the subjects of power and social work, childhood and youth, participatory methods and inter-professional education.

Neil Thompson is an independent writer, educator and adviser and a producer of multimedia learning resources (**www.avenuelearningcentre.co.uk**). His personal website is at: **www.neilthompson.info**.

Sue White is Professor of Social Work (Children and Families) at the University of Birmingham. Her interests include ethnography, interactional sociology, child welfare, systems design and family-minded practice.

Chapter 1

Professional social work and the professional social work identity

Jonathan Parker and Mark Doel

all professions are conspiracies against the laity

(George Bernard Shaw, *The Doctor's Dilemma*, 1906)

Introduction

The title of this book and, indeed, the title of this introductory chapter are not without controversy, as the epigraph at the start of this chapter suggests. The term is contested in multiple ways. *Professional* social work suggests there is such a thing as 'professional' social work, and that it must be distinct from 'unprofessional' social work. In turn, this implies there is a clear and undisputed understanding of what social work itself entails. Even if we restrict ourselves to Western social work or individual countries such as those within the UK, we find fraught and complex definitions, practices and understandings (Horner, 2012). When we add the word 'professional' we extend the complexity and ambiguity of the term, entering the quagmire of sociological argument required to illuminate the concept and its multiple uses.

In this chapter we explore some of the contested meanings and developments in social work and in the understanding of professional practice. We briefly examine some of the history and sociology of professions and professionalism and consider their particular technical uses. We will turn the tables on established meanings.

We have heard much about the closing of ranks within professions to protect their own members, and equally about good, open practice representing 'professional' approaches. For instance, the Francis inquiry (Francis, 2013) into Mid-Staffordshire Hospitals has led to calls for a change in the rules of reporting perceived poor practice (Lamb, 2013). In one of our own careers as a social worker (Parker), there was a situation in which a colleague changed her social work notes to protect herself from blame after a child went missing, and although this was brought to the attention of managers and investigated, it was 'dealt with quietly'. Taking another perspective, we have witnessed the inexorable rise of bureaucracy and managerialism, especially since the 1980s, as a means of both ensuring accountability in practice and controlling those practices, and a concern that this in itself is caus-ing poor outcomes (see Catchpole, 2013). Does this rather unsavoury collec-tion of examples signify what we mean by 'professional' social work? Perhaps it is this common interpretation of professionalism that raises people's suspicions and evokes comments that professionalism tends to exclude the human; that it is more concerned with the completion of impersonal targets and goals than with the creation and maintenance of relationships in difficult circumstances. However, it can be argued that such an interpretation reflects a confusion between manage-rialist and professional practices, when the former concerns impersonalised stand-ards and targets, while the latter focuses on best practice and outcomes for those to whom social workers are accountable and offer services.

What is social work?

When we pose the question 'What is social work?' we expose ourselves to mul-tiple interpretations and associated queries. Does the question imply that there is a single, particular entity, job or profession that we call by the name of social work? And, if so, is social work a global phenomenon or does it relate solely to particular nations at specific periods in their development?

When we come to analyse the questions of definition still further we see that the practices of social work vary, not only across the countries of the world – something that may well be expected given the local circumstances in which social work-ers operate – but also within the UK itself. Within the four administrations in the UK (England, Northern Ireland, Scotland and Wales), the regulation of social work by professional bodies differs, and legislation underpinning social work practice varies especially between England and Wales, and Scotland. If what we do as social workers portrays what we are in the eyes of the public, and if what we do is shaped by legisla-tion that is singular to a country or region, then we have a range of social work types.

It is a fact that social work is not an homogenous entity. The complexities of social work practice and the diverse meanings associated with it across the world, and even within individual nations, are acknowledged in the literature (Hutchings and Taylor, 2007). The acceptance of the broad, and somewhat problematic, IFSW definition of social work (2000) is, however, indicative of similarities and standards in social work globally. Further commonalities are seen within shared approaches to aspects of social work curricula, methods, practices and legislation and administration (see Parker et al., 2012):

> *The social work profession facilitates social change and development, social cohesion, and the empowerment and liberation of people. Principles of social justice, human rights, collective responsibility and respect for diversities are central to social work. Underpinned by theories of social work, social sciences, humanities and indigenous knowledges, social work engages people and structures to address life challenges and enhance wellbeing.*

> (IFSW, 2000)

However, despite broad, if somewhat reluctant, acceptance, even this definition is challenged and, necessarily, under review (Agten, 2012); indeed, it can be argued that shared approaches to the design and delivery of social work stem from colonial histories and now represent neo-colonial actions enacted in indigenous terms (Parker, 2013). It may also be conjectured that social work cannot be reduced globally to a set of anything other than very broad defining characteristics – rather useless when it comes to knowing what action to take, but perhaps this is all the IFSW definition can achieve. So, our focus in this text is to locate social work in the UK, recognising organisational and political alignment with social work structures in the West, and offering, not imposing or assuming, perspectives that may be useful where systems are developing in different ways.

Profession and professionalism in social work: a contested terrain?

Professionalism's unspoken meanings

Contemporary social workers practise in a fraught context, balancing increased disadvantage and marginalisation for some and the needs of society to function constructively. Social workers in the UK apply balm to social and individual troubles, challenge disadvantageous social structures and practices, while, somewhat paradoxically, also being an integral part of those social structures by virtue of being (predominantly) employed by local government.

When we think of a professional, however, we may consider the example of footballers (see Payne, Chapter 2 in this volume), who are 'professional' because they (usually a man) play football as a paid job. The same footballers also may be said to be acting 'unprofessionally' if they swear at the referee over a decision he has made. This suggests that a professional is someone who is *paid* for doing what they do, and who has *certain rules of engagement/practice* to follow. However, it is more complex when one starts to consider such things as the 'professional foul', where it is counted as part of the game to commit an offence, to break the rules, on behalf of the desired outcome – something that reflects, perhaps, current contention over corruption in public life (Brown, 2013), and something we would certainly not countenance in social work.

There are also those instances when social workers are said to have performed a 'good job', meaning perhaps that they have managed their emotions in a highly charged situation, advocated strongly for a service user, and negotiated complex human situations. This might also extend to the service user who states of the social worker, 'she was always very *professional*, you know, she always did what she said, always came on time and kept me informed as things moved along'.

These 'popular' constructions of what it might mean to be a professional social worker are often contested. For instance, the social worker who maintains a 'professional distance', not letting her emotions cloud her judgement and action may not always be acting empathetically with her service users or clients. These definitions raise more questions about the meaning of being or becoming a professional social worker.

Professionalism and power

The history of professionalism and the concept of a 'profession' paint an especially convoluted picture for social work. There has been a drive towards acceptance of social work as a profession sitting equally alongside those from which the term gained sociological meaning; for example, medicine and law. However, social work does not always conform to earlier identified functionalist and trait-based characteristics of a profession. We may ask why would we want our distinct role as social workers to conform to an abstract model? The answer lies partly in power relations, and a wish for social work to have its 'seat at the table' in terms of status.

Professions represent an institutionalised means of controlling an occupation (Johnson, 1972). Functionalist understandings of professions have emphasised the distinctiveness that professions claimed, locating them as a means of maintaining social order through professional ethics and distinctive knowledge or practices.

Witz (1992), a neo-Weberian sociologist, recognised that the strategies employed by professions to retain power in society represented strategies to promote professional elitism and the propensity to close ranks and protect themselves, as well as displaying 'occupational imperialism' (Larkin, 1983), that is, the desire of one profession to occupy the territory and position of others. What she added to the debate, however, is particularly pertinent to our current consideration of social work and professionalism. She highlighted the relationship between gender, power and the professions, locating the 'professional project' – its becoming and its maintenance – within the patriarchal structure of society. This, in itself, necessitates a critique of professional elitism and self-regulation, which would privilege males in a profession in which the majority of practitioners are women, although this critique itself requires caution (Parker and Ashencaen Crabtree, 2012). Social work is also, perhaps, a profession that could be understood as controlling the lives and social position of women, especially evident, for instance, in the child protection and safeguarding practices of social workers (Scourfield and Coffey, 2002).

Interactionist action-focused models differ from functionalist ones. They do not ask what a profession is, but how it operates (the processes) and what the profession did to get here, to assume and preserve its privilege, recognising too that the actions of a profession constructs the social reality in which it operates (Macdonald, 1995). The interactionist approach is pertinent to social work today. *Professional power* is central to understanding the ways in which any profession can control and regulate its own work and gain dominance over others. In contemporary social work this is partly reflected in the struggles for professional body recognition seen in the four UK countries in 2002, following which English social work suffered a blow in 2012 with a move to a more generic and health-based regulatory body (the Health Care Professions Council, HCPC) (Ixer, Chapter 12). Alongside this, a number of reforms of social work stemming from changing social needs (Scottish Executive, 2006) and politically-driven campaigns following well-publicised tragedies have questioned, challenged and curtailed social work-ers' powers to determine their work (Social Work Reform Board, 2012) and to make 'professional' judgements, while others have reasserted the need for such an approach (Munro, 2011). In the UK there is a tension between social work and its dominance over social care, although this itself is further challenged by the increased dominance of health professions over social care work, diminish-ing the stature, perhaps, of social work still further. These examples demonstrate the contested, fluid and mutable understandings of professional work, but show, also, that the actions of organisations are important in defining the position of professions within the broader society. Social work has struggled as a 'poor rela-tion' in contrast to traditional professions such as medicine or law, and those newer 'professions' such as teaching, police and nursing who perhaps enjoy greater public support (Jones, Chapter 11).

The actions of social work to gain acceptance as a profession have suffered somewhat because it is useful in a hierarchical organisational world to have a practice or discipline that is easy to blame for the ills it is, in part, created to address. However, social work does its cause little good when membership organisations set up to champion social work fight amongst themselves for power, influence and control, as has happened recently. The British Association of Social Workers (BASW) claims to act on behalf of social workers covering all four countries in the UK and offers advice, support, insurance and trade-union-type advantages to its members. The BASW operates in a way that protects itself and its members, and its approach appears to mirror more traditional approaches to professional enclosure. The College of Social Work (TCSW), on the other hand, has the backing of recent reforms, claims to be the 'voice' of social work, but covers only England in its brief. The battle for territory between the two organi-sations has given an impression of fragmentation and uncertainty or lack of con-fidence in what social work is about.

Is social work a profession, a semi-profession or para-profession?

We have already hinted that social work's journey towards professionalisation and professionalism has been and remains fraught. Social work, in its twentieth-century development, was conceptualised as a semi-profession, 'almost but not quite' having the status of other professions (Payne, Chapter 2; Thompson, Chapter 5).

Illich (1972/2011) launched a scathing attack on what he considered 'disabling professions' in which professional experts define and legitimate the 'problems' they work with, and he called for a more sceptical approach to the 'diagnose and prescribe' power base of traditional professions. In this more traditional approach to the professions, the social worker controls, identifies and legitimates certain psycho-social needs, and necessarily excludes others by default. This may lead social workers to set an agenda which meets their needs and those of their agencies, such as the completion of assessment tasks according to the set timescales, increasing the number of children adopted or reducing the number of care orders applied for, rather than working at the pace that is required for best practice and outcome in the particular case. Using such an analysis, we may question why social work would want to aspire to a 'professional' status of this nature. Illich's analysis allows us, however, to question what we mean and to consider how we move from the notion of a 'profession' to the idea of the 'professionalism' of the individual social worker.

Social work has striven towards certain traditional brands of 'professionalism', gaining mandatory registration for social workers in 2005 following significant work by the former professional body, the General Social Care Council (GSCC). It requires formal undergraduate qualifications as a minimum (from 2003) and there is an increasingly prescribed curriculum, all of which suggests that social work has been moving rapidly towards a traditional professional status. The degree, however, continued to draw on wide knowledge bases from different disciplines, for instance sociology, law, economics, psychology, anthropology and others, with perhaps the nearest traditional discipline associated with social work being 'applied' social policy. So, it may be questioned whether there is an exclusive knowledge base for social work, which in traditional definitions of the professions remains important; some suggest this exclusiveness may lie in social work's values or in its approach to working alongside those people who use its services. However, all professions have a value base that drives their work (some more explicit and central than others), so this is neither exclusive nor does it necessarily constitute a knowledge base.

The trajectory towards professional status has not been universally endorsed by everyone. Indeed, whether there is anything unique at all about social work has been questioned by one of its own former members, Virginia Bottomley (a former UK government minister), who implied that 'streetwise grannies', those members of the public with common-sense attitudes to caring, could undertake the role (Brindle, 2002). This could perhaps also be said about other professions when people state they can make their communities safe, or police the actions of others, or nurse the sick in informal, everyday ways. Of course this challenges the notion of exclusivity in professions and it is likely that we may wish, as social workers, to reject closed systems which exclude others. However, does this mean prescribed professional qualifications do not form an essential component of a profession?

There is a large voluntary and volunteer workforce that cares for people and people who act as advocates in communities to promote change. Perhaps these complexities mean there is an ambivalence towards professionalism within social work.

Social work's ambivalence towards professionalism

Government at state and local levels increasingly determines who social workers work with and delineates the means by which services are to be delivered. This is happening despite the increased emphasis on the people who use the services being involved in the planning and delivery of their services; perhaps because any expectations of services become jointly constructed by the actions of social workers (what they themselves do) and the subsequent interpretations of those people who receive the services (how the actions are understood). So, social work may not always meet the assessed needs of individuals. Indeed, the delivery of predetermined services according to set eligibility criteria may be understood as defining social work practice today, rather than the building of relationships (Ruch, Chapter 4). The bureaucratic environment in which social work is practised, need not, of course, disrupt social workers' own commitment to professional practice, but it does demand a revision as to what that might mean.

Hugman (1998) critiques the more traditional definitions of profession based on closely guarded, and often self-defined, 'expertise' and the concepts of 'best interests', which may serve to exclude those who use services. He recognises that this is, therefore, challenged by the service user and consumerist focus of recent years:

> *The very existence of occupations which make claims to expertise in areas of health and welfare may be said to have been founded on the exclusion of users from the definition of need or appropriate responses to its remedy.*

> (Hugman, 1998: 137)

Karban and Smith (2010) expand this argument, describing health and social care professions as being in a state of change, or even crisis, as public confidence has been shaken by public challenges, technological and role change, and politically-motivated policy and organisational changes. They also recognise that professional working in health and social care continues to be driven by the need for 'joined-up working' across different disciplines. However, this often blurs 'professional' distinctions and the development of an identity which begins in initial education and training. As such, social work still requires a robust research base to demonstrate its empirical rather than ideological validity. Indeed, the promotion of 'joined-up' approaches or working together across 'professional' groups may represent an evolutionary adaptation of traditional professionalism in which inter- and multidisciplinary approaches are accepted as good, without clear research to back this up.

These changes in our understanding of the professions challenge the utility and moral character of the term 'profession' as applied to social work, and necessitate asking a different question: not 'Is social work a profession?', nor 'How did it get there?', but 'What might professional social work look like?' In this vein, Thompson (2009) charts the journey from a traditional approach to social work as a profession, through the challenges of anti-professionalism and radical perspectives, finally arriving at an empowering 'new professionalism'; something he relates and expands upon in this volume (Thompson, Chapter 5; Doel and Parker, Chapter 13).

Professional identity

Social work education provides and constructs the cultural templates and narratives for becoming a professional; socialising students into the wider culture, tradition and practices of social work. This occurs through class-based and field education (practice placements) in social work agencies. However, this is a complex and, sometimes, tense state of affairs, understandably so given the changes, demands and exigencies of contemporary practice. Claims of alleged inadequacies of preparation for practice through the education system (Brindle, 2013) lead to role conflicts for social workers between the instrumental completion of tasks and the meeting of targets, and the *cri de coeur* for professional autonomy that relies on judgement, criticality and compassion. Munro's (2011) report identifies the titanic rise of managerialism, a stultifying bureaucracy that suffocates human-to-human practices. However, from Baby Peter onwards, through the Social Work Task Force (2009) and the subsequent Social Work Reform Board (2010, 2012), social work has rather meekly accepted criticism that something was wrong with the education of social workers at qualifying levels and onwards. To an extent, it may also be argued that subsequent reforms have inadvertently and paradoxically reinforced the instrumental, technical aspects of learning that have been increasingly required in practice to avert possible blame when tragedies occur; a case, perhaps, of *plus ça change, plus c'est la même chose*. Alongside all these reforms it is still questionable how much other 'professions' accord social work a similar status. Within this context of continuous reform, the chapters of this volume examine what being a professional social worker in today's UK may mean in a variety of situations.

The challenge of specialisms

There are concerns that social work is breaking up into many different sub-professions (childcare workers; mental health workers) in which social work does not even appear in the job title. Historically, was social work more of a profession when it was a unitary occupation with its own large social work departments and budgets?

Reviews and reforms in social work education in the early 1990s, certainly after the Diploma in Social Work was introduced, have seen a frequent call to separate social work into specialisms: for example, child and family work, and social work with adults, with others located in health settings, such as mental health. A recent conversation with a director of adult and children and family social services indicated a concern that social work, as we know it, would disappear if separate education and training routes for adult and children and family workers were brought in. Her concerns seemed to suggest that social work was more of a profession when integrated within local government social services departments.

Social workers often now apply for and work in roles in which the term 'social worker' may not be used, but the roles and tasks undertaken remain broadly familiar. While many would argue they are not 'precious' with respect to the name social worker, there is a tension between having a protected title, requiring registration, and removing that title from people's roles. Of course, political expediency may be responsible for some of these changes in which the removal of a title allows a lower pay scale to be used. However, it brings into question whether social work is, in the UK and England especially, a 'profession' in many of the senses we have used so far. This does not mean, of course, that social workers cannot be 'professional'.

The challenge of managerialism

Given that autonomy is one of the hallmarks of professionalism, how can a profession that is increasingly not in control of its own diary, not in control of how it allocates its time, who it chooses to work with, and in what ways, be seen as a profession?

Lipsky's (1980) classic text comes some way to explaining this contested journey. He describes the ways in which 'street level bureaucrats' or those workers dealing with people on a day-to-day basis are charged with implementing often ambiguous public policies and tasked to do so with inadequate resources. These workers may compromise their original ideals to negotiate this path and develop individualised procedures to do so (Pithouse, 1987). It may be argued, also, that managerialism in social work has demolished any earlier pretensions social work had to being a profession according to the traditional sociological definitions. The culture of managerialism has increased the surveillance, control and 'de-professionalisation' of practitioners and service organisations by demanding compliance and rule-bound behaviours (Singh and Cowden, Chapter 6). For example, as a consequence of system changes made to protect children after the inquiry into the death of Victoria Climbié (see Laming, 2003), social workers face increased recording requirements so that they spend less time with people engaged in undertaking work towards changes in parenting and promoting safe behaviours (Munro, 2011).

There are, then, two competing ideas of work organisation within the sociology of the professions: professionalism and managerialism. The distinction between these sometimes mistakenly conflated concepts is important. Allen's (2001) study of nursing understands professionalism to be organised around moral obligations to care as autonomous and trained experts, whilst managerialism focuses on the nurse as employee within a bureaucratic organisation. This echoes the changes that have already occurred and now permeate social work and underpin the drive towards professionalism within practice. Social workers in the UK are employed, predominantly, within large public bureaucracies and a culture of managerialism pervades; however, the moral obligations of social workers are to work as effectively and ethically as possible, on behalf of people who use their services, aligned with the ethical standards and values of social work practice and updating their skills and knowledge throughout their careers (Higham, Chapter 9).

Social workers have never had the autonomy to define 'private and public ills' in the same way as the medical profession has defined 'diseases' (Foucault, 1973;

Pearson, 1973). Rather, four forms of 'social gaze' have developed: through local governmental power; through media power that 'defines' (or more usually castigates) social workers; through those who use social work services; and through social workers themselves. Thus there is a looser approach to professionalism in social work which steers it away from an exclusive, elitist and self-creating profession to one which focuses on core values and working together with those who use its services.

It is within this environment that any discussion of professional social work is sited: its practice challenging traditional professional and managerial approaches and offering alternative perspectives to follow concerning how social work may best be performed.

The decline of social work methods

While we have seen that the lack of a distinctive knowledge base has been used to question whether social work is a profession, or a semi- or quasi-profession, it is the application of methods that, to an extent, defined what a social worker is – what is it that they do that is somewhat distinct from other professions. Over recent years social work methods have gradually become diluted, even disappeared altogether. Social work specialisms used to be defined as casework, family work, group work and community work. A social worker could explain (to another professional or to the lay public) the method they would use (e.g. group work) and this helped to define their area of expertise as significant to the contribution they could make – but, as noted, methods have experienced a catastrophic decline. Most social workers would describe themselves as 'doing assessments', which can hardly be described as a professional method.

Another disquieting change has been the seeming transfer of areas of 'expertise' to other 'professions' such as therapeutic work with people with mental health problems undertaken by Community Psychiatric Nurses (CPNs), and the removal of probation from social work training in the late 1990s, which led to a decline in group work, intensive treatment, outward bounds and community activities. This also occurred in community and youth work, which, although not social work in the UK, used similar approaches and was often aligned in its role and purposes. From the introduction of the NHS and Community Care Act 1990, and following the specialist assessment role of Approved Social Workers (the former Approved Mental Health Professional AMHP) under the Mental Health Act 1983, the emphasis on the centrality of assessment as a core social work task displaced the application of social work methods. Prescribed assessment tasks are, of course, easier to monitor, audit and regulate, and, therefore, by these means it is easier to control the social work role and diminish its professional status.

The skills and knowledge to use social work methods are still taught on most courses, though with much less emphasis, and it is possible to view this as a counter to some aspects of the profession's contemporary crisis.

Overview of the book and its structure

The title of this book reflects the aspirations of the social work profession in the UK during a time of tumultuous structural and cultural change both globally and locally, and during a continued economic recession and a time of assault on welfare via austerity. The term profession, as we have seen, is used in many different and contested senses and this reflects its problematic nature. However, *best practices*, those that promote social justice, individual, family and community development and a 'new professionalism' (Thompson, 2009) are the focus of this book. Account is taken of the shifts occurring in England as a result of the work of the Social Work Reform Board, the College of Social Work's Professional Capability Framework (PCF) and the Munro Review of children and families social work. However, the discussions in this book transcend local and current changes. Each chapter stands on its own and each author offers their own perspectives on professional social work at this time.

The book argues that good professional practice is built on critical engagement, reflexivity and analysis. It challenges the dominance of rational technocratic approaches, favoured by target setting, while acknowledging that there must be some limits to professional autonomy, as long as these limits are open to question.

The book's chapters cover various aspects of modern, professional social work practice, from concepts and ideas through to the practical realities of everyday social work.[1] The major theme running through all the chapters is professionalism in social work, and this inevitably leads the reader into questions about the role of social work. What are the tensions present in the role of the social worker as functionary of the state and client advocate? This debate draws upon the fundamental importance and centrality of the social work value base to the profession.

Organisation and appeal of the book

The book will appeal to students who are studying on initial qualifying courses and also those studying at Masters level. The book includes frequent references to practice throughout as well as clear links to relevant standards. We hope it will be stimulating to those students engaged in social work courses in all countries of the UK and around the world. We hope, too, that the emphasis on criticality, analysis and engagement with the conceptual and definitional aspects of professional social work will help the book to remain a useful reference into the future.

---

[1] The term 'frontline' is often used to describe everyday practice realities with people who use social work services. In the main, it is avoided in this text because of its erroneous, in this context, associations with military action and its (mis)appropriation by a quasi-governmental body to 'train' social workers almost entirely in the practice setting.

Chapter overview

In Chapter 2, Malcolm Payne argues that understanding the contested definitions of 'profession' offers social workers insights into what it means to be a good 'professional'. He acknowledges the distance created by the mystique of professionalisation, the processes that polarise professionals and service users while constructing expertise that is more concerned with the self-preservation of status than helping, and looks at of some of the mistaken associations with managerialism and overly-bureaucratic practice. Payne counters these concerns by examining 'de-professionalisation', which divides up the roles and functions of social workers and dismantles the generic system we retain in social work practice (something that at the time of writing the Government are again proposing for social work education, see **www.gov.uk/government/news/review-announced-on-social-work-education**), and prevents social workers from genuinely working alongside people to meet their needs in the ways they want. Payne's chapter sets the scene for the sociological debates about professions and professionalisation, contextualising it within the UK regulatory requirements and social work's professional groups.

In Chapter 3, Sue White illustrates the multiple complexities of contemporary social work practice using an account of a social worker's experience of dealing with what appears to be a routine referral from the police domestic violence unit. In this chapter, she promotes the centrality of research for practice and highlights the processes of reflection and reflexivity, as means to explore presumptions and to question 'common-sense' and stereotypical thinking which may lead to poor practices.

Chapter 4 focuses on the primacy of interpersonal relationships for developing constructive and ethical social work with vulnerable people. Gillian Ruch sets out the complexities and problems inherent in practice, recognising it is frequently informed by firmly held and often unquestioned assumptions, with the messier aspects of life 'swept under the carpet'. Her chapter seeks to disturb some of these entrenched assumptions about what social work is and how it is practised, arguing that *effective social work requires approaches that prioritise practitioners developing realistic and holistic relationships with the individuals and families they encounter in everyday practice*. She deals with some of the less palatable realities of social work in dealing with and confronting behaviours and practices that we find abhorrent in others while recognising our own potential complicity and the impacts this has on what we do. This chapter theorises relationship-based approaches, drawing on Hollis' earlier psycho-social approach and informing this with a social, political and cultural perspective that recognises the interaction of environment with the personal. The chapter provides a brief historical overview of social work, explaining the importance of recovering relationships in the professional context. The chapter concludes with recommendations to assist practitioners in making the turn to relationship-based thinking and practice, and the importance of an organisational context which encourages this.

Neil Thompson focuses on emotional resilience in Chapter 5 and notions of practitioner competence. Social workers immerse themselves in the worlds of people made vulnerable and distressed by the contemporary social world. They work with people who have been abused or otherwise traumatised, people who have experienced significant loss, suffering or pain, and those marginalised within or alienated from society as a result of social inequalities and wrongful discrimination. Thompson's exposition of the emotional component of practice allows him to reflect upon the earlier critique of professionalism bound with self-preservation and *occupational closure* and to promote a 'new professionalism' which recognises the emotions and reaffirms good humane practice. Social workers need, in Thompson's view, resourcefulness, robustness and resilience to remain emotionally competent to work within the challenging world of contemporary social work.

Radical social work has excited students and practitioners and also evoked fury and equivocal responses. What is clear, however, and increasingly so as austerity has an impact on welfare and the social world, is that social work operates in a political context, and that this must be acknowledged. In Chapter 6, Gurnam Singh and Stephen Cowden ask whether radical action in professional social work is still meaningful in an age of global neo-liberalism supported by austerity. They also enquire into changes that have occurred in the post-war consensus of the welfare state, which for them heralded contemporary social work in the UK, discussing what it means for social workers to practise as 'radical' practitioners and the need to update the ideas of radical social work. Singh and Cowden chart the toll of neo-liberalism on social work in curtailing autonomy and leading to de-professionalisation and the rise of instrumentalist, controlled practice that has frustrated and demoralised workers. This change is critiqued within an understanding of professional social work and professionalism. Singh and Cowden lay claim to social work ethics as a means of restoring professionalism, autonomy and radical practice in the face of these attacks, and champion a progressive and radical approach to the challenges that social workers face if they are to work effectively and ethically within the contemporary social world.

In Chapter 7, Steven Shardlow identifies two perennial ethical questions about social work; the first asking who should or should not receive social work services and engendering complex political, moral and economic issues that are often influenced by the social climate of the day. The second question relates to the real and gritty everyday ethical challenges that social workers face, and suggests the diversity of these questions can be reduced to a single question, 'How should a social worker behave, if they are to behave as a moral professional?'

In Chapter 8, Roger Smith introduces social work as an applied form of enquiry, focusing on the world of practice. He argues that the application of skilled enquiry depends on actively engaging with research knowledge. However, despite the importance of research knowledge for supporting professional practice, too often repeated as a mantra of 'evidence-based practice', he identifies that research is often ignored or marginalised within the daily practices of social work practitioners. Asking why this might be, he identifies the often problematic and tense relationship between research and practice in UK social work, in which practitioners are not provided with the skills to read, judge, synthesise and apply research evidence. This factor, alongside organisational pressures, time factors and accessibility in research militates to constrain the impact that research has on practice. However, Smith argues cogently that practitioners and social work organisations should strive to change this state of affairs, demonstrating that 'social work is not just applied common sense'. His chapter, therefore, seeks to explore ways in which social workers can be encouraged and enabled to engage with research in a constructive manner that will enhance practice and practice outcomes, while avoiding the pitfalls of a partisan-like approach that may privilege one form of research over another on the basis of ideology rather than whether it can be applied well and appropriately; in other words he argues for the fostering of research-mindedness. The chapter continues with a consideration of core skills in research, and in reading, interpreting and applying research to practice settings. Smith advocates for the importance of practitioner research, especially where this is focused around and inclusive of service users. In arguing for practitioner involvement, he also addresses the importance of that research being undertaken in a 'professional' manner, by which he means in an ethical, beneficent way on behalf of others, pursuing better practice outcomes and aligned with social work standards that promote social justice and emancipation.

Professionalism, being a professional, has traditionally involved pursuing the knowledge of that profession and ensuring currency. This has been a constant theme within social work, especially since the introduction of the DipSW (the UK qualification before social work became a graduate profession) in 1989. While social work emulates other professions here, it perhaps also does so in the difficult relationship practice has had with the need to undertake continuing professional development (CPD). In Chapter 9, Pat Higham provides an historical sweep of the former Post Qualifying Social Work Education and Training requirements and considers changes wrought by the introduction of the Reform Board recommendations, examining how these may have an impact on the professionalism of contemporary social workers. She lauds the development of the Professional Capabilities Framework (PCF) as a means of professionalising English social work in a global context, recognising the demands it lays upon social workers for continuing to develop their knowledge for practice throughout their career. She considers further that this more fully emphasises 'professionalism'. However, the uneasy terrain created by removing the mandate for a university-housed post-qualifying system and promotion of CPD activities creates an uncertain future.

In Chapter 10, Marion Bogo explores how supervision for staff can assist in maintaining and enhancing the professionalism of their work. She reflects on the substantial body of work that has developed on professional development through supervision, drawing on some of that work at a pre-qualifying level but recognising that, while supervision has its advocates, there is a dearth of empirical studies supporting its application. In her chapter, Bogo identifies the concepts and principles for staff supervision and professional development, illuminating the central features that may be employed to develop an integrated approach to staff supervision that can be used in contemporary social work environments.

Ray Jones reflects, in Chapter 11, on the ways in which the media has related to social work, and the portraits it paints of practice and practitioners. He recognises that the media, whether print, radio or television, have often portrayed social work and social workers in a less than salubrious light, focusing on selling copy, engaging with public and political concerns and verging on the sensational. However, Jones argues convincingly for the importance of engaging with the media, especially given the influence the media have on public opinion. He bases much of the chapter on his own substantial experiences of working with the media, building on the positive and proactive aspects of this relationship while guarding against the negative. Jones sees working with the media as central to informing public attitudes and putting right those who dismiss social workers and seek to use them as a soft target to blame for contemporary society's many ills. Like Singh and Cowden earlier, Jones sees the potential of the press as a means of challenging austerity-driven welfare reform and contributing to political argument from an informed stance on behalf of those with whom social workers practise.

In Chapter 12, Graham Ixer reflects on the development and use of regulation in the context of social work, drawing on his unique insight into the history of regulation and the initial registration of social workers within the former professional body, the General Social Care Council (GSCC). Ixer examines the archives of the Central Council for Education and Training in Social Work and the General Social Care Council, finding limited evidence that regulation achieved its objectives of promoting and delivering quality social work education or meeting the public protection agenda. Regulation has been plagued by political interference and conflict as it sought to steer a path between professional, political and public expectations. Ixer is stark in his conclusions, that despite being subject to political whim, without regulation the neo-liberal agenda of market forces risks the gains the profession of social work has so far achieved.

In the final chapter, we bring together some central themes emerging from this book, recognising that there is no single approach to the notion of professional social work. Looking back 30 years and forward 30 years, we consider a possible future for the profession of social work, and suggest a possible and preferred future.

Conclusion

As reform of social work education and practice is set in train in England, following the recommendations of the Social Work Reform Board (2012), 'professionalism' as a social worker is written into the expectations laid upon practitioners, at all stages of their careers. The Professional Capabilities Framework's first capability is *1. Professionalism: Identify and behave as a professional social worker, committed to professional development*, suggesting that professionalism is central to both identity and behaviour (**www.tcsw. org.uk/pcf.aspx**). This capability has links to traditional approaches to the sociology of professions in terms of immersion and socialisation into something almost equivalent to 'closure' in which only the appropriately qualified, registered and fully socialised can be considered as professionals. However, it also focuses on the moral dimensions encompassed by 'behaviour', which not only indicate specific practices undertaken by social workers but also the underlying values from which their practice derives. The ninth capability extends the focus on professionalism and engages with the contemporary discourse of leadership: *9. Professional Leadership: Take responsibility for the professional learning and development of others through supervision, mentoring, assessing, research, teaching, leadership and management*. Again, this capability shares features with more traditional notions of professionalism such as the intrinsic development and transmission of adept knowledge and skills within the select grouping, as well as a concern for promoting practices and behaviours that represent 'good' social work. It is possible to consider these reforms in two ways, either as a cynical manifestation of contemporary discourses in which power is brokered by groups occupying different positions, or as a genuine attempt to ensure the best possible practice of social work alongside those who experience it. It is this tension that runs through discussions of professionalism within social work, and permeates discussion within the chapters in this volume. Our hope is that the reforms will turn on the second possibility, a genuine reflection on practice and the improvement of social work, and that this book will aid that process.

REFERENCES

Agten, J (2012) Personal communication.

Allen, D (2001) *The Changing Shape of Nursing Practice.* London: Routledge.

Brindle, D (2002) Job Centred: Practical Focus for Social Work Degree. *The Guardian*, 29 May, **www.theguardian.com/society/2002/may/29/socialcare.guardiansocietysupplement** (accessed 2 July 2013).

Brindle, D (2013) Social Work Training Reforms: It Takes Five Weeks to Create a Social Worker? *The Guardian*, 21 May, **www.theguardian.com/society/2013/may/21/social-work-training-reforms** (accessed 2 July 2013).

Brown, J (2013) Scandal: Just How Corrupt is Britain? Rotten Banks, Dodgy Cops, MPs on the Fiddle. A Conference on Public Life has Evidence to Topple Long-held Assumptions. *The Independent*, 10 May, **www.independent.co.uk/news/uk/crime/scandal-just-how-corrupt-is-britain-8610095.html**

Catchpole, K (2013) Towards the Monitoring of Safety Violations. *BMJ Quality and Safety*, doi:10.1136/bmjqs-2012-001604, **http://qualitysafety.bmj.com/content/early/2013/04/10/bmjqs-2012-001604.abstract**

Foucault, M (1973) *The Birth of the Clinic: Archaeology of Medical Perceptions.* London: Routledge.

Francis, R (2013) *Report of the Mid-Staffordshire NHS Foundation Trust Public Inquiry*, HC 947. London: The Stationery Office.

Horner, N (2012) *What is Social Work?* (4th edition). London: Learning Matters/Sage.

Hugman, R (1998) *Social Welfare and Social Value*. Basingstoke: Macmillan.

Hutchings, A and Taylor, I (2007) Defining the Profession? Exploring an International Definition of Social Work in the China Context. *International Journal of Social Welfare*, 16(4): 382–90.

IFSW (2000) *Definition of Social Work*, **http://ifsw.org/policies/definition-of-social-work/** (accessed 2 July 2013).

Illich, I (1972/2011) Disabling Professions. In I Illich, IK Zola, J McKnight, J Caplan and H Shaiken (eds) *Disabling Professions*. London: Marion Boyars.

Johnson, T (1972) *Professions and Power*. London: Macmillan.

Karban, K and Smith, S (2010) Developing Critical Reflection within an Inter-professional Learning Programme. In H Bradbury, N Frost, S Kilminster and M Zukas (eds) *Beyond Reflective Practice: New Approaches to Professional Lifelong Learning*. London: Routledge.

Lamb, N (2013) New Rules to Stop Cover Ups in Care, **http://normanlamb.org.uk/wp/2013/ new-rules-to-stop-cover-ups-of-poor-care/**

Larkin, G (1983) *Occupational Monopoly and Modern Medicine*. London: Tavistock.

Laming, H (2003) *The Victoria Climbié Inquiry*, Cm 5730. London: HMSO.

Lipsky, M (1980) *Street Level Bureaucracy: Dilemmas of the Individual in Public Services*. New York: Russell Sage Foundation.

Macdonald, KM (1995) *The Sociology of the Professions*. London: Sage.

Munro, E (2011) *Munro Review of Child Protection: Final Report – a Child-centred System*, CM 8062. London: The Stationery Office.

Parker, J (2013) Active Relationships as Partnerships in Social Work: A Case Study in Social Work Education. In A Azman (ed.) *Contemporary Social Work Education, Training and Practice*. Malaysia: Institut Sosial Malaysia, Ministry of Women, Family and Community Development.

Parker, J and Ashencaen Crabtree, S (2012) Fish Need Bicycles: An Exploration of the Perceptions of Male Social Work Students on a Qualifying Course. *British Journal of Social Work*. Advance access, published 20 July, doi:10.1093/bjsw/bcs117.

Parker, J, Ashencaen Crabtree, S, Chui, WH, Kumagai, T, Baba, I, Azman, A, Haselbacher, C, Ashkanani, HR and Szto, P (2012) WAVE: Working with Adults Who are Vulnerable – a Comparison of Curricula, Policies and Constructions. *Revista de Asistenta Sociala*, XI (3): 1–18.

Pearson, G (1973) Social Work as the Privatized Solution of Public Ills. *British Journal of Social Work*, 3(2): 209–27.

Pithouse, A (1987) *Social Work: The Social Organisation of an Invisible Trade*. Aldershot: Ashgate.

Scottish Executive (2006) *Changing Lives: Report of the 21st Century Social Work Review*. Edinburgh: Scottish Executive.

Scourfield, J and Coffey, A (2002) Understanding Gendered Practice in Child Protection. *Qualitative Social Work*, 1(3): 319–40.

Social Work Reform Board (2010) *Building a Safe and Confident Future: One Year On*. London: Department for Education.

Social Work Reform Board (2012) *Building a Safe and Confident Future: Maintaining Momentum – Progress Report from the Social Work Reform Board.* London: Department for Education.

Social Work Task Force (2009) *Building a Safe and Confident Future: The Final Report of the Social Work Task Force, November 2009.* London: DCSF.

Thompson, N (2009) *Practising Social Work: Meeting the Professional Challenge.* Basingstoke: Palgrave Macmillan.

Witz, A. (1992) *Professions and Patriarchy.* London: Routledge.

Chapter 2

Being a social work professional

Malcolm Payne

Introduction

What does practising as a *professional* social worker mean? I argue that understanding the debates about what a profession is offers you guidance about how to be a good professional. Many people feel that professionalisation, the process of becoming a professional, produces traps for the unwary that may diminish the flexibility of our work, create social distance between practitioners and service users or disadvantage service users inappropriately. But I argue that good practice enables us to overcome many of these problems. Changes in how services are organised has led many social workers to be concerned about de-professionalisation, the process of moving away from practice that treats service users holistically, and instead contributes to dividing up the broad social work task into bite-sized pieces that allows for public accountability, but denies social workers the chance to meet needs in ways that consider service users' preferences.

This chapter starts by reviewing sociological debates about professions and professionalisation, in general and in social work, so that you can understand how these issues affect you in your practice. It moves on to look more widely at the requirements of UK regulators and social work professional groups that help you to use your professionalism to help service users more effectively and combat the downsides of having professional status.

What is a profession?

In everyday conversation, when we say someone is a professional, we usually mean three things:

- A professional is someone whose job falls into a special category of employment that has come to be called a profession.

- A professional is someone who does a job exceptionally well, for example when we say: 'She did a really professional job'.

- A professional is someone who is paid to do their job, the footballer paid for playing in the premier league, for example, as opposed to someone playing as a volunteer in the Sunday league at the local park.

These three things are connected. Among the expectations that people have about professions, compared with other types of work, is that professionals have demonstrated that they are competent to do a job well, and as a result people value what they do more highly and think that it is worth paying them to do it.

For example, many social care agencies, including the hospice I worked at most recently, engage volunteers in their work. We had a group of volunteers as part of the bereavement service. They were trained and supervised by a social worker who referred bereaved people who needed the support of talking to a sympathetic person about their experiences and feelings. Each person who wanted to use the service was assessed by a social worker first. People with complex needs or who were at risk of depression or other serious mental health issues would become the direct responsibility of the social worker. The assumption was that a professional social worker, because of their knowledge base from advanced study and professional qualifications in social work practice, can do a wide range of tasks to a good standard and can act independently, deciding on the appropriate response to new complex situations as they arise. A volunteer, on the other hand, fulfils a planned, restricted role, but does not have this flexibility and is not paid to accept the responsibility of complex work with people who might be at risk in their bereavement.

What is so special, then, about professions? Why are they not just jobs like many other occupations that we pay people for? In the remainder of this section, I outline the main elements of a long history of debate in sociology about the special characteristics and social roles of professions, drawing on Turner (1987: Ch. 7), Freidson (1970, 1994), Brint (1994) and Leicht and Fennell (2001).

Professions were initially seen as being special because they represent the institutionalisation of altruistic behaviour, a commitment to service that benefits individuals and a contribution to community and social well-being. In turn, this benefits general social stability. These positive features of a profession were contrasted with occupations where people work solely to earn money or to generate profits through business or where an occupation has no community or social benefit.

Professions were also distinguished from trades, where the aim was to buy and sell things for profit, craftsmanship, where there were high levels of skill but no academic education, and artistry, where there were again high levels of skill but the aim was to produce a product or outcome that would be stimulating, beautiful or interesting, but not necessarily of social benefit. These distinctions make the point that the traditional view is that a profession is for social benefit, contributing to others' lives, and requires academic learning alongside practical skill.

A 'trait' theory of professions developed from these ideas, proposing that specific characteristics of professions could be identified; to the extent that an occupational group incorporated these characteristics, it could be described as a profession. These features of professions include requirements to comply with a code of ethics, to act in the interests of users of the professional's services, a high level of education in specialised knowledge and control of entry to and discipline by the profession itself.

The 'professionalisation' thesis proposes that as society becomes more complex, some occupations develop towards becoming a profession, as knowledge and skill in certain areas becomes more specialised. Thus, professions accumulate these requirements as they become more valued in society for their specialist knowledge and skill.

A critique of these ideas developed which pointed out that the claims for the altruism of well-established professions were being taken at face value, when it was possible to see that they also gained advantages in social status, money and freedom of action that came from being accepted as a profession.

A socialist and Marxist development of that critique goes further. It points out that professions have become involved with using their specialist expertise in the service of the state, gaining social influence by acting on behalf of the state and the dominant economic interests in society. That power is expressed in social distance between practitioners and service users and also in actions on behalf of the state or powerful interests in society which sometimes disadvantage service users.

A feminist critique also notes that many professions reinforced the hierarchy of relationships in family life, in which women's domestic labour was devalued. Professionalisation reproduced this hierarchy in work life. So, the church, the law and medicine, for example, historically excluded women from taking a full role in the profession, subordinating occupations that are dominated by women, such as nursing, social work and teaching. These professions also practised in a way that reinforced and subordinated the domestic and family role of women in society, rather than seeing them as making valid contributions to roles that had social power. Social work has also been accused of doing this, enforcing traditional ideas about family roles in working-class families, for example.

More recently, changes in work organisations and management ideas in post-industrial workplaces have led to an emphasis on managerial and entrepreneurial roles so that professional work becomes only one of many ways of stratifying the workplace. This leaves professions in an ambiguous position. Their status may be devalued by an emphasis on management objectives or entrepreneurship: some work may become de-professionalised through industrialisation of the work that professionals do. I consider how this has affected social work later in this chapter.

Each of these points tells us about some of the potential advantages and disadvantages of social work being a profession. I argue that good professional practice should aim to enhance the advantages and overcome the disadvantages, as well as contributing to social benefit and also to an academic understanding of a skilful practice that enables the profession to develop.

Social work's professionalisation project

By looking at debates about social work, we can see many of these general trends acted out. Practitioners' concerns about the social and occupational status of social work first arose as it became a source of employment for middle-class women in the late nineteenth and early twentieth centuries. A conference speech by the American educationalist and administrator Flexner (1915) had an important impact. Pursuing a 'traits' perspective, he argued that social work did not display the 'six key elements' of a profession, including a systematic body of theory and knowledge, a professional culture and authority coming from, for example, a professional association, a code of ethics and a mandate from society to practise.

A professionalisation project emerged among American social workers to work towards achieving these markers of professionalism. When a unified professional association was formed in the US in 1955, an influential paper by Greenwood (1957) argued almost half a century on that social work had still not achieved professional status. Nokes (1967) noted that welfare professions often had responsibilities for caring for or managing the behaviour of people with difficulties, rather than 'virtuoso' roles requiring distinctive knowledge and skills, which were more typical of medicine. Also, there were no 'manifest disaster criteria' by which you could tell if the work of welfare professions had failed: again the comparison was with death as the clear consequence of failures of medical practice. Failure in welfare professions was more nuanced and took longer to reveal its consequences.

From these controversies, we can see how concern about whether social work was a profession came about as it became a paid job, and as social workers jockeyed for position in relation to other kinds of work in related areas; in particular they compared themselves with medicine. It is clear that a profession is about how work is organised in relation to other similar kinds of work.

Social work organisations in other countries, including Britain, were aware of this debate and set out on their own professionalisation projects (Payne, 2005a). In the UK, many elements of this were achieved with the formation of a unified professional association, the British Association of Social Workers (BASW) in 1970, which then published a code of ethics and continued to press for the registration and regulation of social workers as a profession (Payne, 2002). The development of the social sciences worldwide began to generate a body of knowledge separate from healthcare and education professions.

Most important was the foundation, in the UK, of unified social services agencies within local government in 1971, with the implementation of the Seebohm Report (1968) on the social services. Similar moves followed across Europe, so that social work appeared to have established an accepted and valued role in the 'European social model' of welfare provision, in which the state took a significant role in meeting the social needs of citizens. This role included the provision of social work particularly with families and abandoned, neglected or ill-treated children, and to a lesser degree with older, disabled and mentally ill people. The Seebohm Report held out the prospect of a universal social work service along the lines of the UK National Health Service (NHS) and social security provision.

It is clear from these events that the social work profession in the UK and Europe is connected with the role of the state in providing services to its citizens: social work is an aspect of those services. Sociological research drew attention to how such professional roles interact with the management and organisation of work and the role of the state. This sociological work led to attacks on social work's professionalisation project because it seemed to be leading to a concern for social workers' own interests in gaining control of their work. In the process, social workers seemed to want to diminish the importance of democratic control of their practice and service users' own ability to make decisions about their lives free from professional interventions. These debates make it clear that being a profession is not only about the organisation of work, it is also about who controls the work. Also, if it is work on behalf of the state, becoming a profession raises questions about whether the state's involvement in controlling that work may lead to the profession also controlling the lives of citizens in the interests of the state.

The North American sociologist Nina Toren (1969) identified a range of occupational groups, among which she counted social work as one of the 'semi-professions', holding that it could never achieve full professional status because social workers were employed by agencies which had the right to direct them in their professional objectives and practices. This analysis focuses on traits such as the professional's right to independent decision-making using their specialist knowledge and expertise as the mark of a profession. However, it also suggests that there may be alternative types of professional occupations, rather than just one model based on expert knowledge, such as that claimed by doctors. The ancient professions of the church, the law and medicine provide a template of individual professional independence, but this may not be relevant to professions in present-day society.

An important sociological critique emerged from the work of Freidson (1970) on the medical profession. He argued that the primary aim of professions is not to achieve altruistic social benefit, but to organise workers to their own benefit by controlling the daily pattern of practice and the organisation of the agencies within which the profession was practised. So doctors control the organisation of clinics and hospitals and dominate how medical work is carried out by subordinate professions. In addition, professional organisations controlled access to the profession through education and professional registration, by this process limiting the number of workers and making access to the profession's expertise scarcer and more valuable. This, in turn, enhances the economic and social status of the profession. Freidson's work led to the recognition that an important aim of professions is to assert and advance their status, rather than the altruistic benefit of the people and society that they serve.

Professionalisation, according to Marxist analysis (Parkin, 1979), is a process in which professions seek to move towards this improvement in status by achieving exclusionary *closure*. By defining the nature of the profession's work, and by controlling the content and process for awarding the credentials required to practise it, they exclude others from it. Connected with this, the control of work and qualifications in an area of work *usurps* or allows the profession to take over the roles of connected or overlapping occupational groups. For example, during the 1970s, social work in the UK began a process of usurping the role of health visitors in family work, except with new-born children, and the potential role of lawyers in advocacy for the welfare rights of poor families.

The risk for social work in these analyses is that practitioners create inflexible ways of doing and managing their work. On the face of it, such inflexibilities protect service users by making sure that the best knowledge is brought to bear on their problems. Often, however, they work to the disadvantage of other professions and service users, because they may make it more difficult to organise help through shared work with other occupational groups. For example, service users often complain that they have to be assessed several times by practitioners with different roles, rather than just one person.

A powerful polemic (Illich et al., 1977) argued that professions were 'disabling', since by limiting access to expertise in dealing with important aspects of their lives, they limit the freedom of patients and clients as individuals to make their own decisions and of communities to pursue their interests. In this way, professions tend to support the interests of powerful elites in society, rather than the poor and socially excluded. Moreover, by controlling understanding of their professional expertise, they exclude the people that they claim to help from improving their understanding and involvement in managing their own problems and disabilities.

The risk for social work of ignoring this analysis is that we denigrate the competence of service users to manage their own affairs and make their own decisions, because they do not have practitioners' knowledge and expertise. Sometimes, practitioners deny users' expertise in the particular way in which problems affect them. For example, care home managers might think that residents will be upset about proposals to change their home, so they do not consult them at an early stage, leaving any discussion until the residents cannot have any worthwhile effect on the changes. This appears to be sympathetic to residents, but actually deprives them of control of their own lives. Sometimes, practitioners think that users and their carers do not have enough knowledge about a complex medical and social problem such as dementia, when the user and their family have daily experience of managing how the dementia affects them in their home and community. That knowledge may not be generalisable to other situations, but it is more expert than generalised professional knowledge in dealing with their own situation.

These points were taken up during the 1970s by the movement for radical social work. Writers in this tradition such as Bailey and Brake (1975) argued that social work's professionalisation project was flawed because it sought the enhancement of its own status and control of its area of work. The large public social services agencies generated by the European social model often possessed legal powers of compulsion, for example in the UK in childcare and mental health. They also focused on the effective management of resources and the bureaucratic control of poor people; it was argued that this was true of the local authority social services in the UK. The radical social work answer to this was that, rather than social workers acting as expert practitioners, they should advocate for service users' rights and demonstrate, in a community approach, co-operative mutual aid to service users. Moreover, radical social workers should ally themselves with the interests of other workers and poor and excluded citizens through membership of trade unions and community organisations, rather than becoming part of a separate professional culture in a professional association. This attacks one of the central tenets of the trait approach to professions.

There have been other attacks on social work's professionalisation project. The sense that there has been a progressive development of knowledge has always been strongly contested. For example, Wootton (1959) and Brewer and Lait (1980) argued powerfully that too much was claimed for social work's exper- tise and knowledge base, and research demonstrated that claims for the effec- tiveness of long-term supportive interventions in family life were unjustified (Fischer, 1973, 1976). This led to movements for more emphasis on empirical research into methods of practice in the 1970s (Reid, 1994), leading to claims for evidence-based practice based on positivist research methods from the 1990s onwards (Otto et al., 2009). These movements, however, are open to the radi- cal charge that they are seeking to reassert expert professional status against the interests of service users.

Many of these issues came to a head in the UK during debates about the Barclay Report (1982) on the role and tasks of social workers. The Report found that there was little support for introducing registration and regulation of social work- ers, a crucial step in the professionalisation project. This was because there were many practitioners, particularly in residential care, who were and would con- tinue to be unqualified. Also, the main mechanism of public accountability was the public mandate for social services, through the local government democratic process. The main employment was in unionised local government jobs, and the local government union was opposed to professional registration, explicitly on the grounds of social work's continuing lack of a definable knowledge base (Barclay Report, 1982: 183–4), but probably also because it sought to leave existing employee–trade union negotiating relationships undisturbed (Payne, 2002). The National Council for Voluntary Organisations also argued that de-professionalisation of social assistance in favour of greater community involvement was preferable. Although this debate is in the past, these comments give us clues to some of the problems for social work practice that becoming a profession might gen- erate. How does professional accountability interact with accountability to the political and social mandate for our service? How does it interact with the responsibilities of other colleagues and the rights of communities and the people we serve?

The issue of professionalisation was raised in the UK again in a report of the Association of Directors of Social Services (SeQueira, 1986), suggesting that lay members of local authorities could not indefinitely be the group to judge standards of social work practice. An action group of interested organisations was established, led by the National Institute for Social Work and funded by the Joseph Rowntree Memorial Trust. This led to an agreed position among the interested parties, and a commitment from the Labour Party to introduce registration when it was elected (Brand, 1999; Parker, 1990): this was achieved by the Care Standards Act 2000 (Payne, 2011). A care council was established to register and regulate social workers in each UK country. This was replaced in England by the Conservative government in the period 2010–12 by registration by the Health and Care Professions Council, as a result of a process of reducing the number of quangos (quasi-autonomous non-governmental organisations) then in existence. Similar processes of licensing exist in most other advanced countries, although on varying legal and administrative principles (Bibus and Boutté-Queen, 2011).

Weiss and Welbourne's (2007) comparative study of the professionalisation of social work in 10 countries pursued a trait approach, adjusted by late-twentieth-century power analysis. They explored the extent to which the knowledge base, public recognition, monopoly of specialist skills and service provision, professional autonomy, professional education, ethical standards, professional organisation and prestige and remuneration indicated that there was broad recognition of a social work profession across the world. Their overall judgement was that social work was increasingly seen as a profession because it required higher education, had official status with many employees working in government jobs, and was seen as complex and skilled. There was wide variation, internationally, in how it was regarded.

This analysis draws attention to the importance of education and training for social work as an aspect of professionalisation. Early trait perspectives within social work focused on professional education being in higher education rather than at lower levels of education. Since the first full-time social work courses in the Netherlands, the US and the UK, social workers established university education as the primary location for social work training (Jones, 1976; Kendall, 2000). In the 1990s, debate emerged about the extent to which global standards of education are possible (Hessle, 2001). Payne and Askeland (2008) argued that attempts to create an agreed curriculum represent cultural influence by Western nations over modes of social work developed in other cultures. On the other hand, international associations of social workers have created global standards to support social workers across the world in establishing the status of the profession (International Federation of Social Workers, 2012).

New public management and deprofessionalisation

I have so far concentrated on the process of professionalisation, but deprofessionalisation also occurs. For example, social workers are often concerned that their knowledge and skills are not seen as specialised and socially valued because many people see the capacity to listen to and help others as a naturally developing social skill. It does not require the same kind of specialist expertise possessed by doctors when they diagnose illness or lawyers when they evaluate a client's legal position and represent them. These are among the reasons for the variation in the status of social work that Weiss and Welbourne (2007) found. Moreover, broad-ranging skills of this kind offer professionals wide discretion in making decisions, because their role is to use their knowledge and skills to evaluate complex one-off situations. Thus, professional work is 'indeterminate', that is, it cannot be specified in detailed sets of instructions that can be carried out by less skilled employees. Indeterminacy has increasingly come under attack both because the work and activity of a professional became less transparent and less amenable to management, and because service users and the public are unable to observe and understand professional decision-making. Because of this, the traditional independent discretion of professions has been challenged; there is less deference towards professional expertise and people have felt excluded from important decisions that affect them because professional expertise had the prime role in those decisions. Part of the problem is the social distance between professionals and service users created by the privileged expertise that goes with professional status.

The development of large government social service organisations in Europe and the UK subjected social work to some of these processes of de-professionalisation. While it was evidence of acceptance of the role of a social work profession, it also led to an increasing bureaucratisation of social work practice. Social workers seemed to have decreasing independent decision-making powers and became primarily local government workers, subject to management and employment conditions standardised across local government, rather than reflecting social work responsibilities. Mintzberg (1979) suggested that in bureaucratised organisations, for example within local government, professionals become *bureau-professionals*, trained in standardised tasks, but operating with wide autonomy in how they do their work. The standardisation means that certainty and consistency are maintained in the bureaucratic organisation. The flexibility of the professionals' autonomy, however, makes an otherwise unreasonably restrictive pattern of work more satisfactory. Social workers began to fit this model, acting as gatekeepers to services and resources for service users, where decisions were increasingly made by local authority managers and politicians.

This process was increasingly managerialised as part of the development of 'new public management' (NPM) in the 1980s (Clarke and Newman, 1987). NPM was a new settlement of relationships between the citizen and the state and between management, political control and professional responsibilities. It arose from the neo-liberal analysis that comprehensive welfare states on the European social model were not economically sustainable. Consequently, new forms of management were required to control the tendency to extend the coverage of the state and to manage professional activities so that they were more financially efficient, in particular using quantitative techniques, such as work study (Pollitt, 1993).

NPM has a view of management as a generic expertise in which management has its own knowledge base and skills. Social work professional knowledge and skill is subordinated to management and financial control. Work activity becomes deskilled as professional tasks are fragmented and industrialised. Initially, this was done by codifying and dividing up tasks into smaller components that could be carried out by separate and less skilled staff. More recently, computerising recording and decision-making also removes professional discretion (Payne, 2000). An example of this process in social work was the development of care–management and purchaser–provider splits in service provision in adult social care in the 1990s. Increasingly, rather than working with clients and their families over wide aspects of their lives, social workers carried out assessments by completing forms and computer programs, putting together packages of standardised services that were contracted for by separate staff in fragmented private agencies. Episodic caring tasks were then completed by less qualified staff managed separately. Long-term relationships between practitioners and service users declined, reducing the possibility of discretionary interpersonal help and support.

Specialisation extends this process of de-professionalisation. The division of labour is increased, so that workers perform fewer tasks, and the organisation of work is determined by higher authority. An example is the division of generic social services into children's and adult social care in the UK, culminating in a formal organisational division during the early part of the twenty-first century (Payne, 2005b).

The critique of welfare professions

We have seen that an important critique of professional power in social work and related professions has emerged, and it was usefully summarised by Wilding (1982):

- Welfare professions make excessive claims for their expertise and can only demonstrate limited achievements.

- There are many failures of professional responsibility, for example in child protection, and the management of mentally ill people in the community, which seem to require external regulation.

- The professional claim of neutrality is challenged because the social work knowledge base does not seem robust enough to demand trust and people feel that decisions are made unfairly or secretly. Parents question decisions to remove their children into public care, for example, and adults question the resource allocation decisions in community care services.

- Professions neglect people's rights to make their own decisions on grounds of professional expertise or responsibility. For example, older or disabled people are not allowed to take the risk of more independence in their living arrangements, in case social services are criticised for not protecting them.

- The service ideal and altruism of professions is challenged: are they seeking to improve their status, income or control of their work environment rather than improve provision for service users?

- Does professional expertise disable the independence and opportunities of service users in favour of security for risk-averse public services or professional control and surveillance of people who are seen as difficult or problematic?

There are three ways in which major professions dominate related occupations: subordination, limitation and exclusion (Turner, 1987: 141). We can see this happening in social care. For example, social care workers such as personal assistants or foster carers are allocated to service users on the basis of assessments by social workers (subordination), do not have responsibility for determining eligibility for services (limitation), and are often not involved in case conferences about the person they serve, even though they often have the closest and most frequent contact with that person (exclusion).

Another attack on the role of welfare professions developed from the NPM emphasis on work study and other private sector management techniques, which emerged, in turn, from a neo-liberal political philosophy concerned about the economic cost of welfare services, and which consequently valued business priorities in managing public services. Bureau-professional management of work was considered to inhibit financial efficiency and imaginative enhancements of practice (Pinker, 1979) and this led to an introduction of business management and language (Harris, 2003). This approach favours financial efficiency over professional discretion in decision-making in social services.

Being a good professional

From this account of debates about the nature of professions and the processes of professionalisation and de-professionalisation in social work, it is clear that being a professional is not only about the expertise of individuals, their altruism, or the social value accorded by the public or the state to their work. It is also closely connected with two important issues of social concern: social stratification and the management of organisations in society. Professions acquire social status as occupations because they are socially valued and possess and control access to specialist knowledge and skill; this in turn gives access to resources for their work. That social status becomes allied to other aspects of social stratification in society, including class and gender. Because a profession is concerned with the organisation of work, professional work inevitably interacts with other organisations and social institutions through which work is organised, including government and the state and the role of the private sector, including entrepreneurial and business thinking. The role of professions has always been questioned, both because the social status accorded to professionals creates a social distance with service users, and the process of professionalisation creates inflexibilities in service which may obstruct democratic control, financial efficiency and co-ordination with other professional groups.

Table 2.1   Acting on and preventing problems with your professional role

	Issue	Positive actions	Preventing problems
1.	Altruism, and the ethic of service	Be clear about your helping objectives and ensure that your work has successful outcomes.	Avoid actions that are only about controlling or surveilling service users.
2.	Specialised expertise gained through research and higher education	Build expertise through qualification and advanced education and use it transparently, helping people to acquire knowledge that will help them in the future.	Avoid social distance, use of jargon, secret decision-making, giving only partial information.
3.	Dealing with complex and difficult situations	Disentangle and explain complexities in people's lives.	Avoid extending your involvement unnecessarily.
4.	Knowledge base	Research and implement the most effective actions.	Explain your understanding and discuss options.
5.	Contributing to social stratification	Aim to enhance equalities and avoid increasing inequalities in services due to ethnicity, gender, disability, sexuality, ageism and other irrelevant social factors.	
6.	Virtuoso professional roles	Explain and justify actions and decisions; encourage challenge.	Avoid claiming a monopoly of areas of work or decisions.
7.	Disabling professions	Empower people to achieve independent control of their lives.	Avoid risk-averse behaviour and help people with procedures.
8	Professional culture	Promote community engagement and mutual aid.	Avoid actions that make people dependent on others.
9.	Rights	Empower people to make their own decisions, strengthening their skills and knowledge to do so.	Respect people's independence, human rights and dignity.
10.	De-professionalisation	Deal with users' needs and social relationships holistically.	Build relationships when tasks are fragmented.
11.	Role of the state	Explain the role of your agency and practice; encourage challenge.	Avoid setting arbitrary boundaries on actions.
12.	Failures of responsibility	Monitor and evaluate your work, get feedback from others involved.	Balance risk and opportunity in users' lives.
13.	Agency and managerialist control	Advocate for users' and carers' needs in your agency	Challenge unnecessary control and surveillance of users.
14.	Subordination	Involve carers, paraprofessionals and volunteers in work and decisions.	Avoid acting unilaterally and without warning or explanation.
15.	Limitation, closure, usurpation	Work jointly and share expertise with professional colleagues.	Avoid trying to control expertise and information.
16.	Exclusion	Involve carers and users in work and decisions.	Be open about aims and plans, discuss your ideas with users and carers.

Good professional practice, therefore, requires practitioners to be aware of the advantages and problems that professional status brings, so that their practice strengthens the advantages and reduces the impact of the problems. In Table 2.1, I have summarised the 16 main points that emerge from this chapter's account of issues around professions and professionalisation. These overlap and connect with each other. In each case, I have suggested a positive way of practising so that you make the best of each issue, and some ways of preventing the downside of each issue.

The first nine issues are all concerned with the nature of professions. Four of these are potentially positive: a profession offers altruistic service, specialised expertise, the capacity to deal with complex and difficult situations and a knowledge base. Good professional practice aims to enhance the benefit of these positives for service users and for the agencies that employ professionals. But there are also potential downsides to the positives, which we can see in the following five issues: the professionalisation of social work might be contributing to social stratification, to developing virtuoso professional roles which exclude colleagues, users and carers from participating in work that should involve them, it may disable people from pursuing independence in their lives and social workers' professional culture may exclude them and prevent them from exercising their rights. Good professional practice tries to prevent these potential problems of professionalism from arising, and uses social workers' awareness of them to correct the disadvantages.

Too much professional power only disadvantages users and carers if social workers allow it to do so. And they cannot empower users and carers unless they have enough independence of thought and action to work alongside users and carers to develop their own power. Professionals cannot give power to users and carers, because if you have the power to give, you also have the power to take away. They can, however, use their professional skills to allow users and carers to take their own power. Social workers also need to be aware that using professional power in any situation does not necessarily take away power from someone else. People taking up opportunities to use their power may lead to more power being used overall, rather than one group's power taking away from another's.

The next group of four issues are about the interaction of professions with the management of the organisations in which professionals operate. De-professionalisation means that we may find ourselves splitting up aspects of our work that should be treated as a whole, social workers' actions on behalf of the state mean that their responsibilities are sometimes oppressive or controlling, their work may fail to meet all their responsibilities, and agency and managerialist control may mean that our work is inflexible and fails to meet users' and carers' needs. Good professional practice means trying to treat individuals as whole human beings, with aspirations and opportunities, and as part of their families and communities. They are not bundles of problems, to be assessed according to official procedures. Every employee is obliged to fulfil the responsibilities of their employment, but every professional is able to use the opportunities of that employment to further the humanity, citizenship and aspirations of the person they are working with. Working in healthcare, with terminally ill people, I have often arrived at the bedside or sat with family members looking at what seems to be a hopeless phase of life. But we all have to live through the worst of times. Someone who puts aside the forms for a few minutes to acknowledge and share distress, someone who asks for people's own perceptions and hopes before starting on the official requirements, someone who explains the processes they are going through and evidently fights for the wishes of users and carers can at least make providing social services a human process and may often make it one which responds better to the needs of the people they serve. That is the minimum role of a professional in an official service, whether its focus is also bureaucratic, political or entrepreneurial.

The final group of three issues is about how we interact with other professions and with other people employed in social care: the processes of professionalisation may mean that they feel subordinated, limited in their work or excluded from our actions. Again, good professional practice means finding ways of preventing that from happening and positively engaging and sharing our work with colleagues in effective partnerships.

UK codes of practice for social workers

An important way in which professionals develop their responsibilities and achieve good professional practice is by working within the requirements of the codes of practice and ethics which govern their work. The organisation of regulation varies in different countries, and is controlled by a combination of setting standards of qualification and education and by registering or licensing individual practitioners, giving them the right to practise. In this section, I discuss the requirements of UK social workers.

The HCPC *Standards of Conduct, Performance and Ethics* (2012) documents 14 standards that represent professional requirements for practitioners in England. These apply to all the professions that the HCPC regulates, and makes no special provision for social care employees. The Codes of Practice of the social services regulatory bodies in Northern Ireland, Scotland and Wales follow the practice of the former English General Social Care Council. I have used the example of the Scottish Social Services Council (2009); the other two countries have similar Codes in place.

In Tables 2.2 and 2.3, I have identified three types of provisions within the Codes. Column 1 in each Table lists the standards directly concerned with how practitioners provide services to service users. Column 2 lists standards concerned with the practitioner's responsibilities for managing their work and professional standards. Column 3 lists provisions concerned with the regulatory process. The HCPC Code is numbered and Table 2.2 retains its numbering.

A notable difference is that the HCPC process in England is independent of employers, while the social services regulatory bodies in the other three countries

Table 2.2   Standards of conduct, performance and ethics

Service standards	Personal conduct	Regulatory requirements
1. You must act in the best interests of service users.	3. You must keep high standards of personal conduct.	4. You must provide (to us and any other relevant regulators) any important information about your conduct and competence.
2. You must respect the confidentiality of service users.	5. You must keep your professional knowledge and skills up to date.	14. You must make sure that any advertising you do is accurate.
7. You must communicate properly and effectively with service users and other practitioners.	6. You must act within the limits of your knowledge, skills and experience and, if necessary, refer the matter to another practitioner.	
9. You must get informed consent to provide care or services (so far as possible).	8. You must effectively supervise tasks that you have asked other people to carry out.	
10. You must keep accurate records.	12. You must limit your work or stop practising if your performance or judgement is affected by your health.	
11. You must deal fairly and safely with the risks of infection.	13. You must behave with honesty and integrity and make sure that your behaviour does not damage the public's confidence in you or your profession.	

Source: Health and Care Professions Council (2012).

Table 2.3   Social work codes of practice

Service standards	Personal conduct	Regulatory requirements
Social service workers must:		To meet their responsibilities in relation to regulating the social service workforce, social service employers must:
Protect the rights and promote the interests of service users and carers	Uphold public trust and confidence in social services	Make sure people are suitable to enter the workforce and understand their roles and responsibilities
Strive to establish and maintain the trust and confidence of service users and carers	Be accountable for the quality of their work and take responsibility for maintaining and improving their knowledge and skills	Have written policies and procedures in place to enable social service workers to meet the Scottish Social Services Council (SSSC) Code of Practice for Social Service Workers
Promote the independence of service users while protecting them as far as possible from danger or harm		Provide training and development opportunities to enable social service workers to strengthen and develop their skills and knowledge
Respect the rights of service users while seeking to ensure that their behaviour does not harm themselves or other people		Put in place and implement written policies and procedures to deal with dangerous, discriminatory or exploitative behaviour and practice
		Promote the SSSC's Codes of Practice to social service workers, service users and carers and co-operate with the SSSC's proceedings.

Source: Scottish Social Services Council (2009).

have a code of practice for employers, which mirrors the requirements of practitioners. The effect of this difference is that the HCPC code is individualistic in its approach: practitioners are given the personal responsibility to maintain their practice. In this way, it reflects a traditional view of the professional as an independent decision-maker. The social services codes recognise that social work is an agency-based profession, and employers are given responsibilities for facilitating practitioners' compliance with the codes and providing an environment suitable for good practice. Column 3 in Table 2.3, therefore, provides for employers to co-operate in the regulatory process, while the HCPC requires practitioners to provide information that enables regulatory interventions to take place. The fact that these aspects of the codes are so prominent draws attention to the difficulty of balancing the interests of the people that social workers serve against the responsibilities of the state, the organisations and the financial and social imperatives of the people who employ practitioners. The power of employers to force social workers to comply with their instructions, possibly oppressing or disadvantaging service users, their families and communities, often seems overbearing. The education, skill and practice wisdom of the professional and the codes of practice and ethics that support their work provide a weak counterbalance. Practitioners can enhance the strength of their professional power, however, by drawing on the education and practice ethics to offer the best quality of service that is possible and being clear when the organisation of the service inhibits their professional performance. They can also enhance the strength of their profession by contributing their experience to research and professional development.

My analysis of the Codes in Tables 2.2 and 2.3 draws attention to how two elements of the nature of professions is applied in the UK context to social workers. The first column emphasises altruistic and ethical standards in working with service users, while the second column emphasises the professional practitioner as 'virtuous person' and responsible practitioner. Alternative ways of seeing ethical practice emphasise different approaches (Banks, 2012). A utilitarian approach emphasises trying to benefit as many people involved in the situation as much as possible, and trying not to disadvantage them, or balancing advantage and disadvantage rationally; many professional codes of ethics take this approach. A relevant factor may also be an emphasis, deriving from the ethics of Kant, on the duties that go with responsibilities for others. A virtuous-person approach focuses on professionals behaving with integrity, looking at debates about what consistently good behaviour in a situation would involve, and trying to follow those virtuous principles in action.

These different approaches reflect a tension which affects many practitioners who work with people who suffer from psychological, emotional or social stresses. How far do they maintain a distance from service users' distress in order to protect their own balanced, rational judgements, or allow their empathy to generate personal involvement in that distress? How far do they disclose their own personal feelings, if a user's concerns touch the practitioner's personal life? There are no easy answers. We have seen that the way in which professionalisation may lead to increasing social distance between professionals and service users may be one of the downsides of being professional, yet independent, thoughtful responses are also often valued by service users. Each situation has to be worked out anew, and practitioners often struggle with appropriately expressing or managing their feelings. Useful guidance can be drawn from the utilitarian and Kantian ethics, that, as professionals employed, and therefore with a duty, to help others, the social worker should focus first on what will benefit the service users, and exclude actions that seem mainly to benefit themselves. Do you seek more information because you are interested in how other people work out their lives? Then stop yourself, because you are doing it for your own curiosity. Stay with the things you need to find out to serve their needs.

These codes are not the only ones that are relevant to UK practitioners' standards of work. The British Association of Social Workers (BASW) publishes a *Code of Ethics* (BASW, 2012) and its International equivalent, the International Federation of Social Workers, publishes a similar code, the *Statement of Ethical Principles* (IFSW, 2012). Its internet site lists similar codes from many other countries: **http://ifsw.org/resources/publications/national-codes-of-ethics/**, and policy statements on good practice in a range of specialist fields: **http://ifsw.org/policies/**. Such codes provide more detailed accounts of the requirements of ethical practice.

Conclusion

In what ways is social work a profession? What does being a professional mean to a social work practitioner? The debates about organising work through incorporating professions into the workplace, and the processes of professionalisation and de-professionalisation in social work reviewed in this chapter, suggest that there is no easy answer to these questions. There is a clear risk that being part of a profession may act to the disadvantage of service users, their families and communities, and that professionalisation advantages the professional rather than the public and the service user. The role of professions in social services may limit the flexible coordination of services, and may lead to the exclusion of non-professionals and service users from engagement in important decisions that affect them. On the other hand, social workers being professional in using their education, knowledge, skill and humanity may also help and empower service users and the people around them and benefit society by enabling and transforming social relationships and social institutions. I have argued in this chapter that awareness of these tensions is an important part of being a professional. It is important not to be dismissive of the advantages of being part of a profession, in particular the strength it gives practitioners in building the quality of their work and in defending their practice when it is questioned. But it is also important to work through the professional conflicts that all social workers face in their practice with a realistic awareness that a too-stubborn adherence to professional proprieties can sometimes lead to disadvantage for the people we serve or the public policy that sets the boundaries of our role.

REFLECTIVE QUESTIONS

1. *Think about situations in your practice where you felt distant from the people you were trying to help. How far do you think your professional role created that social distance? How could you have worked to prevent and respond to these problems?*

2. *Think about situations in your practice where the requirements of your agency's policy and procedures meant that your practice with service users was inflexible or inadequate. What could you have done to prevent or respond to these problems?*

RECOMMENDED FURTHER READING

British Association of Social Workers (2012) *The Code of Ethics for Social Workers: Statement of Principles*. Birmingham: BASW. This Code is an example of comprehensive detailed codes of ethics for social workers that you may find on the internet. As you look through it, try to think of examples in your practice that demonstrate ethical behaviour according to its principles and also where you think your practice was less ethical, according to its precepts. What could you do to practise more ethically and avoid ethical problems?

Weiss, I and Welbourne, P (eds) (2007) *Social Work as a Profession: A Comparative Cross-national Perspective*. Birmingham: Venture. This edited book describes evidence about the extent to which and ways in which social work may be seen as a profession in a range of different countries, including the UK.

Harris, J (2003) *The Social Work Business*. London: Routledge. Harris' book is a readable and thoughtful account of many of the issues affecting social work that come from New Public Management and issues of public accountability.

Etzioni, A (ed) (1969) *The Semi-professions and their Organization: Teachers, Nurses, Social Workers*. New York: Free Press: 141–95. A classic contribution to the sociological debates about non-traditional professions, with a famous chapter on social work.

REFERENCES

Bailey, R and Brake, M (eds) (1975) *Radical Social Work*. London: Arnold.

Banks, S (2012) *Ethics and Values in Social Work* (4th edition). Basingstoke: Palgrave Macmillan.

Barclay Report (1982) *Social Workers: Their Role and Tasks*. London: Bedford Square Press.

Bibus, AA and Boutté-Queen, N (2011) *Regulating Social Work: A Primer on Licensing Practice*. Chicago: Lyceum.

Brand, D (1999) *Accountable Care: Developing the General Social Care Council*. York: Joseph Rowntree Foundation.

Brewer, C and Lait, J (1980) *Can Social Work Survive?* London: Temple Smith.

Brint, S (1994) *In an Age of Experts: The Changing Role of Professionals in Politics and Public Life*. Princeton, NJ: Princeton University Press.

British Association of Social Workers (BASW) (2012) *The Code of Ethics for Social Workers: Statement of Principles*. Birmingham: BASW.

Clarke, J and Newman, J (1997) *The Managerial State: Power, Politics and Ideology in the Remaking of Social Welfare.* London: Sage.

Fischer, J (1973) Is Casework Effective? A Review. *Social Work,* 18(1): 5–20.

Fischer, J (1976) *The Effectiveness of Social Casework.* Springfield, IL: Charles C Thomas.

Flexner, A (1915) Is Social Work a Profession? In Pumphrey, RE and Pumphrey, MW (eds) (1961) *The Heritage of American Social Work: Readings in its Philosophical and Institutional Development.* New York: Columbia University Press: 301–7.

Freidson, E (1970) *Profession of Medicine: A Study of the Sociology of Applied Knowledge.* New York: Dodd, Mead.

Freidson, E (1994) *Professionalism Reborn: Theory, Prophecy and Policy.* Cambridge: Polity.

Greenwood, E (1957) Attributes of a Profession. *Social Work,* 2(3): 45–55.

Harris, J (2003) *The Social Work Business.* London: Routledge.

Health and Care Professions Council (HCPC) (2012) *Standards of Conduct, Performance and Ethics.* London: HCPC.

Hessle, S (ed) (2001) *International Standard Setting in Higher Social Work Education.* Stockholm: Department of Social Work, University of Stockholm.

Illich, I, Zola, IK, McKnight, J, Caplan, J and Shaiken, H (1977) *Disabling Professions.* London: Marion Boyars.

International Federation of Social Workers (IFSW) (2012) *Statement of Ethical Principles.* Geneva: IFSW, **http://ifsw.org/policies/statement-of-ethical-principles/** (accessed 1 December 2012).

International Federation of Social Workers (IFSW) (2012) *Global Standards.* Geneva: IFSW, **http://ifsw.org/policies/global-standards/** (accessed 1 December 2012).

Jones, C (1976) *The Foundations of Social Work Education,* Working Papers I Sociology 11. Durham: University of Durham.

Kendall, K (2000) *Social Work Education: Its Origins in Europe.* Alexandria, VA: Council on Social Work Education.

Leicht, KT and Fennell, ML (2001) *Professional Work: A Sociological Approach.* Malden, MA: Blackwell.

Mintzberg, H (1979) *The Structuring of Organisations: A Synthesis of the Research.* Englewood Cliffs, NJ: Prentice-Hall.

Nokes, P (1967) *The Professional Task in Welfare Practice.* London: Routledge and Kegan Paul.

Otto, H-U, Polutta, A and Ziegler, H (2009) *Evidence-based Practice – Modernising the Knowledge Base of Social Work?* Opladen: Barbara Budrich.

Parker, R (1990) *Safeguarding Standards.* London: National Institute for Social Work.

Parkin, F (1979) *Marxism and Class Theory: A Bourgeois Critique.* London: Tavistock.

Payne, M (2000) *Anti-bureaucratic Social Work.* Birmingham: Venture.

Payne, M (2002) The Role and Achievements of a Professional Association in the Late Twentieth Century: The British Association of Social Workers 1970–2000. *British Journal of Social Work,* 32(8): 969–95.

Payne, M (2005a) *What is Professional Social Work?* Bristol: Policy Press.

Payne, M (2005b) *The Origins of Social Work: Continuity and Change.* Basingstoke: Palgrave Macmillan.

Payne, M (2011) Social Work Regulation in the United Kingdom. In Bibus, AA and Boutté-Queen, N, *Regulating Social Work: A Primer on Licensing Practice.* Chicago: Lyceum: 45–59.

Payne, M and Askeland, GA (2008) *Globalization and International Social Work: Postmodern Change and Challenge.* Aldershot: Ashgate.

Pinker, RA (1979) *Social Work in an Enterprise Society.* London: Routledge.

Pollitt, C (1993) *Managerialism and the Public Services: Cuts or Cultural Change in the 1990s?* Oxford: Blackwell.

Reid, WJ (1994) The Empirical Practice Movement. *Social Service Review,* 68(2): 165–84.

Scottish Social Services Council (2009) *Codes of Practice for Social Services Workers and Employers.* Dundee: Scottish Social Services Council.

Seebohm Report (1968) *Report of the Committee on Local Authority and Allied Personal Social Services* (Cmnd 3703). London: HMSO.

SeQueira, R (1986) *Registration and a Social Work Council? A Discussion Document Prepared for the ADSS Parliamentary Sub-committee.* London: Association of Directors of Social Services.

Toren, N (1969) Semi-professionalism and Social Work: A Theoretical Perspective. In Etzioni, A (ed) *The Semi-Professions and their Organization: Teachers, Nurses, Social Workers.* New York: Free Press: 141–95.

Turner, BS (1987) *Medical Power and Social Knowledge.* London: Sage.

Weiss, I and Welbourne, P (eds) (2007) *Social Work as a Profession: A Comparative Cross-national Perspective.* Birmingham: Venture.

Wilding, P (1982) *Professional Power and Social Welfare.* London: Routledge and Kegan Paul.

Wootton, B (1959) *Social Science and Social Pathology.* London: George Allen & Unwin.

Chapter 3
Practising reflexivity: nurturing humane practice
Sue White

Introduction

Research is inextricably bound to social work's history and yet it is erroneously often seen as separate from practice. Whilst it is routinely conceptualised as something upon which practice should properly draw, research skills and methods are not always constructed as absolutely integral to the social *work* in social work. This chapter explores reflection and reflexivity, characterised as processes of exploring presumptions and presuppositions, and argues for their importance in promoting humane social work practice in 'just' organisations. Such arguments have a long pedigree. Mary Richmond, General Secretary of the Baltimore Charity Organization in the late nineteenth century, is widely acknowledged as an early pioneer of social work. She approached the process of trying to understand the success or failure of the investigations and interventions of particular 'charity visitors' with a social scientific mind and rigorous methods. By analysing each case in fine detail and interpreting and reinterpreting cases which seemed superficially similar and yet had reached very different outcomes, she sought, rather like the evidence-based practitioners of today, to understand 'what works' (Margolin, 1997). She found that sympathy and friendliness rather than form filling and intrusive questioning were key to successful understandings of a family's circumstances and to gaining access to *things not spoken of to others* (Gutridge, 1905: 361).

That families choose to disclose 'things not spoken of to others' only to practitioners with a sympathetic disposition may seem self-evident, but it is a core problematic for social work as profession. Social work occupies a liminal space between the private and the public. The disclosure by an individual of some intimate family secret may leave a social worker with no option but to act in an authoritative way on behalf of their agency, or the state, to protect those who are, or whom society has deemed, vulnerable. This is morally, ethically and emotionally very difficult terrain:

> *The directive, then, was for social workers to give their clients a special type of confidence – a confidence that appears as confidence to clients and feels like*

confidence to the investigators, that does what confidence is supposed to do in terms of eliciting information and trust, but a confidence that does not preclude the continuing recognition that 'a family, under ordinary circumstances well-meaning and honest, under pressure of distress, may be tempted to deceive'.

(Margolin, 1997: 35, citing Birtwell, 1895: 137)

In order to illustrate these interactional, organisational, intellectual and emotional complexities, I would like to begin with a fictional account of one social worker's experience of dealing with a routine referral from the police domestic violence unit. The story is a composite of several cases and is derived from my own detailed ethnographic observations of everyday practice in social work over two decades.

Practice Example
Monday morning in the duty and assessment team

F A S C I M I L E   T R A N S M I S S I O N

Domestic Violence Unit,
73 Silver Street
14/3/05

INCIDENT REPORT:

Responded to emergency call to 53 Waterloo Avenue received at 22.15hrs on 13/3/05. Altercation in progress between adults, Shaun Bailey and Theresa Jenkins. Shaun Bailey (4/8/75) allegedly punched Theresa Jenkins on face causing swelling to nose and eye. Both adults had been drinking. Shaun Bailey arrested at scene, charged with assault. Theresa Jenkins refused to attend for hospital care. Couple have two young children, Maria Bailey (13/8/02) and Thomas Bailey (5/2/04). Both reported asleep during incident.

PC Traynor 34961

Ruth is a social worker in a local authority duty and assessment team and receives this fax from PC Traynor, at the police domestic violence unit. Ruth first checks the system for any previous involvement with the family. She discovers that there had been an assessment six months ago, following a report from the police about another domestic incident. The case was closed after one visit on the grounds that the children were asleep and not in danger and the parents reported that they had resolved the difficulties. Ruth's team manager decides that a further assessment is now required and asks her to visit.

Ruth has been qualified for six months and has some experience of similar cases. She talks to her colleague who had completed the previous assessment. Her colleague reports that Shaun and Theresa make a 'lovely couple when they're sober' and that, although 'things were thrown about' and there was 'a lot of shouting', there had not been any allegations, or any obvious evidence, of physical violence. Ruth's colleague knows Shaun. She had worked with him when he was 14 years old and had been referred by his parents because they were struggling to cope with his drug use and deteriorating behaviour. She says that he has made fantastic progress, and although he can be rather 'excitable', he has 'really grown up' and is now drug free and working as a driver. This is reassuring to Ruth, because sometimes visits like this can be frightening, but she remains apprehensive about the visit. Ruth thinks it might have been better if her colleague had been given the case, as she knows the family better, but Ruth is on duty today, not her colleague.

Ruth has been working in the duty and assessment team since she qualified. She has noticed how many incidents of domestic abuse are referred by the police and, although she knows that the children in the households are at increased risk of harm, particularly when drugs and alcohol are involved, she doesn't think that her team is really helping the families. Ruth is not quite sure what she will say when she arrives at the house, but she has an assessment form to complete which tells her what to ask and she finds that structure helpful: it helps her to remember what to say next when she is under pressure.

Ruth sets out on her visit and arrives at the family home. It is not as she had expected. It is a neat house on a quiet road. Theresa answers the door. She is a young white woman in her early twenties. There is some slight discoloration under her left eye, but she is wearing make-up so it is hard to tell if she has any other injuries. Theresa invites Ruth into the house. She says she is really embarrassed about calling the police and 'making such a fuss over nothing'. Ruth notices, as she passes through the hallway, that there are toys on the living room floor. In the kitchen, children's drawings are attached to the fridge with magnets in the shape of letters of the alphabet. Theresa is cooking scrambled eggs for the children. Maria is sitting at the kitchen table, combing her doll's hair, and Thomas is in a high chair banging his spoon. Both children are clean and well dressed. Ruth asks whether Shaun is at home and is told he is at work and that he 'feels awful' about what has happened. Although she knows she should involve fathers in her assessments, Ruth is relieved he is not around. Theresa reiterates that she wishes she hadn't 'lost it' and called the police. She tells Ruth that she has been with Shaun since they left school and they are getting married next year.

Ruth had anticipated a rather more confrontational meeting in which she would do what she usually does, which is to ask whichever adult is present if they are aware that their behaviour will be impacting on the children's development and to explain that she has a duty to ensure the children are safe by completing an assessment. Ruth says this anyway and Theresa starts to cry, turning away from the children so they do not see. Ruth tells Theresa that she can see she is upset about what has happened and Theresa says again, in hushed tone, so that the children do not overhear, she just wishes she had not called the police, because now children's services are involved and that will make everything worse. Theresa says she doesn't need to be told that they shouldn't drink and argue. She already knows this and so does Shaun. They feel bad enough about it already. Theresa says they have both agreed not to drink in the house any more. They had been arguing over money and things had got way out of hand, she had picked up the phone, threatening to call the police, and Shaun had slapped her in temper, but they love each other and are a happy family. Ruth wonders where to begin raising the issues she needs to address on the assessment form. Best to start at the top, she concludes. Ruth works through the form, but feels embarrassed as it asks questions about the children's health and development and Ruth can see with her own eyes that they are fine. She tries to get through the matter as quickly as possible.

A key turns in the door. Shaun has arrived home. He steps into the kitchen. Maria shouts 'Daddy!'. Theresa tells Shaun that Ruth is a social worker. He sighs and says 'I thought so'. He asks Ruth to step into the other room because he doesn't want to talk in front of the children. Ruth feels anxious about how Shaun might react. Shaun tells her he's really sorry, he can't believe what he's done, but he doesn't want people thinking he and Theresa don't look after the children properly. He says his family is 'his life' and begins to cry. Ruth really was not expecting this. Ruth says she can see he is distressed, but there is really nothing to worry about, she just needed to make sure that everything is OK and the children are safe. Shaun says he had a social worker once and she was great, it's not that he doesn't like social workers. Shaun tells Ruth that drink is to blame and that he and Theresa will definitely not drink at home any more. Ruth wants to ask some more questions, but she is uncomfortable and feels rather useless, so she decides against it and thinks she has enough information to fill in the form.

The children are now eating their lunch. Ruth wishes Theresa and Shaun well, tells them to contact her if they need anything more and leaves them with a leaflet. She goes back to the office, relieved that all went well, and types in the form, concluding her case summary as follows:

> *Domestic violence incident on 13/3/05 police called. Theresa punched in face by Shaun. Both very upset by incident and say it will not happen again. They had been having an argument about money and it got out of hand. No previous violent incidents. Both children were asleep during incident and not disturbed. Both children are up to date with their immunisations and appear well cared for. Both parents seemed concerned that children's services were involved and upset when informed about the impact of domestic violence on children. Information given about local domestic violence support services.*

Ruth's team manager agrees that 'no further action' is necessary and the case is closed. As a newly qualified social worker, Ruth has 12 other active cases and her attention quickly shifts to those.

During the ensuing five years, two further referrals are made to the team by the police. They relate to heated verbal arguments between Theresa and Shaun. The children were not present in the house at the time of the incidents, and therefore the case was not allocated to a social worker. Maria's nursery also makes a referral because they are concerned about Maria's deteriorating behaviour. After some telephone contact and advice it is felt that the nursery could continue to manage this without any involvement from children's services. In 2010, the following fax is received:

F A S C I M I L E   T R A N S M I S S I O N

Domestic Violence Unit,
73 Silver Street
8/2/10

INCIDENT REPORT:

Responded to emergency 999 call 53 Waterloo Avenue. Arrived at scene at 11.25hrs on 8/2/07. On arrival Theresa Jenkins (16/4/75) and Shaun Bailey (4/8/75) had been arguing. He had accused her of seeing another man. She became very upset and he attacked her to 'teach her a lesson'. He pinned her against the wall and attempted strangulation. Theresa has red marks on her neck and a cut lip. During the incident Thomas Bailey (5/2/04) attempted to intervene by running between his mother and father. He was pushed to the floor by Shaun Bailey. Thomas knocked his head on a kitchen cupboard and has facial bleeding and a graze above his left eye. Thomas was distressed and crying at the scene. Shaun Bailey then punched the wall injuring his right hand and breaking some plates that fell to the floor. Maria Bailey (13/8/02) witnessed the assault and ran out of the house to a neighbour who called the police. The couple have 2 other children, Scarlett Bailey (23/1/05) and Rhiannon Bailey (16/12/07) who were also in the house when the alleged assault took place. Alleged assailant Shaun Bailey arrested at scene. Photos taken of Theresa's injuries to neck and eye area and of kitchen area where alleged assault took place. Theresa and Thomas were taken by ambulance to Central Hospital. WPC Johnson remained at property until arrival of Theresa's mother Deirdre Jenkins, of 52 Cross Road, Winterton who will look after Maria, Scarlett and Rhiannon over the weekend.

PC Smith

What are we to make of this story and what can it tell us about humane practice? Clearly many opportunities to help this family were missed and what of Ruth's visit to the family as a newly qualified social worker?

In the hurly burly of everyday practice, it is easy for an outcome like this to occur. Many of the errors were a product of the very brief encounter with the family. For a variety of reasons, our intrinsic characteristics as human beings operate as both friend and foe in social work decision-making (White, 2009). At an individual level, we are equipped with an innate apparatus to assess our fellow human beings on an intuitive/emotional level (Haidt, 2001; White, 2009). Ruth was easily reassured by the appearance of the house and the children, the presence of toys, the cooking of lunch and the emotionally appropriate reaction of the parents. At times, she was just plain scared and uncomfortable and wanted to get out of the home as quickly as possible (Stanley and Goddard, 2002).

These personal, interpersonal and social factors were compounded by the organisational systems and institutional imperative to act quickly and decisively and to close the case (Broadhurst et al., 2010a, 2010b). The duty system precluded the involvement of a social worker who had a much more thoroughgoing understanding of the family, particularly Shaun, and would have been able more successfully to accomplish a friendly, but cautious and respectfully doubting position. Ruth had an institutional script stressing to the parents the harm they were likely to cause. Her encounter was driven in substantial part by the form she was required to complete; as a novice in a difficult situation she found this comforting (Gilligan, 2011), yet the form also imposed a particular order on the conversation and focused attention on some areas at the expense of others (Hall et al., 2010; White et al., 2009).

If we are to turn the very human practice of social work described above as *humane* practice we need to reflect on some of the features of our own reasoning processes. Careful, judicious, research-minded and humane practice requires particular organisational environments in which to flourish. These environments need to facilitate debate and dialogue. They need to be oriented to conversation and communication. At present social work agencies are focused on workflow and outputs, artificially cloaking ambiguity and uncertainty in habit and routine. If we want good decisions, we need to design organisations paying due regard to the 'human factors' which influence thinking. To this end, let us examine in more detail some of the human factors at play in social work sense-making and judgement.

The importance of relationship

It is not important only that the expert should have a clear and comprehensive idea of the user's difficulty from the latter's point of view; it is also and equally important that the user should have a good idea of his/her difficulty as it has taken shape in the expert's mind. ... Creating this shared basis is often a difficult task. ... It is a task whose purpose is paradoxically to create the problem, rather than – as it might seem to the practitioner – to resolve it.

(Folgheraiter, 2004: 40)

[Professionals] should never forget that they graft their action onto a process that has already been set in motion, and perhaps a long time previously. Their own action is always preceded by that of the people directly involved in the problem, belonging to the pre-scientific world of daily life. Social coping – defined as an ability to manage or eliminate a living difficulty – is often a battle already begun elsewhere: who knows when, who knows by whom.

(Folgheraiter, 2004: 92)

In these two quotations, Folgheraiter is making a case for 'relational social work'. The extracts underscore the limits of our own potency as professionals and remind us that we will not be permitted to know very much about a person's life if we cannot make a relationship with them and hear and assimilate their version of the circumstances. The sorts of institutional responses discussed in the case example above radically compromise the conversations to which Folgheraiter refers. The rapid throughput of cases, processed to tight timescales, using standardised assessment schedules, seriously compromise 'relational social work' (Munro, 2011).

Of course, there are some situations where such a relationship may be easier to forge. For example, a social worker in a children with disabilities team, working with a family over many years, where there are no concerns about the parenting and the focus is on emotional support and service provision, may have to deal with some emotionally gruelling matters, such a child's serious illness or death, but establishing a genuine relationship with the parents may be relatively straightforward. However, even when social workers are involved with complex families where there are concerns about risk, the importance of providing a dependable professional relationship, in particular with those families who conceal or minimise their difficulties, has been conclusively demonstrated (Knei-Paz, 2009; Thoburn et al., 2009). Furthermore, it has been shown that 'uncooperative' people can be encouraged to become engaged with professionals if the services provided seek to meet all their needs and do not focus narrowly on risk factors alone (Morris et al., 2009).

Relationship, human judgement and the problem of certainty

So, forging a relationship, albeit under challenging conditions, is key to safe, humane practice, but there are particular features of our human sense-making apparatus which mean that, on its own, this relationship, may also be a source of error. In 2007, Peter Connelly (Baby P) a toddler aged 17 months, who was subject to a child protection plan supervised by the London Borough of Haringey Children and Young People's Service, was brutally killed having suffered months of abuse, while in the care of his mother, her boyfriend and their lodger. In her evidence to a UK House of Commons Select Committee on 15 September 2010, Sharon Shoesmith, the former Director of Haringey Children and Young People's Service who was sacked as a result of Peter's death, remarked:

> *I think one of the lasting issues of this case surrounds why all those professionals – police, doctors, consultants, nurses, health visitors and social workers – were caught in the trap of feeling that the mother was being genuine. Why did they not question that more? I think that has to be the overriding question ... I was in the room when the police officer came in and said that the mother had been charged with murder ... I was in the room when that happened and those who knew Peter Connelly and the mother were*

completely taken aback and said, 'That couldn't possibly be the case. You must have it wrong: this couldn't be the case.' That was their reaction, having known this person.

(www.publications.parliament.uk/pa/cm201011/cmselect/ cmeduc/465i/10091502.htm)

It would seem that the professionals involved in this case were distracted and misled precisely because they felt they *had* forged a good relationship with Peter's mother, who was, in reality, deceiving them.

The errors were exacerbated by other human factors. Human beings have particular cognitive biases. We tend to reach conclusions quickly and develop a 'psychological commitment' to our first formulation (Dowie and Elstein, 1988). This is confounded by a tendency to seek out evidence that confirms a hypothesis, rather than searching for 'disconfirming' evidence. This is known as 'confirmation bias' (Wolf et al., 1985). Peter Connelly was observed to be injured very frequently with a variety of bruises and bumps which became increasingly serious over time. However, Tracey Connelly, Peter's mother, alleged that he would frequently injure himself and had behavioural disturbances such as head banging, which were also observed by the social worker. A strong (but *wrong*) hypothesis thus took hold that Peter had a behavioural disorder. In his last few months of life, Peter's weight was falling dramatically. His father had also raised significant concerns and told agencies that Tracey Connelly had a new boyfriend. Many agencies were involved with Peter, but, as Sharon Shoesmith observed above, the different professionals seemed to be failing to notice or to respond to the deterioration in Peter's health and development and to act appropriately in relation to his injuries. Tracey Connelly had been apparently co-operative with services, frequently presenting Peter at the doctor's surgery for example, seeking help with what she said was his difficult behaviour. The serious case review conducted after Peter death notes:

> *There was too ready a willingness to believe Ms A's accounts of herself, her care of the children, the composition of the household, and the nature of her friendship network. The appropriate mode of relationship with the parent/carer should be at first an observing/assessing one; and where there are indications of possible harm a questioning and even sceptical one. Her account may well prove to be accurate when tested over time but at this stage it should have been assumed that it may be self serving. The danger is an over-identification with the service user in a wish to support and protect the child's place in the family. There was already reason to believe that she was not being truthful about the injuries to her child.*

(Department for Education, 2010: 28)

The intuitive judgements the professionals had made about Tracey Connelly's character, and their cognitive commitment to the 'behavioural disturbance' hypothesis, led them to pay insufficient attention to clear signs that Peter was being abused. So, humane practice is not just about getting along with people and having what appears to be an easy, conflict-free relationship. If we are to avoid the sort of catastrophic error that contributed to Peter Connelly's death, we need to understand the role that our relationships and feelings for and beliefs about other human beings play in our judgements and find a way to question and test them.

For a long time, emotions were seen as distinct from our capacity to reason. Emotions were things to be tamed, allowing reasoning to take place uncontaminated. There is now clear evidence that a good deal of 'rational' decision-making relies on our capacities as human beings to make sense of the world using our emotions (e.g. Damasio, 1994; Haidt, 2001; Printz, 2007). Apparently, we cannot do without our emotions.

> At their best, feelings point us in the proper direction, take us to the appropriate place in a decision-making space, where we may put the instruments of logic to good use.
>
> (Damasio, 1994: xiv–xv)

As co-operative *social* animals, we are equipped with abilities for making intuitive judgements about each other, often of a moral nature. Gut feelings are not impeccable guides to judgement but neither are they dumb and 'irrational'. They are not inferior to reason. they rely on the capacities of our evolved, social brain and exist to enable us to act quickly, often with a high degree of accuracy in many different situations (Gigerenzer, 2002).

However, our intuitive judgments are vulnerable to particular types of error and so critical debate with others is vital so that social workers, and indeed other professionals, learn to recognise and interrogate such biases and choose whether they feel they need to correct them – in this *particular* case, in these *individual* circumstances. We make judgements routinely about people we meet and we are usually rather good at them. If we were not, then the social order would quickly break down. Furthermore, when we make evaluations of others we tend to feel rather sure of ourselves (White, 2009; White and Stancombe, 2003). Intuitive reasoning produces a feeling of certainty – very comforting for social workers operating in highly ambiguous and uncertain territory!

When we pronounce that someone is cold, aloof, arrogant, shifty, kind, or genuine, the grounds for these feelings are not routinely interrogated, rather these properties seem self-evident – simply to be so. Social work practice takes place in the realm of human relationships, so it both relies on, and is at risk from, these feelings of certainty. When these evaluations are shared with others who have similar cultural norms to our own, we are likely to feel even more sure of ourselves. The intoxicating cocktail of unambiguous judgements about our fellow human beings, produced by our innate wiring, is more potent when taken in the company of like-minded friends. So, our judgements about other each other normally stay in the realm of what we think of as common sense (Green, 2000), and that is a problem for social work. A 'gut feeling' can make an individual particularly resistant to change or challenge (Payne and Bettman, 2007), especially if that gut feeling is masked by a 'technical' vocabulary, using, for example, psychological theory of one sort or another – so a 'cold' mother becomes re-described as a mother who has failed to bond with her child, but the judgement is made on intuitive grounds, not through systematic scientific observation and critical self-questioning.

The presence of other human actors in the right atmosphere of circumspection, challenge and debate may properly work to 'trouble' the intuitive reading of a case, but it will not do so unless the organisational cultures encourage this kind of critical questioning. Without such a culture we all too frequently remain in an unquestioning, comfortable collective settlement about the reality of a family's circumstances – which may often prove to be right, but is sometimes *strong but wrong*.

Our emotions and the social world, the cultures in which we live and work, are connected:

> *Because people are highly attuned to the emergence of group norms, the model proposes that the mere fact that friends, allies and acquaintances have made a moral judgement exerts a direct influence on others, even if no reasoned persuasion is used.*

> (Haidt, 2001: 819)

This means that the cultures in social work teams and the dominant ideas of the profession at a particular point in time will affect the emotional/intuitive responses of individual social workers. These tendencies are amplified still further when practitioners, like Ruth whose practice we examined at the beginning of this chapter, are under pressure to categorise and make decisions quickly, as Eraut notes:

> *The process of becoming a professional involves learning to handle cases quickly and efficiently, and this may be accomplished by reducing the range of possible ways of thinking about them to manageable proportions. This leads to intuitive reliance on certain communal practitioners' concepts*

> (Eraut, 1994: 43)

Social work is concerned with human relationships and at the same time relies on human relationships to get the job done. If social workers are to practise humanely, they will need to find ways to stand back and analyse their own thoughts and assumptions. For this, they need something more than good relationships, they need to become good social scientists.

Research for and as practice

> Research: n. *a careful search: investigation: systematic investigation towards increasing the sum of knowledge.*

> *(Chambers Dictionary)*

I have argued that humane practice requires relational skills, but also demands that social workers are able to stand back from their relationships. Research and research skills can help them to do this in three ways:

1. Social workers need to draw on published research studies to help them to understand individuals' and families' needs, matters of safety and risk, and to plan their interventions.

2. Social workers need to develop research skills, such as observation, synthesis of information and analysis, so that they can 'increase the sum of knowledge' about a particular set of circumstances

3. Social workers need to use research skills to examine their own assumptions and as a check on the essential but fallible intuitive judgements discussed above.

Hence, research is helpful *for* practice, but in many ways it also *is* practice.

Let us take the three aspects of research-minded practice in turn. Attending to the first point, it is important that published research findings are used appropriately. For example, they should not be consulted simply to shore up a set of assumptions a social worker has made about a case. This is a tendency I have observed in many pieces of work I have assessed on post-qualifying programmes, where the literature has been searched simply to find a paper, any old paper will do, which appears to confirm the social worker's own reading of a case. Rather, research should be consulted with the potential to generate new understandings or shake up old ones.

The second point in our list of research skills underscores the need for careful and systematic observation and data gathering. Working mechanically through a form, as Ruth, our novice social worker, felt compelled to do, is not likely on its own to yield very thorough understandings. Here is where the two aspects of humane practice – relationship and research – coalesce. A humane practitioner must show humility about their ability to 'know' a family's circumstances – a humility eloquently described below:

> As a social work student, I was confused by professional ways of talking, writing, analysing and describing people's lives ... Even after graduating and working as a front line social worker, I remained unable to muster the authority of my education and the power of my organizational mandate to make 'true' pronouncements, to produce unequivocal case 'facts' and to work with certainty and confidence in my authority and power. I remained confused by the worlds of my clients ... Perhaps it was my own sense of being confused, and thereby of being fallible, that continued to make me angry when I heard the pretentious authority and certainty that accompanied the pronouncements of experts and officials.
>
> (de Montigny, 1995: 5)

The third aspect of research mindedness postulates that, in order to practise with care and humility, it is important for social workers to attend to how their own work gets done in everyday situations. What is the impact of organisational procedure?

What kinds of analysis and thinking seem to dominate the team? How have I as an individual social worker tested my assumptions? Have I diligently undertaken the activities described under points one and two? If not, why not? Here, the way social work organisations function becomes a crucial factor.

Humane practice and the learning organisation

There have been some attempts to theorise about what characteristics an organisation should have to create the conditions for the sort of practice I have tried to promote above. The term 'organisational learning' was first coined by Argyris and Schön (1996) and the related notion of the 'learning organization' (Senge, 1990), has been defined as follows:

> *At the heart of a learning organization is a shift of mind – from seeing ourselves as separate from the world to connected to the world, from seeing problems as caused by someone, or something 'out there' to seeing how our actions create the problems we experience. A learning organization is a place where people are continually discovering how they create their reality. And how they can change it.*

(Senge, 1990: 12–13)

In our example at the beginning of this chapter, if Ruth had been working in a learning organisation, she would have been able to articulate her disquiet about conducting the assessment and perhaps to suggest that her colleague, who knew the case better, was the more appropriate person to undertake the work. The team may have been able to reflect on the reasons why the case had been re-referred, quickly assessed and closed so many times. In Senge's terms, these kinds of repetitive, but unhelpful organisational practices are known as defensive routines.

> *To retain their power, defensive routines **must remain undiscussable**. Teams stay stuck in their defensive routines only when they pretend that they don't have any defensive routines, that everything is all right, and that they can say 'anything'. But how to make them discussable is a challenge.*

(Senge, 1990: 255, original emphasis)

Social work has its defensive routines and, if our agencies are to become learning organisations, we are going to have to develop ways to make them visible. Research can help us to do this, by shaking up what we take for granted:

> *[T]here is a need for professionals to retain critical control over the more intuitive parts of their expertise by regular reflection, self-evaluation and a disposition to learn from colleagues. This implies from time to time treating apparently routine cases as problematic and making time to deliberate and consult. It is partly a matter of lifelong learning and partly a wise understanding of one's own fallibility.*

(Eraut, 1994: 155)

50

There is no doubt that these taken for granted dimensions of practice are often very difficult to extract and articulate, particularly perhaps for experienced practitioners. For this to take place there need to be spaces and places where reflection upon the everyday can take place. Activities like professional supervision provide essential opportunities to bring 'the learning organisation' to life, but the learning organisation needs more than this. An atmosphere of respectful dialogue and debate is necessary for humane practice. It shows us the fallibility of our own reasoning processes, it makes them discussable and hence makes error less likely. The last two decades in the UK have seen the dominance of rule-bound practice. There are signs that the tide is turning (Munro, 2011), but there is a long way to go and we wouldn't want to start from here. It is time to promote a 'just culture' (Dekker, 2007) in social work organisations, and this requires, at the very least, that practitioners are able to say when they think they have made, or may have made, mistakes, but it also requires us to recognise when our preferred ways of knowing, our habits and routines are themselves mistaken. For this, social workers must always be social scientists of their own domains.

REFLECTIVE QUESTIONS

1. *When did you last make a decision or perform an action which you felt was unhelpful to a family?*

2. *Think carefully about the 'root causes' which led you to make this decision or perform this action. For example, were you following procedures, were you limited by the range of available options and services?*

3. *How could you make these effects knowable to managers and others in the organisation?*

4. *What would have to change in your organisation for these things to be routinely debated?*

Broadhurst, K, White, S, Fish, S, Munro, E, Fletcher, K and Lincoln, H (2010) *Ten Pitfalls and How to Avoid Them: What Research Tells Us*, NSPCC Inform, **www.nspcc.org.uk/Inform/research/findings/tenpitfalls_wda78613.html**

Dekker, S (2007) *Just Culture: Balancing Safety and Accountability.* Aldershot: Ashgate.

Margolin, L (1997) *Under the Cover of Kindness: The Invention of Social Work.* Virginia: University Press of Virginia.

Argyris, C and Schön, D (1996) *Organizational Learning II: Theory, Method and Practice.* Reading, MA: Addison Wesley.

Birtwell, ML (1895) Investigation. *The Charities Review*, 4: 129–37.

Broadhurst, K and Holt, K (2009) Partnership and the Limits of Procedure: Prospects for Relationships Between Parents and Professionals under the New Public Law Outline. *Child & Family Social Work*, 15(1): 97–106.

Broadhurst, K, Wastell, D, White, S, Hall, C, Peckover, S, Thompson, K, Pithouse, A and Davey, D (2010a) Performing 'Initial Assessment': Identifying the Latent Conditions for Error at the Front-Door of Local Authority Children's Services. *British Journal of Social Work*, 40(2): 352–70.

Broadhurst, K, White, S, Fish, S, Munro, E, Fletcher, K and Lincoln, H (2010b) *Ten Pitfalls and How to Avoid Them: What Research Tells Us*, NSPCC Inform, **www.nspcc.org.uk/Inform/ research/findings/tenpitfalls_wda78613.html**

Damasio, AR (1994) *Descartes' Error: Emotion, Reason and the Human Brain*. New York: Avon Books.

Dekker, S (2007) *Just Culture: Balancing Safety and Accountability*. Aldershot: Ashgate.

de Montigny, G (1995) *Social Working: An Ethnography of Front Line Practice*. Toronto: University of Toronto Press.

Department for Education (2010) *Haringey Local Safeguarding Children Board, Serious Case Review 'Child A'*. Department for Education.

Dowie, J and Elstein, A (eds) (1988) *Professional Judgement: A Reader in Clinical Decision Making*. Cambridge: Cambridge University Press.

Eraut, M (1994) *Developing Professional Knowledge and Competence*. London: Falmer Press.

Folgheraiter, F (2004) *Relational Social Work: Toward Networking and Societal Practice*. London: JKP.

Gigerenzer, G (2002) *Reckoning with Risk*. London: Allen Lane, The Penguin Press.

Gilligan, P (2011) Decision Making Tools and the Development of Expertise in Child Protection Practitioners: Are We 'Just Breeding Workers Who are Good at Ticking Boxes'? *Child and Family Social Work*, 16(4): 412–21.

Green, J (2000) Epistemology, Evidence and Experience: Evidence Based Health Care in the Work of Accident Alliances. *Sociology of Health and Illness*, 22(4): 453–76.

Gutridge, AW (1905) Investigation. In *Proceedings of the National Conference of Charity and Correction*. Portland, OR: 359–62.

Haidt, J (2001) The Emotional Dog and its Rational Tail: A Social Intuitionist Approach to Moral Judgement. *Psychological Review*, 108(4): 814–34.

Hall, C, Parton, N, Peckover, S and White, S (2010) Child-centric ICTs and the Fragmentation of Child Welfare Practice in England. *Journal of Social Policy*, 39(3): 393–413.

Humphreys, C (1999) Avoidance and Confrontation: Social Work Practice in Relation to Domestic Violence and Child Abuse. *Child & Family Social Work*, 4(1): 77–87.

Kahneman, D, Sloveic, P and Tversky, A (1982) *Judgement under Uncertainty: Heuristics and Biases*. New York: Cambridge University Press.

Knei-Paz, C (2009) The Central Role of the Therapeutic Bond in a Social Agency Setting: Clients' and Social Workers' Perceptions. *Journal of Social Work*, 9(2): 178–98.

Margolin, L (1997) *Under the Cover of Kindness: The Invention of Social Work*. Virginia: University Press of Virginia.

Morris, K, Barnes, M and Mason, P (2009) *Children, Families And Social Exclusion: Developing New Understandings*. Bristol: The Policy Press.

Munro, E (2011) *The Munro Review of Child Protection: Final Report – A Child-centred System.* London: Department for Education.

Payne, J and Bettman, J (2007) Walking with the Scarecrow: The Information Processing Approach to Decision Research. In Koehler, D and Harvey, N (eds) *Blackwell Handbook of Judgment and Decision Making.* Oxford: Blackwell Publishing.

Printz, JJ (2007) *The Emotional Construction of Morals.* Oxford: Oxford University Press.

Senge, PM (1990) *The Fifth Discipline: The Art and Practice of the Learning Organization.* London: Century Business.

Stanley, J and Goddard, C (2002) *In the Firing Line: Violence and Power in Child Protection Work.* Chichester, West Sussex: Wiley.

Thoburn, J and members of the Making Research Count Consortium (2009) *Effective Interventions for Complex Families Where There Are Concerns About, or Evidence of, a Child Suffering Significant Harm,* **www.c4eo.org.uk/themes/safeguarding/files/safeguarding_ briefing_1.pdf**

White, S (2009) Fabled Uncertainty in Social Work: A Coda to Spafford et al. *Journal of Social Work,* 9(2): 222–35.

White, S, Hall, C and Peckover, S (2009) The Descriptive Tyranny of the Common Assessment Framework: Technologies of Categorization and Professional Practice in Child Welfare. *British Journal of Social Work,* 39(7): 1197–217.

White, S and Stancombe, J (2003) *Clinical Judgement in the Health and Welfare Professions: Extending the Evidence Base.* Maidenhead: Open University Press.

Wolf, FM, Gruppen, LD and Billi, JE (1985) Differential Diagnosis and Competing Hypotheses Heuristic: A Practical Approach to Judgement Under Uncertainty and Bayesian Probability. *Journal of American Medical Association,* 253: 2858–62.

Chapter 4

Understanding contemporary social work: we need to talk about relationships

Gillian Ruch

Introduction

The allusion in the title of this chapter is to the novel by Lionel Shriver, *We Need to Talk about Kevin*. The story comprises a series of letters from a mother to her ex-husband that address the challenging subject matter of their son who has grown up to commit a mass murder. In the novel Shriver tackles fundamental assumptions about motherhood and presents some challenging perspectives that are not always easy to digest. While the subject matter of this chapter – the relationships social workers establish with vulnerable people – is not quite as disturbing, it is nonetheless difficult, informed by firmly held and often unquestioned assumptions, and an aspect of our everyday lives that many would prefer to overlook. Much as Shriver's book challenges deeply held assumptions about motherhood and makes disturbing reading, this chapter seeks to unsettle some deeply embedded assumptions about what social work is and how it is conducted. In the course of the chapter I argue that effective social work requires approaches that prioritise practitioners developing realistic and holistic relationships with the individuals and families they encounter in everyday practice. Such a statement might seem self-evident but sadly the current state of affairs in the social work profession in the UK necessitates the centrality of relationships in social work practice being made explicit. For effective relationship-based practice to be realised requires us to honestly confront, not only difficult aspects of the behaviours and circumstances of those with whom we work, but also unpalatable dimensions of our own professional responses and stance. And this is not easy.

In order to understand the contemporary context and professional significance of relationship-based practice the chapter begins with a brief historical overview to explain how we have arrived at this point where the importance of relationships in professional context needs to be recovered. With this historical backdrop established, a theoretical framework for relationship-based practice is outlined which provides the context for an exploration of what is required of practitioners if they are to be effective in championing relationship-based approaches. In focusing on practice an emphasis is placed on the importance of thoughtful and feeling-ful interventions that are attentive to detail. Being mindful of affective responses and able to incorporate them into the practice encounter in the present moment – thinking on your feet or, as Schön (1983) refers to it, 'reflecting in action' – are fundamental skills practitioners need to develop if relationship-based practice is to take hold. The essence of relationship-based practice resides in such respectful responses to human encounters. The chapter concludes with suggestions for support mechanisms for practitioners that enhance the likelihood of them acquiring and maintaining these skills, underlining that realising the potential of relationship-based practice is contingent on practitioners being located in relationship-based organisational settings.

Where have we got to and how did we get here? Contemporary configurations of social work practice

At a conference on inter-professional working a social worker, in response to a presentation about policy developments and their impact on practice, outlined the following practice incident. A social work colleague was on annual leave and in her absence the team manager requested another team member who did not know the family (the social worker presenting this account) to undertake a routine visit with a police officer colleague to a family with two children who were subject to a child protection plan. During the allocated social worker's absence the children were monitored. They were attending school and also had been seen playing outside their home. There were no untoward concerns at the point at which the routine visit by the social worker and police officer was undertaken. On arrival at the home no one answered the door. The social worker attempted to contact his line manager, who was unavailable, for advice and guidance. The police officer rang his inspector who advised that they knock the door down to gain access, which they duly did. No one was at home.

The social worker outlining this practice incident described his feelings of disbelief about the way the circumstances had unfolded and escalated, of distress at having betrayed the family's trust, and of concern about the serious damage that had been done to the relationship of the allocated social worker with the family. How, in light of these excessive and violent interventions, could the social worker on her return from annual leave re-establish a meaningful relationship with this family? The incredulity in the audience on hearing this account was palpable. The incident powerfully illustrates how, in a relatively short space of time, practice has evolved. Where once the care–control dichotomy that is an integral component of social work practice would have been weighted towards the 'caring' end of the continuum, it is now much more aligned with the 'controlling' aspects of practice, characterised by authoritative, potentially or actually aggressive, and punitive behaviours that appear to disregard the vulnerable circumstances in which people find themselves. We need to have the conversations, much as take place in Shriver's novel, to explore and understand how this set of affairs that we are deeply implicated in has developed, in order to tackle the unpalatable aspects of professional social work that appear to be burgeoning in the current social and political climate. Unless we face these dark, shadow sides of our professional existence, both the unbearable circumstances of service users and our unexpected, often undesirable, professional responses to them, we run the risk of them becoming increasingly pervasive as they are allowed to grow unchecked and unchallenged.

An incidental conversation with an academic colleague (Sue White, personal communication), in which she commented on the shift she had observed in local authority social work responses to incidents of domestic violence, served to reinforce to me that the preceding incident was not unrepresentative of contemporary practice dynamics. As a practitioner in the 1980s Sue remembered visiting women who were experiencing domestic violence and how it was common practice to adopt a supportive, 'caring' professional position, that both acknowledged the complex dynamics in such relationships and endeavoured to empower and enable the women concerned to find a way out of their difficult situation. In contrast, her observations of contemporary responses to similar situations were of practitioners adopting an authoritative stance which essentially threatened the removal of children if the mother did not 'sort the situation out'. These responses, she noted, appeared to lack compassion and placed the responsibility for resolving the difficulties being encountered squarely on the shoulders of the vulnerable women. What has happened to escalate the circumstances of everyday social work to such a level that these kinds of disproportionate reactive responses are not uncommon in frontline practice?

While there has been a complex web of social, political and economic forces at work over the past two decades, at its simplest these current configurations of professional practice can be understood as a response to the growing societal awareness of the impact of risk and uncertainty on social structures and behaviours and the emergence of what has become known as New Public Management, with its concomitant understandings of how people function (Broadhurst et al., 2010; Parton, 2008; Power, 2004; Warner and Sharland, 2010). Adopted from the world of private business, New Public Management is premised on enhancing efficiency, effectiveness and economy through the application of performance management strategies that involve high levels of surveillance, inspection and regulation (Skinner, 2010). Embedded within these foundational principles is an understanding of human behaviour that privileges cognition, rationality and predictability and marginalises the emotional, irrational and unpredictable dimensions of human beings. It is this restrictive perspective on human behaviour that enables vulnerable individuals to be naively construed as consumers, and practitioners as service commissioners or providers. Both configurations ignore the affective dimensions of human beings and the powerful and often profound impact of emotion on the encounters and exchanges that take place. They allow for the operation of rationally determined, economically driven transactions, with no reference to the vulnerabilities and often understandably irrational responses of the individuals concerned (both service users *and* practitioners) to difficult and distressing circumstances. This stance stands in stark contrast to the holistic understanding of human beings that is integral to professional social work practice (Ruch, 2005, 2010). It is the tension between these seemingly incompatible professional and managerialist understandings of social work that is shaping contemporary practice and accounts for the practice scenarios outlined above.

Relationship-based approaches to social work practice seek to unsettle the prevailing orthodoxies about how people behave to allow for consideration of the affective dimensions of human behaviour. We all enter social work with a mixture of motivations, but invariably embedded within them is a deep-seated desire to 'help people' and to 'make a difference'. While not wishing to diminish the importance of these ideals, for professional motivation to be sustained and effective professional practice realised requires practitioners to develop the capacity to acknowledge their ambivalence towards vulnerable people and entrenched social problems. Such ambivalence can be identified by the internal, private conversations and judgemental thoughts we all on occasions, I would suggest, harbour about people 'bringing their situation on themselves', or needing to 'accept their circumstances' and 'get on with it'. The inherently unpredictable and messy nature of emotional responses to human circumstances, particularly in challenging or distressing situations, makes it quite understandable why rational models of professional practice, that allow practitioners to overlook the more difficult aspects of life, are attractive. It is for these reasons that the emphasis of this chapter is on the need to talk about relationships, so that we can fully engage with their complexity and our ambivalence about them. Indeed this recognition of the multi-faceted dimension of relationships highlights the need for these conversations to be even more specifically focused – we need to talk psycho-socially about relationships. What does this mean and how might we do it?

What is relationship-based practice? A theoretical framework

It is a cliché to state that there is nothing new under the sun, but it is certainly true that relationship-based practice is by no means an entirely 'new' conceptual framework for social work. Rather it builds on existing psycho-dynamically informed approaches, most notably the psycho-social model associated with Hollis (1964), and updates it in response to wider developments in social, political and cultural understanding. In particular relationship-based practice has sought to respond to critics of the psycho-social approach who considered it to be pathologising of service users and biased towards the expertise of the professional. With the emergence in the 1980s of anti-oppressive perspectives these criticisms gained momentum and the subsequent demise of relational approaches to social work can be attributed to these conceptual developments.

As a consequence the contemporary configuration of relationship-based practice has incorporated an anti-oppressive dimension which seeks to make more transparent the power dynamics that are integral to all professional exchanges. In so doing it acknowledges the distinctive, but equally valuable, perspectives that service users and practitioners bring to the professional relationship. Alongside this particular feature of the relationship-based approach being advocated here, the following characteristics are core ingredients:

- Human behaviours and the professional relationship are an integral component of any professional intervention.

- Human behaviour is complex and multifaceted. People are not simply rational beings but have affective (both conscious and unconscious) dimensions that enrich but simultaneously complicate human relationships.

- The internal and external worlds of individuals are inseparable, so integrated (psychosocial), as opposed to one-dimensional, responses to social problems are crucial for social work practice.

- Each social work encounter is unique, and attention must be paid to the specific circumstances of each individual.

- A collaborative relationship is the means through which interventions are channelled, and this requires a particular emphasis to be placed on the 'use of self'.

- The respect for individuals embedded in relationship-based practice involves practising in inclusive and empowering ways (Ruch, 2010).

When referring to a relationship-based approach it is all too easy to fall into the trap of perceiving it with the warm cosy glow conventionally associated with the term 'relationship' and adopting a 'rose-tinted spectacles' perspective that overlooks the harsh realities of practice that working with people in vulnerable and distressing situations encompasses. It is precisely because of these 'harsh realities' that an holistic and realistic relationship-based approach is so important if we are to avoid the perverse sorts of practice outlined earlier. Practitioners need to be willing and able to engage with the whole range of emotional challenges that social work encompasses and have the professional wherewithal to withstand their impact.

What do relationship-based practitioners look like? Identifying professional competencies and capabilities

To date empirical research into relationship-based practice is negligible and an aspect of practice ripe for further research. One notable exception is a Canadian research study which explored 'good helping relationships' in the field of child protection (the Canadian child protection context being broadly comparable with the UK context) (de Boer and Coady, 2007). The study identified two broad categories of professional qualities that service users (parents) and practitioners considered to be central to the creation and maintenance of effective helping relationships – the soft, judicious use of power and a humanistic attitude and style that stretches traditional professional ways of being.

According to de Boer and Cody (2007), the soft, mindful and judicious use of power includes:

- *being aware of one's own power and the normalcy of client fear, defensiveness and anger;*
- *responding to client negativity with understanding and support instead of counter hostility and coercion;*
- *conveying a respectful and non-judgemental attitude;*
- *providing clear and honest explanations about reasons for involvement;*
- *addressing fears of child apprehension and allying unrealistic fears;*
- *not pre-judging the veracity of intake, referral or file information;*
- *listening to and empathising with the client's story;*
- *pointing out strengths and conveying respect;*
- *constantly clarifying information to ensure mutual understanding;*
- *exploring and discussing concerns before jumping to conclusions;*
- *responding in a supportive manner to new disclosures, relapses and new problems;*
- *following through on one's responsibilities and promises.*

The humanistic attitude and style that stretches traditional professional ways of being includes:

- *using a person-to-person, down-to-earth manner (versus donning the professional mask);*
- *engaging in small talk to establish comfort and rapport;*
- *getting to know the client as a whole person – in social and life history context;*
- *seeing and relating to the client as an ordinary person with understandable problems;*
- *recognising and valuing the client's strengths and successes in coping;*
- *being realistic about goals and patient about progress;*

(Continued)

(Continued)

- *having a genuinely hopeful/optimistic outlook on possibilities for change;*
- *using judicious self-disclosure towards developing personal connection;*
- *being real in terms of feeling the client's pain and displaying emotions;*
- *going the extra mile in fulfilling mandated responsibilities, stretching professional mandates and boundaries.*

On reviewing these two broad categories and the specific qualities encompassed within each of them it is possible to identify two professional skills that practitioners need to acquire if they are to effectively practise in ways that are capable of generating good helping relationships: firstly, the capacity to observe and engage with intimate and uncomfortable physical and emotional experiences (their own as well as those of others); secondly, their ability to think emotionally and to feel thoughtfully. In so doing practitioners will be developing a range of professional competencies – vulnerability, a 'not knowing' stance, compassion – that are currently under-recognised within, or even absent from, the existing professional competency model of professional development and from the newly devised professional capabilities framework currently being introduced under the auspices of the College of Social Work in England (www.collegeofsocialwork.org/pcf.aspx).

Learning to observe

Relationship-based practice requires us to engage holistically with not only all aspects of the functioning of vulnerable individuals but also all aspects of our own professional behaviours and responses. This is not easy to do as it requires us to confront aspects of others, and more particularly of ourselves, that are not always palatable or expected. In his policy paper *The Heroic and the Stoical* Tim Dartington provides a painful, but insightful, vignette of the needs of an elderly woman being misunderstood.

> *Barbara tries to get up out of her chair. She flops down in her chair but later tries to get up again. She manages to stand up just when a carer comes in and says, 'Sit down Barbara, you'll break your back'. Barbara sits immediately. The carer leaves. Barbara tries again. Another carer comes in and says to Barbara, 'Sit down or you'll fall'. Once again Barbara tries. The carer says impatiently, 'Sit down! What's the matter with you?' and then, looking more closely, as though talking to a naughty child, 'Oh you've gotten yourself wet.' The carer brings a wheelchair and takes Barbara away. (From an observation of the day room in a dementia unit, reported by Paul Terry, Working with Old People conference, 2006.)*

(Dartington, 2012: 6)

It is not that Barbara's circumstances are ignored. This interaction is neit... intentionally abusive nor deliberately neglectful, but Barbara's circumstances are inadequately observed and attended to, resulting in her experiencing avoidable humiliation and distress. Such examples are commonplace in the accounts of infant observation where young children in daycare settings who have similarly wet themselves frequently go unnoticed by staff for considerable periods of time, as their attention is on other, often less child-centred, activities, for example, making items to go on wall displays. Such oversights raise important questions about how daycare institutions, whether for the elderly or young, prioritise what staff do and how they train staff to notice the needs of individuals. Clearly the prospect of changing nappies or wiping bottoms on a daily basis is not an attractive proposition and it is not difficult to see how alternative tasks get prioritised over those associated with our fundamental human dependency needs. The focus in a number of recent enquiries into shortcomings in the care system has been on the failure of professionals to adequately feed patients and service users and poignantly reinforces this point in relation to help with toileting, another equally fundamental, but perhaps less palatable, human need.

Social workers, as opposed to social care workers, are less likely to find themselves involved in this level of intimate personal care, but this capacity to attend to the detailed interactions and experiences of individuals is pivotal to being an effective relationship-based practitioner. Recent tragedies in childcare social work are, in part, attributable to the inability of practitioners (for all the reasons outlined here) to see what was in front of them (Cooper, 2005; Department of Health, 2002). It is the attention paid to this level of detail that is central to relationship-based approaches and that enables practitioners to see and relate to individuals as ordinary people with understandable problems and to demonstrate the empathic responses that de Boer and Coady (2007) identify as important for good helping relationships. Unless we can tolerate understanding what it feels like to be vulnerable and dependent we cannot begin to conceptualise and operationalise our professional roles accurately, respectfully or effectively. Developing such observational skills requires practitioners to adopt a disciplined and unfamiliar approach to learning. It requires them, in the first instance, to learn to 'be' rather than to 'do'. Learning to 'be' increases the likelihood of more accurately observed and fully informed interventions that are responsive to and respectful of the specific needs of an individual. The current shifts in the configuration and curriculum of qualifying and post-qualifying social work programmes provide fertile terrain for promoting relationship-based practice through the development of modules that incorporate observational learning (Le Riche and Tanner, 1998; Miller et al., 1989; Ruch, 2007a).

Thinking emotionally and feeling thoughtfully

Associated with this need for attentiveness to detail is the capacity to tolerate the reactions that vulnerability, dysfunction, distress and dependency create in us. Learning to observe requires us to tolerate the thoughts and feelings elicited by distressing situations, which can be surprising and run contrary to the ideals that are frequently articulated as the motivating factors in taking up the social work profession. The motivations for entering a caring profession referred to earlier – our desire to help people, to empower individuals, or even more ambitiously our wish to make the world a better place – are unequivocally laudable. At the same time we cannot afford to overlook, as the practice scenarios vividly illustrate, the impact of the shadow sides of professional practice, by which I mean the less altruistic, less tolerant aspects of our psychological make-up which can be powerfully and often unexpectedly triggered by exposure to human vulnerability and dependency needs. Practitioners need to be able to demonstrate the paradoxical quality of competent vulnerability, that is the capacity to know what they don't know and to acknowledge what they find unbearable and intolerable. Unless we can explore our limitations and our less acceptable traits, we run the risk of denying and repressing them, only to discover them being displaced and re-emerging in potentially more perverse and damaging ways. Acceptance that we can be repulsed by the living conditions of someone with mental health problems or judgmental of the actions of a perpetrator of sexual abuse, for example, is part and parcel of developing a relationship-based approach. To deny these reactions is to deny the full humanity with which we are all endowed.

Alongside our capacity to judge others or to defend ourselves against the emotional demands of practice, we need to recognise how as practitioners we can become unhelpfully caught up in the lived experience of individuals who are encountering difficulties. Parkinson's (2010) account of working with service users who are experiencing depression and hopelessness vividly recognises the emotionally demanding nature of such work. She acutely captures the importance of attending to the detail of interactions in order to avoid becoming drawn into the depression and hopelessness being experienced and to be able to empathise with and accurately respond to the circumstances service users find themselves in.

> *Social workers are drawn to empathise with service users. Learning about the importance of empathy and how to differentiate empathy from sympathy is an early aspect of most social work training. To empathise with someone who is themselves feeling desperate requires preparedness from the practitioner to be alive to a burdensome, suffering state of mind. It is no small matter to commit to maintaining contact with a person who is in anguish for the length of time that this is helpful to them.*

> (Parkinson, 2010: 118)

She goes on to say:

> *If a social worker can be helped to make their own sense of the possible origins of feelings of hopelessness, depression and despair, he or she is less likely to jump into pathologising or labelling a depressed service user and more likely to set out to establish a therapeutic relationship with them. Although someone prone to depression is not usually in a depressed state all of the time, social*

workers need to expect and be ready to work with periodic recurrences of depression, along with the intense disappointment and sense of failure that these may bring both to the service user and to those who are trying to help.

(Parkinson, 2010: 119)

In particular, Parkinson underlines the need to be not only mindful of what is said in encounters but how it is said, a skill that embraces the two core relationship-based characteristics highlighted here – the ability to think emotionally and to observe accurately.

A dimension of professional relationships that has received less attention, but one that equally needs to be carefully and emotionally thought about, is the capacity to over-identify positively with service users. Turney (2010) in her exploration of how practitioners, in their relationships with service users, negotiate the boundary between intimacy and professional distance poses an important question:

... But are relationships which appear to be working well subject to the same scrutiny? This may seem a strange question, but an absence of attention to 'good' working relationships and interactions with 'cooperative' service users may mean that we fail to recognise situations where the positive aspects of the relationship have become almost a hindrance – when they can perhaps be too much of a good thing, which may then distract the worker and distort the work.

(Turney, 2010: 134)

In order to minimise the professional hazards associated with professional relationships practitioners need to develop the capacity for emotionally informed thinking by paying attention to the thoughts and the feelings that are generated by practice encounters. The literature on emotional intelligence (Goleman, 1996; Howe, 2008; Morrison, 2007) is helpful in outlining the interrelated nature of thoughts and feelings, and the work of the psychoanalyst Wilfrid Bion is particularly instructive in this regard. For Bion (1962), thinking and feeling were inextricably interlinked. In order for infants to develop their full developmental potential it was crucial they had adequate 'containers' (carers) who could help them process the normal but powerful, primitive feelings of early development associated with being hungry, tired, afraid etc. In the absence of such containers emotional responses are experienced as overwhelming and other aspects of the infant's development, most notably their cognitive capabilities, risk being impaired as a consequence. You only have to observe a parent sensitively responding to a baby who is crying inconsolably and making what is unbearable to the baby bearable, to see containment in action. Equally, social workers are often exposed to the painful encounters of parents who are unable to offer such a containing experience to their infant, often because they themselves have been inadequately contained and lack the resources to model it for their own child. When translated into the domain of social work practice it is possible to see how Bion's ideas can also apply to practitioners, who when facing uncertain, unfamiliar, potentially hostile circumstances need to resort to external safe containing spaces, for example supervision, or internalised ones, such as the reflective space associated with the skills of reflective practice, in order to be able to respond accurately and empathically (Bower, 2003, 2005; Ruch, 2005, 2007b). The incapacity to tolerate difficult circumstances and the feelings associated with them, creates the risk of these feelings being 'acted out' rather than 'thought about'. For both service users and practitioners safe spaces where such potentially destructive feelings can be confronted in a thoughtful manner are crucial for balanced psychological (and professional) development and the promotion of constructive behaviours that derive from it.

This does not make for easy reading as none of us likes to admit to our frailties and shortcomings, but unless we do so our professional competence and capacity to practise in relationship-based ways will be impaired. Rather than perceiving vulnerability as weakness, however, these insights can inform how the newly constructed professional capabilities framework (referred to earlier) that is being introduced in England for assessing and facilitating social workers' professional development across their career trajectory, is interpreted and operationalised. To engage with the difficult issues that social work encompasses requires tenacity, honesty and vulnerability, professional characteristics that need to be seen as integral to the new framework. From this somewhat unorthodox perspective, vulnerability can be construed as an important thoughtful and emotionally intelligent professional capability that contributes to the development of relationship-based practice and robust professional capabilities.

There is a rapidly growing interest too in mindfulness within the human service professions (Duncan and Bardacke, 2010; Williams et al., 2007). Mindfulness in mental health contexts is being widely promoted as an effective intervention for people suffering with depression. As an approach that advocates the benefits of meditation, mindfulness is in keeping with core ingredients of relationship-based practice with its emphasis on being present to the dynamics of the moment and on the ability of practitioners to reflect in action in order to respond to these dynamics in the here-and-now. Developing self-awareness through mindfulness, as well as promoting mindful practice for the benefit of others, is a very current and immediate configuration of relationship-based practice that is worth exploring further.

How can we promote it? Supporting and sustaining relationship-based practice

Within psychodynamic theoretical circles it is widely recognised that our capacity to respond empathically is dependent on the extent to which we have experienced empathy (Bower, 2005). This notion of mirroring experiences is well established within social work thinking but all too often under-represented in everyday education and practice. Mattinson's seminal study on reflection processes in supervision, first published in 1975 and still entirely relevant today, explores how within the supervision process practitioners are inclined to re-enact the dynamics of the practice encounter they are discussing. Being alert to these unconscious exchanges is the responsibility of competent supervisors and a skill which enables them to effectively act as containers, that protect and promote the well-being of practitioners.

In light of these well-established understandings of practice dynamics it is not an overstatement to claim that the existence of relationship-based practice is contingent on practitioners experiencing relationship-based organisational contexts. Practitioners need 'safe spaces' in which they can confidentially expose their professional frailties in order to allow them to develop their vulnerable competence and draw on all their relational resources in the best interests of the individuals and families with whom they work. An example of such a model is reflective case discussions (Ruch, 2007b). Once again these are by no means an entirely new phenomenon, but build on the work discussion models of the Tavistock Centre (Rustin and Bradley, 2008) and the reflective teams familiar in systems therapy. In essence these forums provide a space in which a practitioner can present a current practice preoccupation to a group of peers and then observe the group discussing the issue. The ground rules of the model encourage the group to engage in a dialogue that is curious about what is and is not said and how it is said. How the presenter and the group conduct themselves – that is, the process – is considered as informative as the content of the discussion, and the overall aim is not to problem-solve but to provide the presenter with multiple perspectives on the issue in order for them to come to a more informed decision about how they will subsequently act. In keeping with the unorthodox professional characteristic of vulnerable competence referred to earlier, this model encourages such professional vulnerability and construes it as a strength as opposed to a professional shortcoming.

Concluding thoughts

It is not unreasonable to suggest that relationships with service users are the essence of social work and, therefore, social work would not exist if it were not relationship based. What I have sought to explore in this chapter, however, is that what is meant by a 'relationship-based' approach, and the effectiveness (or otherwise) of a relationship-based model of social work, depends on how the nature of relationships is understood. It is only by embracing all aspects of human behaviour within a relationship-based approach that such a framework for professional practice will resonate with the realities that practitioners face on a daily basis. That this is not easy to do has been reiterated throughout the chapter. But, going full circle, we need to keep talking about the challenges that relationships present us with, in the practice contexts of supervision, reflective case discussion forums, informal collegial conversations and in academic contexts such as this chapter, in order to keep our thinking alive and open to the complexity and richness of which interpersonal relationships are composed.

RECOMMENDED FURTHER READING

Bower, M (ed) (2005) *Psychoanalytic Theory for Social Work Practice: Thinking Under Fire.* Abingdon: Routledge.

Howe, D (2008) *The Emotionally Intelligent Social Worker.* Basingstoke: Palgrave.

Ruch, G, Turney, D and Ward, A (2010) *Relationship-based Social Work: Getting to the Heart of Practice.* London: Jessica Kingsley.

REFERENCES

Bion, W (1962) *Learning from Experience.* London: Heinemann.

Bower, M (2003) Broken and Twisted. *Journal of Social Work Practice*, 17(2): 143–52.

Bower, M (2005) Psychoanalytic Theory for Social Work Practice. In Bower, M (ed) *Psychoanalytic Theory for Social Work Practice: Thinking Under Fire.* Abingdon: Routledge: 3–14.

Broadhurst, K, Hall, C, Wastell, D, White, S and Pithouse, A (2010) Risk, Instrumentalism and the Humane Project in Social Work: Identifying the Informal Logics of Risk Management in Children's Statutory Services. *British Journal of Social Work*, 40(4): 352–70.

Cooper, A (2005) Surface and Depth in the Victoria Climbié: Inquiry Report. *Child and Family Social Work*, 10(1): 1–10.

Dartington, T (2010) *Managing Vulnerability: The Underlying Dynamics of Systems of Care.* London: Karnac.

Dartington, T (2012) *The Heroic and the Stoical: The Integration of Health and Social Care.* London: Tavistock Centre.

De Boer, C and Coady, N (2007) Good Helping Relationships in Child Welfare: Learning from Stories of Success. *Children and Family Social Work*, 12(1): 32–42.

Department of Health (2002) *The Victoria Climbié Inquiry.* London: The Stationery Office.

Duncan, L and Bardacke, N (2010) Mindfulness-Based Child Birth and Parenting: Promoting Family Mindfulness During the Perinatal Period. *Journal of Child and Family Studies*, 19(2): 190–202.

Goleman, D (1996) *Emotional Intelligence: Why it Can Matter More than IQ.* London: Bloomsbury.

Hollis, F (1964) *A Psycho-Social Therapy.* New York: Random House.

Howe, D (2008) *The Emotionally Intelligent Social Worker.* Basingstoke: Palgrave.

Le Riche, P and Tanner, K (eds) (1998) *Observation and its Application to Social Work: Rather Like Breathing.* London: Jessica Kingsley.

Mattinson, J (1992) *The Reflection Process in Casework Supervision* (2nd edition). London: Tavistock Institute of Medical Psychology. (Originally published 1975.)

Miller, L, Rustin, M, Rustin, M and Shuttleworth, J (eds) (1989) *Closely Observed Infants*. London: Duckworth.

Morrison, T (2007) Emotional intelligence, Emotion and Social Work: Context, Characteristics, Complications and Contribution. *British Journal of Social Work*, 37(2): 245–63.

Parkinson, C (2010) Sustaining Relationships: Working with Strong Feelings II: Hopelessness, Depression and Despair. In Ruch, G, Turney, D and Ward, A (eds) *Relationship-based Social Work: Getting to the Heart of Practice*. London: Jessica Kingsley Publishers.

Parton, N (2008) Changes in the Form of Knowledge in Social Work: From the 'Social' to the 'Informational'. *British Journal of Social Work*, 38(2): 253–69.

Power, M (2004) *The Risk Management of Everything: Rethinking the Politics of Uncertainty*. London: Demos.

Ruch, G (2005) Relationship-based Practice and Reflective Practice: Holistic Approaches to Contemporary Child Care Social Work. *Child and Family Social Work*, 10(2): 111–23.

Ruch, G (2007a) 'Knowing', Mirroring and Containing: Experiences of Facilitating Child Observation Seminars on a Post-Qualification Child Care Programme. *Social Work Education*, 26(2): 169–84.

Ruch, G (2007b) 'Thoughtful' Practice in Child Care Social Work: The Role of Case Discussion. *Child and Family Social Work*, 12(4): 370–9.

Ruch, G (2007c) Reflective Practice in Contemporary Child-care Social Work: The Role of Containment. *British Journal of Social Work*, 37(4): 659–80.

Ruch, G (2010) The Contemporary Context of Relationship-based Practice. In Ruch, G, Turney, D and Ward, A (eds) *Relationship-based Social Work: Getting to the Heart of Practice*. London: Jessica Kingsley Publishers.

Rustin, M and Bradley, J (eds) (2008) *Work Discussion: Learning from Reflective Practice in Work with Children and Families*. London: Karnac.

Schön, D (1983) *The Reflective Practitioner*. New York: Jossey Bass.

Shriver, L (2003) *We Need to Talk about Kevin*. New York: Counterpoint.

Skinner, K (2010) Supervision, Leadership and Management: Think Piece. In van Zwanenberg, Z (ed) *Leadership in Social Care*. London: Jessica Kingsley.

Trevithick, P (2003) Effective Relationship-based Practice: A Theoretical Exploration. *Journal of Social Work Practice*, 17(2): 163–76.

Turney, D (2010) Sustaining Relationships: Working with Strong Feelings III: Love and Positive Feelings. In Ruch, G, Turney, D and Ward, A (eds) *Relationship-based Social Work: Getting to the Heart of Practice*. London: Jessica Kingsley Publishers.

Warner, J and Sharland, E (2010) Editorial. *British Journal of Social Work*, 40(4): 1035–45.

Williams, M, Teasdale, J, Zindel, S and Kabat-Zinn, J (2007) *The Mindful Way through Depression: Freeing Yourself from Chronic Unhappiness*. New York: Guilford Press.

Chapter 5

The emotionally competent professional

Neil Thompson

Introduction

Social work involves working with people in distress and difficulties, people who have perhaps been traumatised by abuse or other life experience, people who have encountered major loss, suffering and pain. In addition there can be immense feelings of alienation and disaffection rooted in social inequalities and the discrimination and oppression associated with them. It would therefore be extremely naive not to recognise that there is a strong emotional component to social work.

It would also be naive not to recognise that, as professionals, we bring our own emotional issues into our work. The idea of the 'objective' professional as someone who can leave their feelings at the office door as they arrive for work is, of course, not one that is tenable in reality. Social work is, by its very nature, a challenging occupation (Thompson, 2009a), and we must count among the challenges being able to deal effectively with the emotional elements involved. Failure to do so can mean that our interventions are insensitive and therefore potentially counterproductive or even oppressive, and that our own emotional needs go unmet, potentially resulting in significant problems for us – stress, burnout, anxiety, depression or any combination of these.

This chapter therefore explores what is involved in the emotional challenges of social work. In particular, it relates these to what it means to be a professional, particularly in terms of what I shall refer to as the 'new professionalism', and the emotional implications of that. The concept of 'emotional competence' will be introduced and its significance explored. This will lead to a consideration of the 'three Rs' and how each of these relates to the emotional challenges of social work. Finally, there will be a discussion of the crucial role of self-care – exposing ourselves to high levels of emotionality without proper strategies in place for protecting ourselves is a very dangerous and foolhardy undertaking.

The chapter will not provide easy answers or formula solutions. As Howe comments: 'We are creatures saturated by feelings' (2008: 1). Emotions are part and parcel of being human, part of the existential territory we occupy and the existential challenges we face. Emotion is not some form of illness or pathology for which we should seek a cure. Rather, it is a dimension of how we relate to other people and how we relate to ourselves (or, more specifically, our sense of self – how we maintain a coherent identity). It is therefore something we need to wrestle with throughout our lives, not something that can be resolved once and for all. There are, however, strategies that can help us in this regard, and the need to develop our own strategies is a key message of this chapter.

Emotional challenges

Emotions are traditionally thought of as psychological phenomena, with a strong biological basis. However, this can be misleading, as it neglects other, equally important aspects of emotion, namely the sociological and the spiritual (or existential). As Fineman puts it, emotions are: 'intersubjective, a product of the way systems of meaning are created and negotiated between people' (2000a: 2). Parkinson et al. reinforce the need to adopt a broad perspective on understanding emotion when they argue that:

> *Although emotions are often seen as intensely personal experiences, it also seems clear that most of them have an intimate relationship to other people's thoughts, words, and deeds and bring direct consequences for how social life proceeds. Further, our position within groups, subcultures, and the broader society helps to determine our emotional outlook on the world.*

> (2005: 2)

So, what constitutes an emotional challenge? I would identify the following as important examples of what can reasonably be interpreted as emotional challenges within the context of this broader, more holistic understanding of emotion:

- *Anxiety:* Although anxiety is not contagious in a literal sense, if we are not careful, being exposed to other people's anxieties can make us feel anxious too. In addition, if we approach the demands of social work in an unconfident way and without the appropriate supports in place, then we can find ourselves becoming anxious in our own right. Here a vicious circle can develop in which our own anxiety can make our client(s) more anxious, while also making us more prone to being caught up in their anxiety. Being able to manage anxiety (our own and other people's) is therefore an important part of the social worker's repertoire.

- *Depression:* Depression can be similar, in the sense that the feelings of hopelessness and helplessness that characterise depression can also drag us down. In social work we are likely to encounter depressed people fairly often even if we do not specialise in the mental health field. The challenge is to be able to work towards lifting the depressed person's spirits (carefully, sensitively and at their pace), rather than allowing their low spirits to have an adverse effect on us.

- *Aggression:* Sadly it is not uncommon for social workers to encounter verbal abuse and aggression. Such situations are likely to generate a fight or flight response as a result of our bodies pumping adrenaline into our blood stream to prepare us for responding to the perceived threat. Thankfully, most aggression does not lead to actual violence, but our bodies do not know that and react accordingly. This can leave us feeling tense and agitated and therefore prone to reacting rashly and unwisely. We therefore have to make sure that we are able to train ourselves to respond to such situations as calmly as we can, difficult though that may be.

- *Grief:* Grief is a very powerful phenomenon that can generate very intense emotions and therefore significant challenges (Thompson, 2012a). Working with someone who is deep in the thrall of grief can: (i) leave us feeling overwhelmed by the sheer intensity of the experience; and (ii) open up old wounds of our own. When working with grief we therefore need to make sure that we have access to appropriate support, what Schneider (2012) calls a 'healing community'.

- *Emotional overload:* At times we can face a situation where we are encountering different emotions from different directions (and, of course, we will not be free of emotions coming to us from our personal lives outside of work), all combining to produce a sense of emotional overload – just too many emotional plates to keep spinning. Once again, this is a time when support can be significant and we should not be afraid to ask for it.

- *Mind games:* Unfortunately, some clients and carers can play 'mind games' at times, by which I mean they can attempt to manipulate situations by playing on our heart strings – for example, trying to evoke pity; testing our patience; and/or trying to get 'under our skin'. We therefore need to be aware of this possibility and make sure that we do not allow ourselves to be naive enough to be taken in by such games. 'Disguised compliance' (Reder et al., 1993) in a safeguarding context in children's services would be a further example.

This is by no means an exhaustive list, but it should paint a sufficiently vivid picture to clarify that we need to take the emotional dimension of social work very seriously and be alert to the challenges involved and the potential dangers associated with it.

Developing the new professionalism

Traditional professionalism is characterised by a hierarchical relationship ('doctor's orders') and an assumption that the professional's expertise holds the answers. This type of professionalism was at one time associated with UK social work until the radical social work movement presented a major critique of how disempowering such a relationship is likely to be. Unfortunately, this much needed critique produced a period of anti-professionalism, rather than a new professionalism that avoided the problems of the traditional elitist approach while retaining a commitment to the positive aspects of professionalism (see Thompson, 2009b, for a detailed discussion of this).

The 'new professionalism', however, is intended to be a means of reaffirming the positives of professionalism while avoiding a reliance on elitist assumptions. In an earlier work, I argued that professionalism can, and should be, rooted in partnership and empowerment (Thompson, 2007) and this was further developed in Thompson (2009b). It is worth exploring these two key concepts in a little more detail:

- *Partnership:* Traditional ideas of professionalism are based on a hierarchical power relationship. It is as if the client has the questions and problems and the professional, with his or her expertise and access to resources, has the answers and solutions. The expectation, according to this model, is that the role of the client is a fairly passive one, submissive even. Clearly such a model is incompatible with the social work value of working in partnership, which emphasises the importance of participation and involvement and an active role in shared planning, goal setting and working towards achieving those goals (or 'outcomes', to use the current parlance).

- *Empowerment:* A significant danger with the traditional model of professionalism is that it can encourage passivity and thus dependency. This is inconsistent with the traditional social work value of self-determination and the more recent emphasis on empowerment as part of the development of anti-discriminatory practice (Thompson, 2012b). Unfortunately, empowerment is a term that is often misunderstood and oversimplified. For example, it is often assumed to involve professionals 'giving away' their power. It is more helpful to understand empowerment as a process of helping people gain greater power over their lives (using our power constructively to help clients become more powerful). Provided that we do not oversimplify empowerment, then, there is no inconsistency between empowerment and professionalism.

In relation to emotional challenges, developing more partnership-based, empowering forms of professionalism can be seen to be significant in two main ways:

1. It enables us to move away from traditional notions of professionalism rooted in the idea that professional knowledge should be derived from positivistic science that produces objective facts disconnected from 'irrational' matters of emotion. If we are to work genuinely in partnership with the people we are seeking to help, then emotional issues need to feature as part of our interactions and, indeed, our assessment work and all that flows from it.

2. Reaffirming professionalism provides a platform for developing a much stronger professional identity and the professional pride that can and should be part of that. Motivation and morale are important (emotional) issues, and so the capacity for a renewed and enhanced sense of professionalism to make a positive contribution to our emotional well-being is a major factor – and with the potential for significant consequences in terms of how well equipped we are to face the emotional challenges we are likely to encounter.

The 'new professionalism' therefore needs to be understood to have an emotional component, in the sense that it recognises that, while the term 'professionalism' is often associated with the notion of rational objectivity, there has to be scope for addressing irrational and emotional dimensions of human experience. This argument could apply across the helping professions, but it is especially applicable to social work which so often involves working with people who are anxious, distressed, vulnerable, grieving, traumatised, discriminated against, alienated and disaffected. There is a very real danger that, if we do not acknowledge and accept the emotional dimension of social work, our practice could be dehumanising and oppressive.

Why emotional competence?

The concept of 'emotional intelligence' became very popular in the 1990s, largely due to the work of Goleman (1996, 1999). Despite its immense popularity, it has been criticised for, on the one hand, being 'commodified' (that is, used as a basis for superficial commercial enterprises that seek to make a profit from helping people increase their 'EQ', the emotional intelligence equivalent of IQ [Fineman, 2000c]) and, on the other, for misusing the term 'intelligence' by overextending it (Murphy, 2006). For these reasons I will use the term 'emotional competence' to refer to our ability to respond appropriately to the emotional aspects of social work practice.

Emotional competence can be divided into three sets of skills:

* *Reading other people's emotions:* We generally learn basic non-verbal communication skills as part of growing up, but there is much to be gained from taking those skills to a more advanced level in terms of becoming much more sensitive to the subtle nuances of emotional expression (Navarro, 2008). It is quite significant how many clues can be missed if we rely on our everyday level of skill in reading body language and do not take our skills and sensitivity to a more advanced professional level. It can take time to develop these skills, but it is certainly worth the effort. It involves increasing our level of self-awareness and being able to tune it to the subtleties of what our senses are encountering. This is consistent with the idea of reflective practice which entails not operating on automatic pilot or just following set patterns of behaviour. It involves a degree of reflexivity and being attuned to what is happening around us and how we can use our professional knowledge base to help us respond appropriately (Thompson and Thompson, 2008).

* *Managing our own emotions:* Being able to regulate our emotions is a key skill. This does not mean that we are expected to be unfeeling automata, but it does mean that we have to be able to balance head and heart and not simply react in an entirely emotional way without any sort of counterbalance. An important part of this is the distinction between empathy and sympathy. Being sympathetic means sharing the other person's feelings – if they are sad, we are sad; if they are disappointed, we are disappointed. Clearly, this would be very debilitating in social work – we would very quickly become emotionally drained and unable to function. At the other extreme we have apathy, which

means having no feelings at all, and not being attuned to feelings, which is also clearly not appropriate for social work. In between these two extremes we have empathy. Being empathic means being able to recognise other people's feelings and their significance, but without necessarily experiencing them ourselves. Of course, pure empathy is not always possible, and it is inevitable that we will at times actually share the feelings we are encountering in others – but that is where the balance of head and heart comes in. We need to be able to 'regulate' our feelings – that is, not suppress them, but subject them to a degree of rational control, hence the idea of balancing head and heart. Research undertaken by Singh (2006) concluded that the effective regulation of emotion is an important factor in professional efficacy in social work.

- *Communicating emotion appropriately:* This is the other side of the coin from 'reading' body language. We also have to be skilled in conveying emotion in a helpful and constructive way. This will involve language (what we say), paralanguage (how we say it, pitch, tone and so on); and non-verbal communication (what our body and our behaviour are saying). These need to be congruent (that is, consistent with one another and with the emotional message we are trying to convey). Some people are very skilful indeed at this sort of communication of affect, to use the technical term, while others can really struggle to convey emotion in helpful ways, and by helpful I mean ways that help to 'connect' with the other person(s), to form a meaningful and constructive rapport and to form the basis of further communication and interaction.

To these three components of emotional competence I would also want to add the need to be aware of emotional issues in the first place. For example, I have argued elsewhere (Thompson, 2012a) that it is very easy for professionals to miss the significance of grief in people's lives. This is largely because we tend to make a strong association between grief and bereavement. This means that in situations where a death has not occurred we may not be alert to the significance of grief. This is a particularly worrisome danger in social work where so many of the situations we encounter are likely to contain a significant element of loss. Consider the following:

- a child being abused – there are various losses involved here, not least the loss of innocence and trust (Thompson, 1999);

- a child being received into care – the loss of family home is only one of many in such circumstances (Thomas and Philpot, 2009);

- an older person giving up their home to enter residential care – losing many connections and aspects of their sense of self at the same time (Renzenbrink, 2004);

- becoming disabled – although disability is not necessarily a loss in itself, it can bring many losses (Sapey, 2002);

- divorce or family breakdown – this can produce both extensive and intensive losses, with potentially profound and far-reaching consequences (Kroll, 2002);

- becoming homeless or being forced to give up one's home – this can, of course, involve losing far more than just the familiar building we call home (Robinson, 2005).

This is a far from complete list. For example, there is now a growing literature which links mental health problems in adulthood with losses in earlier life, particularly traumatic losses (Rogers and Pilgrim, 2005). It should therefore be clear that a sensitivity to loss in the lives of the people we seek to help should be seen as an essential component of emotional competence.

Kinman and Grant support the importance of developing emotional competence when they comment that:

> *The findings of this study indicate that trainee social workers whose emotional and social competencies are more highly developed are more resilient to stress. More specifically, evidence has been found that emotional intelligence, reflective ability, aspects of empathy and social competence may be key protective qualities in the social care context. The importance of helping social work students to develop their emotion management and social skills in order to enhance well-being and protect them against future professional burnout has been highlighted.*

> (2011: 270)

The three Rs

In a previous discussion of the importance of professionalism (Thompson, 2009b) I introduced the notion of the three Rs. These are very relevant to our discussion of emotional competence. It is therefore worth highlighting in turn each of the three Rs:

- *Resourcefulness:* This refers to our ability to be imaginative and creative, to move away from being simply managerialist rationers of scarce resources (welfare bureaucrats). Being resourceful involves recognising that: (i) we are, in ourselves, an important resource (Hamer, 2006), as captured by the traditional term 'use of self'; and (ii) a creative approach to problem solving is likely to be far more empowering and effective than a narrow focus on service provision (Thompson, 2012c). Being resourceful can also bring greater job satisfaction (West, 1997) and, of course, greater opportunities for learning and development (Thompson, 2006). By contrast, a tramlines approach where we make little use of resourcefulness is highly unlikely to produce much by way of job satisfaction or learning. Resourcefulness can therefore be seen to have emotional consequences, in so far as its presence or absence will have a bearing on our overall well-being and thus our potential for happiness and positive emotions at work.

- *Robustness:* Social work is a challenging undertaking, and so we need a certain amount of robustness to withstand its pressures and demands. This includes a degree of emotional robustness. This takes us back to the notion of empathy, being able to find the balance between a debilitating sympathy and a dehumanising apathy; being strong and hardy without being unfeeling. Robustness, then, is not a matter of being 'macho' and stoic, but, rather, having the personal resources to see us through some difficult times. For me, this is closely related to values, as it is our values that will generally motivate and sustain us through the sticky patches (Moss, 2007). It can also be related to the wider notion of spirituality which includes being clear about who we are and how we fit into the wider world, including having a sense of being part of something bigger than ourselves, of being committed to a worthwhile venture (alleviating distress and hardship, tackling social problems and promoting social justice), as discussed by Moss (2005) and Holloway and Moss (2010).

- *Resilience:* This refers to our ability to bounce back from adversity. It is what enables us to get back up after we have been knocked over. This is clearly a key part of emotional competence, as it is an essential requirement for dealing with the setbacks we will inevitably encounter in social work. If the first time we encounter a setback we go down and stay down or take an inordinate amount of time to recover, we will struggle to be effective and to gain any real job satisfaction by making a positive difference. Of course, we will not always be able to get back up again immediately, but the sooner we are able to do so, the stronger the position we will be in. One important factor in relation to resilience is the recognition that, while experiencing a setback may be construed as a form of failure, that does not mean that we are failures. It is essential that we do not allow experiencing failures from time to time (which is only to be expected in an undertaking such as social work) to affect our self-esteem. Most people experience some form of failure most days (failing to be on time on every single occasion, for example), but that does not make them failures as people. This is an important point to emphasise, as internalising a sense of failure can be a significant barrier to developing resilience.

My focus here has been on the three Rs as they relate to social work staff. However, it is also important to recognise how these factors are often present in clients but not recognised or nurtured and therefore not seen as important potential resources for empowerment. This fits well with the idea of the strengths perspective which has developed as a reaction against the tendency to focus on negatives and to fail to counterbalance these with strengths, including resilience factors.

Where the three Rs are present they can be built *on* and, where they are absent, they can be built *up*. That is, if our assessment indicates strengths in relation to one, two or all three of the three Rs, we can explore how to capitalise on these in order to make progress. Where there is evidence of little strength in relation to any of the three Rs, efforts could perhaps usefully be geared towards building these up in order to help the client(s) be better equipped to deal with the challenges they face.

Self-care

It is not without significance that Sue Thompson entitles her e-book on self-care *Don't Be Your Own Worst Enemy* (S Thompson, 2012). Sadly, it is not at all uncommon for social workers (and, indeed, other members of the helping professions) to invest huge amounts of effort and energy (including emotional energy) into helping others, but do relatively little to ensure their own health, well-being and safety. For example, being exposed to the demands of social work for 37 hours a week is challenging enough, but many people work much longer hours than this and do not reclaim the time owing (time off in lieu). They are, in effect, receiving a salary for their basic hours and then doing a number of unpaid hours on top of that. While it has to be recognised that the nature of social work means that it is often not possible to stick rigidly to a 37-hour week, it also has to be recognised that: (i) there should be the opportunity for taking the time back without becoming unduly behind schedule in terms of our overall workload; and (ii) having to work more than 37 hours per week should not be happening as a matter of routine – it should be the exception not the rule.

If (i) is not the case, then it strongly suggests that there is something seriously wrong in terms of workload management, either in terms of how the individual worker is managing their pressures or the level and amount of work the organisation is allocating to them – or, indeed, a combination of the two. It is not uncommon for excessive work allocation to lead workers to become overloaded and then enter a vicious circle in which they do not manage their work as effectively as they otherwise could have. If (ii) is not the case, then it suggests that either the same issues I have just identified in relation to (i) apply or the whole team is overloaded. In either case, steps need to be taken – individually and collectively – to address the issues in whatever ways possible. Deciding not to address the issues or being defeatist about the possibility for change can be very dangerous. For example, it could lead not only to levels of stress which are harmful to health, but also to dangerous practices that could put the worker's professional registration (and thus career) in jeopardy (I have met many practitioners – for example, on training courses about report writing and record keeping – who have told me that their records are weeks if not months out of date).

If a department were to advertise a post in the following terms I cannot imagine they would get many applicants:

> *Social worker: 37 hours per week paid, plus several additional hours unpaid. Anyone raising concerns about the hours will be made to feel they are letting the side down. If, however, anything goes wrong as a result of excessive hours being worked, the individual worker will be blamed and the department will take no responsibility for the situation.*

Social work by its very nature is a pressurised endeavour. If we do not take self-care concerns seriously and we allow situations to develop in which we are being stretched beyond safe limits and we do nothing about this, individually or collectively, we place ourselves in a very invidious position. Those pressures can easily cross the line and become dangerous, health-affecting stress. For me, being able to pull together to address constructively any concerns about unrealistic and dangerous levels of pressure is a key part of professionalism. It is not an easy thing to do, which is why, in my writings, I have referred to the need to 'meet the professional challenge' (Thompson, 2009b). Social work (and social workers) is too important to be allowed to suffer as a result of a combination of managerialism at a macro level and defeatism about influencing organisational practices at a micro level.

It is also important to note that levels of pressure are not the only consideration when it comes to self-care. There is also the nature of the pressure to be considered. For example, it is well documented that professionals working with people who have been traumatised can experience what has come to be known as 'secondary' (or 'vicarious') trauma – that is, exposure to the intensity of emotion a trauma situation generates can have a potentially traumatic effect on others, including well-trained, experienced and competent professionals (Kaul and Welzant, 2005). We should therefore not be complacent about such risks. We need to be clear about what support is available to us – both formally and informally – and ensure that: (i) we have sufficient sources available to us; and (ii) we are prepared to use them. This may seem an obvious statement, but my experience has taught me that any combination of macho stoicism (and women can be macho and stoic too, of course), stress, burnout, defeatism, cynicism and not wanting to 'let the side down' can lead people not to seek the support they need.

Conclusion

Emotion is a key part of what makes us human. Dealing with emotional matters can be very satisfying and rewarding – quite joyful and enriching in fact. However, we also need to be aware of the other side of the coin and recognise that working in an emotionally intense atmosphere can be potentially quite harmful if we are not conscious of the risks involved and fail to take appropriate steps to protect ourselves from harm. Not handling emotions well can harm our health (through stress), wreck our confidence, make us ineffective or even dangerous in our practice, contribute to a destructive and counterproductive culture of low morale for groups of staff and burnout, defeatism and cynicism for individual staff members.

Being emotionally competent, however, is not just a matter of avoiding the negatives of emotionality. By developing our emotional competence to the full we can become highly skilled in responding sensitively, compassionately and effectively to people's needs; we can achieve very high levels of expertise in handling highly sensitive emotional situations in positive and constructive ways (boosting our own credibility in the process); we can develop a strong foundation of knowledge, skills and confidence that can be used within our own workplace to respond to the emotional challenges of organisational life; and we can develop leadership skills that can be of benefit to us (and to our clients and colleagues) at work and, indeed, in our personal lives outside of the workplace. Developing our emotional competence can therefore enrich the lives of many people, including our own, while neglecting emotional competence can leave us vulnerable to a wide range of problems and dangers.

This chapter has examined emotional competence in the context of professionalism and explored a number of key issues as I see them. It is to be hoped that it has helped to lay a foundation of understanding that can be built on over time, so that social work can play an important in tackling emotional problems in families and communities, rather than add to them in the workplace.

REFLECTIVE QUESTIONS

1. *Why is emotional competence an important part of an effective social worker's repertoire?*

2. *How confident do you feel about your own abilities in this area?*

3. *In what ways do you feel you could improve?*

4. *Who would be the best person to support you in this?*

RECOMMENDED FURTHER READING

Howe, D (2008) *The Emotionally Intelligent Social Worker.* Basingstoke: Palgrave Macmillan.

Parkinson, B, Fischer, AH and Manstead, ASR (2005) *Emotion in Social Relations: Cultural, Group, and Interpersonal Processes.* New York: Psychology Press.

Thompson, N (2009) *Practising Social Work: Meeting the Professional Challenge.* Basingstoke: Palgrave Macmillan.

Thompson, N (2009) *People Skills* (3rd edition). Basingstoke: Palgrave Macmillan.

REFERENCES

Bates, J, Pugh, R and Thompson, N (eds) (1999) *Protecting Children: Challenges and Change.* Aldershot: Arena.

Fineman, S (2000a) Emotional Arenas Revisited. In Fineman, S (ed) *Emotion in Organizations* (2nd edition). London: Sage.

Fineman, S (ed) (2000b) *Emotion in Organizations* (2nd edn). London: Sage.

Fineman, S (2000c) Commodifying the Emotionally Intelligent. In Fineman, S (ed) *Emotion in Organizations* (2nd edition). London: Sage.

Goleman, D (1996) *Emotional Intelligence* London: Bloomsbury.

Goleman, D (1999) *Working with Emotional Intelligence.* London: Bloomsbury.

Hamer, M (2006) *The Barefoot Helper.* Lyme Regis: Russell House Publishing.

Hen, M and Goroshit, M (2011) Emotional Competencies in the Education of Mental Health Professionals. *Social Work Education*, 30(7): 811–29.

Holloway, M and Moss, B (2010) *Spirituality and Social Work*. Basingstoke: Palgrave Macmillan.

Howe, D (2008) *The Emotionally Intelligent Social Worker*. Basingstoke: Palgrave Macmillan.

Kaul, RE and Welzant, V (2005) Disaster Mental Health: A Discussion of Best Practices as Applied After the Pentagon Attack. In Roberts, RA (ed) *Crisis Intervention Handbook* (3rd edition). Oxford: Oxford University Press.

Kinman, G and Grant, L (2011) Exploring Stress Resilience in Trainee Social Workers: The Role of Emotional and Social Competences. *British Journal of Social Work*, 4(2)1: 261–75.

Kroll, B (2002) Children and Divorce. In Thompson, N (ed) *Loss and Grief: A Guide for Human Services Practitioners*. Basingstoke: Palgrave Macmillan.

Morrison, T (2007) Emotional Intelligence, Emotion and Social Work: Context, Characteristics, Complications and Contribution. *British Journal of Social Work*, 37(2): 245–63.

Moss, B (2005) *Spirituality and Religion*. Lyme Regis: Russell House Publishing.

Moss, B (2007) *Values*. Lyme Regis: Russell House Publishing.

Murphy, KR (ed.) (2006) *A Critique of Emotional Intelligence: What Are the Problems and How Can They Be Fixed?* Mahwah, NJ: Lawrence Erlbaum Associates.

Navarro, J (2008) *What Every Body is Saying*. London: HarperCollins.

Parkinson, B, Fischer, AH and Manstead, ASR (2005) *Emotion in Social Relations: Cultural, Group, and Interpersonal Processes*. New York: Psychology Press.

Reder, P, Duncan, S and Gray, M (1993) *Beyond Blame: Child Abuse Tragedies Revisited*. London: Routledge.

Renzenbrink, I (2004) Home is Where the Heart Is: Relocation in Later Years. *Illness, Crisis & Loss*, 12(1): 63–74.

Roberts, RA (ed) (2005) *Crisis Intervention Handbook* (3rd edition). Oxford: Oxford University Press.

Robinson, C (2005) Grieving Home. *Social & Cultural Geography*, (6)1: 47–60.

Rogers, A and Pilgrim, D (2005) *A Sociology of Mental Health and Illness* (3rd edition). Maidenhead: Open University Press.

Sapey, B (2002) Disability. In Thompson, N (ed) *Loss and Grief: A Guide for Human Services Practitioners*. Basingstoke: Palgrave Macmillan.

Schneider, J (2012) *Finding Your Way* (2nd edition). Traverse City, MI: Seasons Press.

Singh, SK (2006) Social Work Professionals' Emotional Intelligence, Locus of Control and Self-efficacy: An Exploratory Study. *South African Journal of Human Resource Management*, 4(2): 39–45.

Thomas, M and Philpot, T (2009) *Fostering a Child's Recovery: Family Placement for Traumatized Children*. London: Jessica Kingsley.

Thompson, N (1999) Responding to Loss. In Bates, J, Pugh, R and Thompson, N (eds) *Protecting Children: Challenges and Change*. Aldershot: Arena.

Thompson, N (ed) (2002) *Loss and Grief: A Guide for Human Services Practitioners*. Basingstoke: Palgrave Macmillan.

Thompson, N (2006) *Promoting Workplace Learning*. Bristol: The Policy Press.

Thompson, N (2007) *Power and Empowerment*. Lyme Regis: Russell House Publishing.

Thompson, N (2009a) *Understanding Social Work: Preparing for Practice* (3rd edition). Basingstoke: Palgrave Macmillan.

Thompson, N (2009b) *Practising Social Work: Meeting the Professional Challenge*. Basingstoke: Palgrave Macmillan.

Thompson, N (2012a) *Grief and its Challenges*. Basingstoke: Palgrave Macmillan.

Thompson, N (2012b) *Anti-discriminatory Practice* (5th edition). Basingstoke: Palgrave Macmillan.

Thompson, N (2012c) *The People Solutions Sourcebook* (2nd edition). Basingstoke: Palgrave Macmillan.

Thompson, N and Thompson, S (2008) *The Social Work Companion*. Basingstoke: Palgrave Macmillan.

Thompson, S (2012) *Don't Be Your Own Worst Enemy: Self-Care for Busy People*, e-book published by Avenue Media Solutions: **www.avenuemediasolutions.com**

Thompson, S and Thompson, N (2008) *The Critically Reflective Practitioner*. Basingstoke: Palgrave Macmillan.

West, MA (1997) *Developing Creativity in Organizations*. London: BPS Books.

Chapter 6

The new radical social work professional?

Gurnam Singh and Stephen Cowden

Introduction

This chapter asks whether radical possibilities are still meaningful within professional social work in an age of neo-liberalism and 'austerity'. More fundamentally, at a time when the post-war welfare settlement that was instrumental in the establishment of the state social work appears to be unravelling, one needs to ask what it means to be radical today. Many practitioners would largely agree that the predominance of neo-liberal managerialism has seriously stifled radical possibilities within state social work (Ferguson and Woodward, 2009; Garrett, 2012; Harris, 2003; Lavalette, 2011; Singh and Cowden, 2009). There is little doubt that for the social work profession as a whole the last decades have seen a significant loss of professional status and autonomy, and this has undoubtedly contributed to an atmosphere of widespread demoralisation and frustration at the front line (Carey, 2008; Jones, 2001). Historically, the notion of autonomy has characterised the way professionals, through a combination of public sanction underpinned by statute, were afforded a high degree of control over their own affairs. In other words, professionals are groups of 'experts' who are able to exercise power and influence to make independent judgements free of political interference. In exchange for being invested with considerable power, professions in return are required to base their actions on a set of ethical precepts, a continuous commitment to critical evaluation of ethics and procedures from within the profession itself.

For many social workers, this idealism associated with professional autonomy built on an absolute commitment to ethics – which inspired them to enter professional work, and which is still taught on social work courses – tends to disappear all too quickly under the pressures one experiences in practice. The following account of those pressures, which appeared within a 2010 Ofsted report on social work with children and families, is one many would recognise:

> *Workloads, expectations and demands on social workers are unmanageable. The majority of us are working long hours to simply keep up. This issue of long hours is 'hidden' due to the expectations of management and the ethos of disciplinaries. We are frightened to say that we cannot manage our workloads.*

> (Ofsted, 2010: 13)

At the level of the public representation, social work seems to lunge from one crisis to the next. While the public at large is blithely unaware of the pressures facing front-line staff, it seems we never stop hearing about social work's inability to protect the people whose safety should be its *raison d'être*; and instances like the tragic death of Peter Connelly ('Baby P') in 2007 only confirm this perception. The predictable policy response to this resulted in yet another major overhaul of social work in the form of the Social Work Reform Board and the *Munro Review of Child Protection* in England and Wales (Munro, 2011), and while this work does sincerely seek to affirm social work's strengths, it is hard to escape the fact that these recommendations will do little to change the everyday conditions in which social work is carried out. It is even less likely that they will change the wider perception of social work, and the low esteem and status which mark the profession. And so, as well as illuminating some of the political, ideological and social challenges confronting radical social workers in times of austerity and cuts, we will seek to offer what new possibilities may emerge, not least given that the need for progressive 'social work' is likely to become even greater.

Understanding the present crisis

Bill Jordan (2004) provides a revealing perspective on the present crisis of social work. Rather than being simply marginalised, he suggests that many concepts, practices and approaches that were first developed in social work – and arguably characterised in part the 'radicalness' of the profession – have now generalised to the point where they are located in 'other fields, not merely in human services, but also in business, marketing and politics itself' (2004: 7), and they are now having major influence across society. One might ask how it can be possible that ideas once associated with radical or at least progressive social work (e.g. service user empowerment, diversity, equality, creativity, etc.) could have apparently become adopted by capitalism. In this regard, Luc Boltanski and Eve Chiapello's (2005) work on *The New Spirit of Capitalism* offers a compelling understanding of the underlying processes that have induced people, who may otherwise be opposed to it, to accept the logic of capitalism. The central argument is that without some kind of consent from the wider public, it is very difficult for capitalism to impose a social order that is sustainable; and to do so it needs to seduce people to accept the 'spirit of capitalism'. It does this through 'audacious acts of appropriation, colonisation and annexation' (Boltanski and Chiapello, 2005: 20) of existing popular ideas associated with being virtuous, but using them to entirely different ends. A good example of this is the way that the discourse of 'service user involvement' has been appropriated to promote a privatisation agenda (Cowden and Singh, 2007; Ferguson, 2007). This appropriation of language and ideas offers a 'power of persuasion capable of exciting and persuading those who may otherwise be hostile to neo-liberalism' (Boltanski and Chiapello, 2005: 20).

And so, while the underpinning values of social work may have become, according to Jordan (2004), incorporated into the mainstream, social work practitioners remain marginalised, stigmatised and seen as untrustworthy. Interestingly, in a strange kind of twist, while the general public appear to have benefited from more 'sensitive treatment' from agencies in the public and private sphere – which have, at least superficially copied from social work ('I'm really hearing your concern there Mr Smith') – the people that social workers deal with, namely, the disempowered, oppressed, poor and most marginalised sections of society, have become subject to increased levels of demonisation (Jones, 2011). And, ironically, it has been social workers who have become those increasingly required to deploy new and insidious forms of control and surveillance against service users, characterised so clearly for example, in the way that 'eligibility criteria' are subjectively applied in 'community care assessments' (Fernandez and Snell, 2012).

How is it that social workers themselves have come to accept these shifts in their role? And more profoundly, at a time when *social work's value base and own lexicon ... is now being symbolically deployed to promote privatization and job cuts* (Garrett, 2012: 8), what does it mean to be a radical social worker today? In a media-driven world clearly one of the key failures of social workers has been an inability to effectively present to the wider public the argument for the importance of the work they do. In some senses, the caring professions more generally have become presented as being out of touch, having a silo mentality and being 'conservative'. In contrast, those advocating neo-liberal reforms have managed to project a dynamic new spirit of capitalism of *conviviality, openness to others and novelty, availability, creativity, visionary intuition, sensitivity to differences, listening to lived experience and receptiveness to a whole range of experiences* (Boltanski and Chiapello, 2005: 97).

Indeed, one of the key challenges of the Munro Review was to develop a strategy for improving the image of social work that was so badly damaged in the face of the Peter Connelly case and in particular the apparent inability of social workers to develop and transform their own practice, which, as Garrett (2012: 13) points out, *was portrayed as moribund*. This was to be done through a range of measures, including: the establishment of robust systems of continuous professional development; the formation of The College of Social Work to provide an independent voice for social work; and the appointment of a Chief Social Worker bridging the gap between government and the profession. The government response to the professional 'failings' in the 'Baby Peter' case points to a dangerous paradox for social work, which is that public perceptions of social workers remain largely negative, yet simultaneously public concerns around the need to protect vulnerable children from abuse, that is, the duties of social work, have never been greater.

One has only to consider the revelations in 2012 of the child abuse carried out by former TV celebrity Jimmy Savile over a 30-year period to see this. What is so frustrating from the perspective of social work's public image is that the very way in which the public opinion has shifted from denial to outrage over issues like this derives in a large part from the efforts made by social work, and in particular feminist currents within that, to put the issue of child abuse on the agenda. This was work carried out in the face of an official indifference and public taboo on discussion, which was itself a significant reason why Savile was able to abuse with impunity for as long as he did. Yet the outrage which now greets these revelations is conducted in an atmosphere in which social work (and one might add feminism more generally) has no voice.

An entirely different and yet strangely similar example of this same process of denying the importance or relevance of social work while at the same time appropriating social work concerns is evidenced by the recent report into Health Inequalities in 2010 by Professor Marmot: *Fair Society, Healthy Lives*. At a time when health inequalities are inexorably widening, Marmot's admirable work seeks to promote some fundamentally positive ways forward in tackling these. In the face of the public discourse, which is increasingly seeking to blame the victims of health inequalities for their situation, Marmot has argued that health inequalities must be tackled first and foremost as *a matter of fairness and social justice*. He is admirably unequivocal in his view that health inequalities are a direct result of social inequalities (Marmot, 2010). While this work is extremely important in the current environment, one might ask why such an intervention comes from health rather than social work, particularly so since historically it has been social work that has argued for these general principles to a far greater degree that any of the medically based health professions. Indeed Marmot proposed working alongside communities using *participatory decision making*, which was a technique developed and championed by radical social work (Cowden and Singh, 2007; Ferguson and Woodward, 2009). So despite the way social work has played such an important role in developing the kinds of structural and holistic approaches envisaged by Marmot, social work itself does not rate a single mention in his 2010 report.

In search of an identity

The above discussion expresses a key problem for social work and that is a question of identity, that is, social work's capacity to recognise its importance to society and at the same time be true to its own radical legacy. It is as though, as Garrett (2012) has suggested, the radical ideas, concepts, language and innovations, which not only social work but the Left more generally once subscribed to, have been adopted by neo-liberals. Along with this we have the real ongoing dismantling of the welfare state and with it very many public sector organisations that traditionally employed social workers. In a situation like this it is as if social workers are suffering from what the sociologist Emile Durkheim called 'anomie'. Durkheim defined the moment of 'anomie' as one where ... *the limits are unknown between the possible and impossible, what is just and unjust, legitimate claims and hopes and those which are immoderate* (cited in Dillon, 2010: 103). Durkheim saw anomie as something that occurred during periods of rapid social change, which resulted in the expectations and hopes that people had of themselves and their lives suddenly becoming trounced and traduced.

While social work has arguably been the midwife for so many important shifts in social attitudes and practices, it suffers not just a lack of public recognition, but also a lack of a belief in itself. Where new initiatives exist, they are manifested in policies such as the development of *personal budgets* and *personalisation*, where in spite of a rhetoric of choice, user-led services and even liberation, these are presented in an atmosphere which demonises past practice in social work and ignores the legacy of radical practice which has been fought for within the profession (Cowden and Singh, forthcoming). Additionally, in spite of the promise of new initiatives like personal budgets, evidence demonstrates that the constant tightening of eligibility criteria, which is taking place at the moment, simply excludes an increasing number from receiving a service at all (Daly and Woolham, 2010). Indeed, many have asked whether this entire initiative was simply a Trojan horse for the destruction of state services, which were highly valued by many service users (Ferguson and Woodward, 2009). In the face of this neo-liberal onslaught that has left many social workers in a state of despair, it may seem like madness or utter *naïveté* to try and put the argument for radical social work. In other words, at a moment in which social work in its most mainstream and respectable garb is just surviving, how would radical social work even get a hearing? In putting these arguments we are not unaware of this view. Rather it is precisely because of radical social work's place at the *limits* of debate, on the recalcitrant fringe of neo-liberal 'common-sense', of what is 'realistic' in times of austerity, that we want to argue the case for why radical social work is more important than ever.

The challenge of neo-liberalism

A central argument of this chapter is that the fundamental crisis in social work, and public services more generally, cannot be understood without seeing its cause within the logic of the economic and political arrangements known as *'neo-liberalism'*. David Harvey has defined this as:

> *A theory of political economic practices [which] proposes that human well-being can best be advanced by liberating individual entrepreneurial freedoms and skills within an institutional framework characterized by strong private property rights, free markets, and free trade.*

> (2007: 1)

Harvey has gone on to characterise the way neo-liberalism has come to present its logic *as an ethic in itself, capable of acting as a guide to all human action, and substituting for all previously held ethical beliefs* (2007: 3).

To see the truth of this one only needs to look at the way this mode of thinking has captured all major political parties and mainstream social commentary, successfully marginalising the social democratic and welfarist political institutions that have held such sway since in the post-war period. Take for instance the idea of 'choice', which on face value appears to be a desirable and wholly apolitical consideration for professionals. However, as John Clarke so appositely points out, 'choice' is one of the key ideas driving neo-liberal social policy (Clarke et al., 2000, 2007; see also Daly and Woolham, 2010; Ferguson, 2007). The choice agenda has been central in undermining the concept of collective provision within social work.

As Marion Barnes notes, choice constructs a society of individuals, rather than seeing the way people's lives are framed by the relationships they are in. Viewing the circumstances of people who are in positions of dependence through this lens has a hugely distorting impact, creating a situation where 'care and protection' come to be seen as 'the booby prize' if people can't exercise 'choice and control' (2011: 160). In other words, services come to be seen as a negative judgement on those seen to lack entrepreneurial capacity to engage in the prize of consumer society. It is through the acceptance of neo-liberal individualist 'ethics' like this, which deprives social work of the capacity to represent itself positively.

Neither is this situation likely to change or improve within the foreseeable future; indeed the current economic recession in the UK is currently seen by the political class as proof that we must have even less welfare. Following the collapse and crisis of the banks in 2007–8, we are now into what Slavoj Žižek has called a period of 'Permanent Economic Emergency':

> *...when after decades of the welfare state, when cutbacks were relatively limited with the promise that things would soon return to normal, we are now entering a period in which an economic state of emergency is becoming permanent.*

> (Žižek, 2010: 86)

Accompanying this state of affairs in the UK, there has been an almost unprecedented attack on those who rely for any reason on the welfare state. Announcing this policy in 2010 the Conservative Chancellor George Osborne stated that *people who think it is a lifestyle to sit on out-of-work benefits … that lifestyle choice is going to come to an end* (*Guardian*, 2010). This has been the harbinger of a whole series of cuts to a wide range of welfare benefits. Indeed, after attacks to Housing Benefit in 2012, Jim Strang, Chair of the Chartered Institute of Housing in Scotland, described the government's attacks on welfare as a *totally unjust and ideological attack on those with the least power and influence in society* (*Housing News*, 13 March 2012). However, the present reality is that such outspoken opposition to government policy and defence of the importance of public welfare is unusual, and again this reflects the way that the ground is made fertile for privatisation and the destruction of services through an ongoing denigration of the achievements and possibilities within public institutions – the regular attacks on social work are one of the many examples of this.

'Old' radical social work – problems and possibilities

So far we have sought to offer an insight into the contemporary crisis of social work under the onslaught of neo-liberalism, which we have suggested is a particularly insidious manifestation of capitalism that has the uncanny ability to present itself as progressive to the extent that old progressive Left rhetoric has been largely subsumed within a new rhetoric of 'empowerment'. And, so, while critique is important, the challenge for reconstructing a new radical social work project is predicated on the capacity to imagine a new and progressive alternative to the neo-liberal status quo. We suggest this requires two key things: first we need to understand why the prescription proffered by 'old' radical social work seems to have little purchase amongst professionals, that is, we need to learn from history; and second, as a means of overcoming the anomie talked about earlier and restoring confidence, there is, in a very practical sense, a need to identify a new praxis from which radical possibilities can grow. We use the idea of praxis here to refer to actions which, in the broadest sense, have the capacity to transform social life from conditions of powerlessness and oppression. And it is out of such actions, which can be manifest in many forms, that new insights and knowledge become generated.

Mary Langan has noted that one of the great ironies of ('old') radical social work was that though as a political movement it had died out by the mid-1980s, as noted earlier, its language and rhetoric have lived on; indeed *the paradox of the 1990s [was] the apparent ubiquity of the rhetoric of radicalism at a time when the radical spirit seemed to have long evaporated* (Langan, 1998: 214). In similar terms Fred Powell has argued that though the radical social work movement was small and short lived, it *exercised an influence ... totally out of proportion to its minority status* (2001: 68). And so in these perplexing times two key questions emerge: how can we develop a clear appreciation of the significance of radical social work and how do we understand the way that its previous prescriptions seem to have been so inadequate in mobilising the profession in our current crisis?

We would argue that in order to understand both of these questions we must understand radical social work first and foremost as a critique of models of scientific rationality and professional authority that were central to a Fabian socialist vision of the welfare state (Powell, 2001). While the institutionalisation of social work that took place throughout the 1950s and 1960s in the UK has brought about significant growth and development of the profession, questions about its role and allegiances loom large. John Harris has noted that while the 1968 Seebohm Report is often regarded as representing the high water mark of British social work, the underlying conception of public service on which it was based did not conceive the power which those public servants had over 'the public' as in any way problematic, hence what was missing within Seebohm was:

> *a consideration of the authority dimension present in bureau-professional regimes or any explicit discussion of the rights service users might need to safeguard their position when faced with bureau-professional authority.*

> (Harris, 1999: 920–1)

It was this scientific rationality and professional authority that was challenged by community activism and social movements in the 1970s and 1980s, and this was very significant as it emerged from the very people that the British welfare state was set up to serve. In social work these were manifest by concerns about the supposed neutrality of the casework model and of the dominant concept of professional expertise, with the more radical elements in the profession asking whether these were in fact tools for individualising and pathologising what were actually social and structural problems. In the book *Radical Social Work*, Bailey and Brake argued strongly against 'professionalism', suggesting that it:

> ... isolates the social worker from the population at large. ... Social workers come to see themselves ... on a par with doctors and lawyers [and this] encourages the introduction of businesslike career structures where 'correct' and 'professional' behaviour (such as detachment and controlled emotional involvement) is rewarded with advancement.

(1975: 145)

It became clear that radical social workers were seeking to break down the professional distance between themselves and the communities who were somewhat problematically seen as the 'clients' of social work. They wanted social workers to be involved with service users as citizens through collective action, instead of sitting on the sidelines as expert professionals. This 'anti-professionalism' was similarly embodied in the title of the radical social work magazine *Case-Con*, implying that casework's individualising 'professional knows best' assumption was an ideological smokescreen which prevented people understanding the underlying causes of social problems.

It is also important to note that 'old' radical social work did not emerge in a vacuum; it was rather one expression of dissatisfaction within the post-war welfare state settlement – the so-called 'crisis of labourism'. One of the most significant manifestations of this was the emergence of the new social movements around the politics of gender, 'race' and sexuality in the late 1960s and 1970s (Lewis,1998).

The book *In and Against the State* (CSE, 1980) was one of the most cogent expressions of the conflicted attitude which many on the Left felt towards the welfare state at this time. While the authors supported public welfare, they also felt that the problem with state provision was not just that it was *...under-resourced, inadequate, and on the cheap... [but] the way it is resourced and administered to us doesn't seem to reflect our real needs* (1980: 9).

Radical social work emerges out of exactly this process of questioning whose 'real needs' social workers were supposed to be serving – were they supposed to be looking after the interests of the state, or the nation, or should their focus be the needs of service users themselves?

We have noted that this critique of professional authority was an important theme in the re-emergence of community activism on the Left during the 1970s, but it was also crucial in the re-emergence of anti-statist ideas on the Right in the 1980s. The neo-conservative columnist David Marsland expressed this point of view succinctly when he argued:

> State welfare is causing grave damage in the United Kingdom ... and throughout the free world. It is impeding the dynamism of global economic

competition and thus slowing global economic growth. Through bureaucratic centralism and underclass dependency, which it mentally creates, it poses a serious long-term threat to liberty and to the stability of democracy.

(cited in Powell, 2001: 4)

This quote demonstrates the way challenging the authority of 'professionals' also became part of the way the New Right was articulating their political vision in support of the 'freedom' of the individual defined against the 'bureaucracy' of the state; represented crucially by public sector professionals. It was, of course, this view which triumphed over that of the community-based radicals, but much of this rationale, as discussed earlier, was derived from an appropriation of the language of the new social movements. The project of 'reform' of the welfare state, which went on to have continuity beyond the Thatcher years and into the New Labour years, was represented in social work by the removal of the supposedly patronising term 'clients', but instead of citizens with rights, they became 'service users' and 'customers'. Accompanying this was the growth of managerialism, which heralded a dramatic expansion of auditing mechanisms and the introduction of 'competence-based' notions of professional learning. It has been processes like these which have been central not just to undermining the critical element within professional practice, but to the commodification and privatisation of large sectors of social care, that have taken place (Harris, 2003; Jordan and Jordan, 2000). So, while the concepts of 'liberation', 'empowerment' and 'anti-oppression' were oppositional in the moment in which they were articulated within 'old' radical social work, today they now sit comfortably within a managerial discourse, albeit shorn of the critique of unequal distribution of power and resources in society, that inspired them.

An example from the field of education demonstrates the way the capture of language has become so significant in establishing neo-liberal consumerism as an alternative 'common-sense' to welfare-based entitlements. One important campaign waged by the black community in Britain in the 1970s concerned the disproportionate number of children from African-Caribbean backgrounds who were classified as 'educationally subnormal' and placed in special schools, popularly known as 'sin-bins' (CCCS, 1982). This was a significant community-based campaign which sought to contest ideas of professional expertise and concerned the demand by parents to have a say in their children's education, rather than this being primarily determined by Local Educational Authorities (LEAs) and educational professionals.

If we cut to the present what we are seeing now is the gradual dismembering of LEAs under the rubric of 'parental choice', and nothing expresses this more than the flagship policy of 'free schools' as espoused by the Secretary of State for Education, Michael Gove. These schools are set up by groups of parents, are funded by LEAs, but are placed outside the constraints and 'bureaucracy' of the LEA. It is interesting to note the way this language of 'free schools' echoes the counter-cultural anti-establishment alternatives of the 1960s–1970s, except that in our contemporary version, 'free schools' are most likely to be enclaves of the socially privileged, built on the demand of the better educated and more articulate for alternatives to what they see as inferior state schools. If we consider these two instances (this and the previous example of parents campaigning against the disproportionate number of African-Caribbean children placed in special schools) as both concerned with parents seeking the right to control aspects of their child's education, what we see in the first instance is a campaign driven by an anti-discriminatory and inclusive imperative; in the second a campaign driven by an individualist logic of simply wanting the 'best for my child', but whose social dimensions operate to the benefit of the already privileged at the expense of the least privileged. This example demonstrates the way neo-liberal social policy has both adopted and appropriated the anti-professional rhetoric of movements or service user movements and radical professional groups, particularly through the language of choice. As John Clarke has noted:

> *Neo-liberalism locates the consumer as a 'willing self': a subject capable of self-direction who has, hitherto, been unreasonably constrained by state or regulatory conditions. 'Liberating' the consumer provides one critical imperative for dissolving the state/market distinction by enlarging the reach of the market. ... 'Choice' in schooling gave parents (the proxy consumers of education) the non-cash mediated right to express preferences about the school that they wished their children to attend. As a result, parents attempted to choose schools – and schools got to choose children (and their parents).*

(Clarke, 2007: 122)

If the moment of radical social work was defined by the *crisis of Labourism*, what we seem to have now is the *absence of Labourism*, that is, the absence of a political party whose stated aim was to defend the interests of working people. This is because the New Labour 'modernisation' project, rather than representing a return to, or even a modernisation of, the principles of the welfare state, was essentially a continuation of a free-market 'common-sense'. Stuart Hall makes the point that *New Labour came closer to institutionalising neo-liberalism as a social and political form than Thatcher did*, particularly as Blair's language found ways of making these ideas acceptable *to Labour voters as well* (Derbyshire, 2012). In the face of the current savage attacks on social welfare, as well as the gradual privatisation of the NHS and education, the current Labour leadership appear signally unable to articulate a defence of the welfare state, or an alternative to the ever-increasing rule of the market. Mark Fisher uses the term 'Capitalist Realism' (Fisher, 2009) to express this condition: one in which we are led to believe there are no alternatives to the capitalist free market. The hold that this has in the current period is shown in the way that for the majority of people it is *easier to imagine the end of the world than the end of capitalism*, and Fisher suggests that:

> *for most people under twenty in Europe and North America, the lack of alternatives to capitalism is not even an issue. Capitalism seamlessly occupies the horizons of the thinkable.*

(2009: 8)

This facilitates what he calls a *pre-emptive formatting and shaping of desires, aspirations and hopes* to fit a *'business ontology' in which it is simply obvious that everything in society, including health care and education, should be run as a business* (2009: 13–16). The takeover and destruction of public institutions, the removal of rights, the privatisation of space, thus meet with a mood of resignation and despair, rather than anger and activism; the anomie that we see afflicting social work is a part of this.

New radical social work and its possibilities – 'Ya Basta'[1]

Having offered a somewhat depressing analysis of the demise of 'old' radical social work in the face of the ongoing onslaught of neo-liberalism we now turn our discussion towards thinking about developing new possibilities. We begin with Fisher, who notes how important it is to focus on the vulnerabilities in this system. He argues that capitalist realism can best be destabilised by exposing its inconsistency and demonstrating that its 'ostensible realism' and 'apparent naturalness' are themselves imposed fantasies resting on utterly fictitious premises (Fisher, 2009: 16–19). We see this fictitiousness residing both in the way neo-liberal finance capital appeared to offer a world of unlimited money, which then turns out not to exist, but equally fictitious is the way it obscures the high price we are paying – in our bodies, in our minds, and in our relations with each other – for the maintenance of the idea that there is 'no alternative' to dehumanising relations which increasingly dominate everyday life. It is in this sense that we need most of all to start talking again about 'capitalism' and that most hoary of topics, the ownership of the means of (social care) production.

In a discussion of the impact of neo-liberalism on the social care sector, Carey notes the growing influence of business whose primary motive was to make profits.

> *Within the private sector dominated market of residential and nursing home care, complex and convoluted rituals of mergers, take-overs, sales and closures have continued ... As a consequence such markets have helped to generate unstable (and therefore potentially unsafe) living and 'support' environments for many residents. For example, recent research has highlighted how many private sector providers have failed to meet basic standards of care ... Also recent plans by the Commission for Social Care Inspection to reduce the number of care home inspectors, including children's homes, suggests that presently unacceptable standards may fall even further.*
>
> (2008: 923)

Private ownership means that banks and financiers are now making key decisions about how social care organisations operate on a day-to-day basis. The

---

[1]A term meaning 'enough is enough' coined by the Zapatista freedom fighters in Mexico and other parts of Latin America in their struggles against capitalism.

very organisations which should have been reined in after their collapse in 2008, not to mention demonstrations of their ongoing corruption, are being given ever more power over our social institutions. This was clearly demonstrated by the collapse of Southern Cross Care homes in June 2011, which occurred after the private equity firm Blackstone separated out the property value of the homes from their actual running. This allowed company directors and shareholders to enrich themselves as the value of the company multiplied to four times its original value, but this financial engineering caused the collapse of the same company three years later, leaving 31,000 older people and 44,000 care staff as pawns in the machinations of stock market. An instance like this demonstrates the ways in which ownership really *does matter*.

Similar dynamics were demonstrated in another scandal that broke around the same time when appalling abuse at the Winterbourne View care home was exposed in May 2011 by the BBC *Panorama* programme. This home was run by a private care organisation, Castle Beck, and following its exposure in the media it was revealing to see the way politicians were quick to claim that the appalling abuses which took place were not in any way related to private ownership as such. In a discussion that took place on the BBC panel programme *Question Time* (2 June 2011), the Conservative MP and former Health Secretary Stephen Dorrell sought to deal with this argument saying that the abuse of people with learning difficulties has happened in all institutions, state run and private. While there have always been abuses of power in institutions for vulnerable people, the key point is that allowing for-profit operators and financiers to take over this area of care does not in any sense reduce that possibility, and, indeed, in an era where regulation of these institutions is characterised as the 'dead hand' of the state versus the thrusting entrepreneurialism of the private sector, abuse is in fact made *more likely*. In addition, the BBC documentary revealed that numerous care staff had contacted the Care Quality Commission to report abuse over several years, but no action had been taken; and this points to the essentially collusive arrangement which exists between private care operators and their so-called regulators.

This, we suggest, is the terrain on which new radical social work now needs to build. The Coalition government's changes to the NHS have made the role of private providers central to the commissioning process, where they will be competing with state-run services on cost. We know from experience that this will be a 'race to the bottom' – with the regime of 'low pay–low skill–no training' that was used by Castle Beck in Bristol, and is used throughout the Adult Social Care sector to an even greater extent.

At the level of rhetoric, while remaining steadfast to the need to work in creative, innovative ways, as the neo-liberal reforms appear to demand, the new radical social worker needs to be rooted to a social justice and human rights agenda and not one determined by the logic of markets. As Carey and Foster (2011: 3) suggest, this will inevitably mean that the new radical social worker will need to engage in acts of 'resistance, subterfuge, deception and even sabotage' and this runs the risk of being seen as difficult, uncooperative and 'deviant'. The key challenge here is not simply to refuse to co-operate for its own sake, but rather to remain steadfast to professional social work values, which if understood and implemented fully provide a crucial position upon which to practise social work in and beyond the welfare state.

An instance of this was provided by an action that was organised by the Social Work Action Network (SWAN) in the West Midlands over a cut of £1.2 million from the budget for Unaccompanied Asylum-seeking Children. The council was attempting to carry this out by asking social workers to 'encourage', in their words, migrant and undocumented young people to leave their foster placements at 16. SWAN responded by saying that it understood the financial pressure which Solihull Council was facing (which itself is a consequence of cuts to the Local Authority by the UK Border Agency) but they argued that this policy was taking *social work services for such a vulnerable group to a particularly low level … By upholding basic social work values, following a 'rights' based anti-discriminatory approach, and asserting the new regulations that will come into force in April this year, the policy can and should be challenged* (SWAN, 2011). They described how this could be done using the law, by using the GSCC Code of Practice and by acting collectively.

For us this illustrates the kind of initiatives that need to be developed. The new radical social worker has to 'dance cleverly'. Rather than engaging in gestural refusals, radicals have to be the *best* social workers, with an absolute commitment to social work values and to developing their skills. The new radical social worker realises that neo-liberal structures cannot be wished away, but that they can be challenged by groups of individuals who decide that 'enough is enough' and act on the basis of those values. John Holloway calls this 'the method of the crack'. In a time when public space is Being walled in and taken from us, Holloway argues that we need to:

> … understand the wall not from its solidity, but from its cracks; we wish to understand capitalism not as domination, but from the perspectives of its crisis, its contradictions, its weaknesses, and we need to understand how we ourselves are those contradictions.

> (2010: 9)

As we noted at the beginning of this chapter, many social workers feel trapped by the consequences of neo-liberal policies, but there are always cracks in those policies, and by seeking these we, at the same time, can discover new possibilities for challenging and transcending the current realities. Through critique we can recognise the way neo-liberalism has appropriated the anti-oppressive language of social work. Through acting together, new radical social workers will engage in a similar re-appropriation of language, but one which rejects the cynicism of neo-liberalism and talks unashamedly about a project of collective emancipation.

To argue for a new radical social work is in no way to suggest that 'old' radical social work was wrong or a failure, but it is to recognise that times have changed. It is crucial to notice the way many of the ideas of 'old' radical social work have had a tremendous influence on the kinds of perspectives social workers as a whole would now adopt, particularly in areas such as rejecting the medical model in disability services, promoting the importance of diversity in practice, opposing racist and sexist practices, rejecting the demonising of the poor and arguing for the importance of involving service users and carers in shaping and delivering services. There remain critical lessons for us from this period, particularly in the need to see the importance of education and critical consciousness for both workers and clients; of linking people with systems and networks within families and communities; of building counter systems by recognising the double-edged nature of existing systems; of seeking to engage at both the individual and structural level with clients' need and suffering, that is, to utilise personal power but to build autonomous power bases.

Further, in confronting a particular 'common sense' notion that professionals should be 'non political' and that their practice should be governed by 'evidence', as if evidence is devoid of ideology, a new radical social work seeks to develop politically conscious practitioners and service users. This can be done by incorporating the language of politics and nurturing the skills for both practitioners and service users/clients, etc. to locate themselves, as Gramsci suggests, in history as subjects. So, as we have argued elsewhere (Cowden and Singh, 2007), the relationship between services users and professionals is not based on a consumerist model of 'customer knows best' but a dialogical approach that characterises the approach taken by Paulo Freire (1972). It also extends the idea of 'citizenship' to the global level. The implication for social work education is clear; the curriculum, in addition to fulfilling professional body and regulatory requirements, needs to enable students to develop capabilities in relation to political activism, advocacy and campaigning.

Conclusion

To formulate a new radical social work one needs to begin by developing a critical understanding of the mechanisms for the production and reproduction of material inequality and power differentials within and between different social groups. One then needs to understand the kinds of group and individual responses that such circumstances of powerlessness and social exclusion tend to produce. In other words, one need, to address cultural, economic, psychological and political issues simultaneously, and we acknowledge that this not an easy task. But this difficulty is exacerbated by the fact that, while the underpinning values of the 'old' radical social work remain just as relevant today – as Bailey and Brake put it, *radical social work is essentially understanding the position of the oppressed in the social and economic context they live in* (1975: 9) – the social and political movements that embodied those forms of politics have either disappeared or become extremely fragmented. Then the project was clear, but today the absence of a positive utopian vision of human emancipation makes it much harder to organise and to act. Yet in spite of this, as Slavoj Žižek argues:

... we have to act now because the consequences of non-action could be disastrous ... We will have to reinvent aspects of the new, just to keep the machinery going and to maintain what was good in the old – education, healthcare, basic social services ... As Gramsci said ... 'the old world is dying, and the new struggles to be born: now is the time of monsters'.

(2010: 95)

REFLECTIVE QUESTIONS

1. Can state social workers maintain a radical perspective in today's social work world that is characterised by cuts, privatisation and personalisation of services?

2. Should social workers engage in political activism? If not, why not? If yes, what form can/should this take?

3. Social workers are defined in many ways, but rarely are they talked about as 'intellectuals'. Can you think of arguments for and against seeing social workers as intellectuals?

4. Radical social workers have historically been suspicious of attempts to 'professionalise' social work. Can you think of why this may be the case?

RECOMMENDED FURTHER READING

Bailey, R and Brake, M (eds) (1980) *Radical Social Work and Practice.* London: Edward Arnold.

Ferguson, I and Woodward, R (2009) *Radical Social Work in Practice: Making a Difference.* Bristol: Policy Press.

Lavalette, M (2011) *Radical Social Work Today: Social Work at the Crossroads.* Bristol: Policy Press.

Singh, G and Cowden, S (2009) The Social Worker as Intellectual. *European Journal of Social Work*, 12(4): 1369–457.

REFERENCES

Bailey, R and Brake, M (1975) *Radical Social Work.* London: Edward Arnold.

Bailey, R and Brake, M (eds) (1980) *Radical Social Work and Practice.* London: Edward Arnold.

Barnes, M (2011) Abandoning Care? A Critical Perspective on Personalisation from an Ethic of Care. *Ethics and Social Welfare*, 5(2): 153–67.

Boltanski, L and Chiapello, E (2005) *The New Spirit of Capitalism.* London, Verso.

Carey, M (2008) Everything Must Go? The Privatisation of State Social Work. *British Journal of Social Work*, 38(5): 918–35.

Carey, M and Foster, V (2011) Social Work, Ideology, Discourse and the Limits of Post Hegemony. *Journal of Social Work*. Advance access 27 September: 1–19, doi: 10.1177/1468017311412032.

CCCS (1982) *The Empire Strikes Back: Race and Racism in 70s Britain.* London: Hutchinson.

Clarke, J, Gewirtz, S and McLaughlin, E (eds) (2000) *New Managerialism, New Welfare?* London: Sage Publications.

Clarke, J, Newman, J and Westmarland, L (2007) Creating Citizen-consumers? Public Service Reform and (Un)willing Selves. In Maasen, S and Sutter, B (eds) *On Willing Selves: Neoliberal Politics and the Challenge of Neuroscience.* Basingstoke: Palgrave Macmillan: 125–45.

Cowden, S and Singh, G (2007) The 'User': Friend, Foe or Fetish? A Critical Exploration of User Involvement in Health and Social Care. *Critical Social Policy,* 27(1): 5–23.

Cowden, S and Singh, G (forthcoming) User Involvement: Now You See It, Now You Don't. In Cocker, C and Letchfield, T (eds) *Rethinking Anti-Discriminatory Practice, Diversity and Equality in Social Work.* Basingstoke: Palgrave.

CSE (1980) *In and Against the State.* London: Pluto Press.

Daly, G and Woolham, J (2010) *Do Personal Budgets Lead to Personalisation?* London: Social Policy Association.

Derbyshire, J (2012) We Need To Talk About Englishness: New Statesman Profile of Stuart Hall. *New Statesman,* 24–30 August.

Dillon, M (2010) *Introduction to Sociological Theory.* Oxford: Wiley-Blackwell.

Ferguson, I (2007) Increasing User Choice or Privatizing Risk? The Antinomies of Personalization. *British Journal of Social Work,* 37(3): 387–403.

Ferguson, I and Woodward, R (2009) *Radical Social Work in Practice: Making a Difference.* Bristol: Policy Press.

Fernandez, J and Snell, T (2012) *Survey of Fair Access to Care Services (FACS) Assessment Criteria Among Local Authorities in England.* PSSRU Discussion Paper 2825, Economics of Social and Health Care Research Unit.

Fisher, M (2009*) Capitalist Realism.* London: Zero.

Freire, P (1972) *Pedagogy of the Oppressed.* London: Penguin.

Garrett, PM (2012) Re-Enchanting Social work? The Emerging 'Spirit' of Social Work in an Age of Economic Crisis. *British Journal of Social Work.* Advance access, published October 11: 1–19, doi:10.1093/bjsw/bcs146.

Guardian (2010) George Osborne to Cut £4bn More from Benefits, 9 September. Available at: **www.guardian.co.uk/politics/2010/sep/09/george-osborne-cut-4bn-benefits-welfare** (accessed 12 December 2012).

Harris, J (1999) State Social Work and Social Citizenship in Britain: From Clientelism to Consumerism. *British Journal of Social Work,* 29(6): 915–37.

Harris, J (2003) *The Social Work Business.* London: Routledge.

Harvey, D (2007) *A Brief History of Neo-Liberalism.* Oxford: Oxford University Press.

Holloway, J (2010) *Crack Capitalism.* London: Pluto Press.

Jones, C (2001) Voices From the Front Line: State Social Workers and New Labour. *British Journal of Social Work,* 31(4): 547–62.

Jones, O (2011) *Chavs: The Demonization of the Working Clas*s. London: Verso.

Jordan, B (2004) Emancipatory Social Work? Opportunity or Oxymoron. *British Journal of Social Work*, 34(1): 5–19.

Jordan, B and Jordan, C (2000) *Social Work and the Third Way: Tough Love as Social Policy.* London: Sage.

Langan, M (1998) Radical Social Work. In Adams, R, Dominelli, L and Payne M (eds) *Social Work: Themes, Issues and Critical Debates.* Basingstoke: Palgrave.

Lavalette, M (2011) *Radical Social Work Today: Social Work at the Crossroads.* Bristol: Policy Press.

Lewis, G (1998) Coming Apart at the Seams: The Crisis of the Welfare State. In Hughes, G and Lewis, G (eds) *Unsettling Welfare: the Reconstruction of Social Policy.* London: Routledge/ Open University: 38–79.

Marmot, M (2010) *Fair Society, Healthy Lives.* University College London Institute of Health Equity. Available at: www.instituteofhealthequity.org/projects/fair-society-healthy-lives-the-marmot-review/fair-society-healthy-lives-full-report

Munro, E (2011) *The Munro Review of Child Protection: Final Report – A Child-centred System.* London: Department of Education. Available at: **www.education.gov.uk/ publications/standard/publicationDetail/Page1/CM%208062** (accessed 18 January 2013).

Ofsted (2010) *Safeguarding and Looked After Children: National Results for Children's Social Work Practitioners Survey 2010* (NAT '10). Manchester: Ofsted.

Powell, F (2001) *The Politics of Social Work.* London: Sage.

Singh, G and Cowden, S (2009) The Social Worker as Intellectual. *European Journal of Social Work*, 12(4): 1369–457.

Social Work Action Network (SWAN) (2011) Practice Notes from the Frontline: Cuts to the UASC budget in Solihull. April. Available at: **www.socialworkfuture.org/ attachments/article/68/solihul%20practice%20notesv8.pdf**

Žižek, S (2010) A Permanent Economic Emergency. *New Left Review*, 64 (July–August): 85–95.

Chapter 7
Ethical tensions in social work

Steven M. Shardlow

Introduction

There are two long-standing and enduring sets of ethical questions about social work: 'Who should be helped?' and 'How should social workers behave?'. The first set of questions is centred upon debates about either who should receive social work help or who should be the recipient of an intervention in their lives by social workers. These debates, while they may appear similar, are not of necessity grounded in the same principles, as some people that may not want to receive help are legally required to accept social work involvement in their lives, by virtue of the legal requirement to protect others or the individual in question! By asking questions about who should or should not receive social work, complex political, moral and economic principles come into play. These principles construct answers to these questions that depend upon understandings about the nature of responsibility for self and others and the nature of relationships between individuals in society. Further investigation reveals embedded fundamental questions, such as: 'For what is the *individual* responsible, as opposed to the state or the family?' Responses to such questions, then, pivot on the nature of formal and legally enforceable obligations or informal expectations that are socially constructed between the individual, state and family. Answers to such questions are likely to be highly contextually specific, given the nature of social work practice, which is grounded in the social and cultural roots of any given society. Fascinating though these broad philosophical and policy concerns are, they are not the primary focus of this chapter. Rather it is the second of the two sets of enduring questions that will be put under the microscope in this chapter. This set of questions address the very real ethical challenges that social workers face in their day-to-day practice. The scope and range of these questions could be summarised as 'How should a social worker behave, if they are to behave as a moral professional?'. This chapter is an exploration of that question and its ramifications. The approach taken begins with a consideration of current ethical codes and requirements, which is followed by an exploration of 'seven tensions'. These tensions illustrate some of the day-to-day professional ethical concerns that social workers are likely to face. Conventionally, many explorations of social work ethics begin by reviewing different fundamental philosophical approaches to the resolution of ethical dilemmas, such as: deontology (see for example the work of Kant); consequentialism (classically found in the utilitarian principles elegantly proposed by Mill); virtue ethics (dating back to the work of Plato, and currently enjoying something of a revival); and post-modern and post-structuralist approaches (found in thinkers such as Foucault) a different approach has been adopted here.

Guides, codes and requirements

Professions socialise their members to adopt normative behaviours, as required or expected of members of the profession. One of the mechanisms used by professions to achieve that objective is to publish a code of ethics that states required, expected and prohibited behaviours for members. This promulgation of explicit requirements can only be achieved if there is a legislative structure for the regulation of members' behaviour by the relevant profession. A great many countries have codes of ethics that govern the conduct of social workers, for example: Australia (AASW, 2010), Canada, Finland, France, Hong Kong, the USA (NASW, 2008). However, in not all of these countries is there a legal obligation on social workers to adhere to the code of ethics. In some countries, for example Australia, compliance with the code by social workers is a voluntary matter. In addition to these nationally based codes there is an international code of ethics published by the International Federation of Social Workers (IFSW, 2012). Compliance with this code is not obligatory.

In the United Kingdom, since 1 April 2005, the occupation of *social work* has been designated a 'regulated profession'. Being a regulated profession implies that the title *social worker*, that is, a member of that particular profession, can only be used by those that meet the conditions set by the government's approved regulatory bodies, which followed the implementation of the Care Standards Act (2000). In the years prior to the designation of social work as a regulated profession, different regulatory bodies were established for England (The General Social Care Council), Northern Ireland (Northern Ireland Social Care Council), Scotland (Scottish Social Services Council) and Wales (Cynor Gofal Cyrmru/Care Council for Wales). On 1 August 2012, the Conservative/Liberal Democrat Government led by David Cameron, as part of a national programme to reduce the number of quangos, abolished The General Social Care Council and transferred the responsibilities for the regulation of the social work profession in England to a renamed Health and Care Professions Council (HCPC).[1] As of 2013, HCPC regulates 16 professions, of which two – art therapy and social work – would fall under the rubric of social care, while the majority would be termed healthcare professions.

These various regulatory bodies across the UK have been charged with a duty to hold a register of all those who meet their requirements to be admitted to the profession of social work (similar arrangements would require such bodies in many other countries to hold lists of suitably qualified practitioners). These requirements stipulate that to be registered as a social worker it is necessary to

---

[1]Previously known as The Health Professions Council.

hold an academic award in social work (that included the completion of specified amounts of supervised professional practice), that a required amount of professional updating is undertaken over given time periods, and that the social worker agrees to, and in day-to-day professional practice adheres to, the professional codes of the regulatory body. Failure to comply with these requirements would entail that an individual would not be admitted to the profession, or would be in breach of the professional codes and could be disciplined. In extreme cases, this could mean removal from the register, which would entail no longer being able to practise as a social worker. The underlying purpose behind these structures for registration is to provide a mechanism that promotes the maintenance of professional standards to protect the public from poor practice.

It is now possible to explore some of the consequences of the transfer of regulation from the GSCC to the HCPC. There is one immediate difference in the present arrangements for regulation of the profession of social work. The GSCC required that students, as soon as they commenced a course that led to a professional qualification in social work, were registered as *student social workers*. The HCPC does not require registration of students of a profession: registration is only required at the point of qualification and when the person intends to engage in professional practice. The Health and Care Professions Council does, however, provide guidance for students in the professions for which it is the regulator (HCPC, 2012). In Northern Ireland, Scotland and Wales the regulatory bodies for social work still require students to register as student social workers. Whether this change entails that the general public and users of social work services are less well protected from unacceptable levels of practice by social work students remains to be seen. This change in regulation is not the only consequence of the HCPC assuming regulation for social work that has led to differences in practice across the United Kingdom.

When the regulatory bodies were set up in 2001 they developed codes of practice for both social care workers and employers. These codes placed expectations about desired and required behaviour upon both employers and employees in the social care workforce. In this sense they are different from approaches taken in many other countries which have a code of ethics that provide a requirement for staff to follow, but no linked set of requirements for employers. In addition, the codes apply to a broad group of staff that work in the human services, and in the UK fall under the generic title 'social care workers'. Hence, in these two respects, the UK has adopted a significantly different approach to that found elsewhere. The first iteration of these codes was almost identical across England, Northern Ireland, Scotland and Wales. However, with the assumption by the HCPC of responsibility for the regulation of social work, the approach to the regulation of social work has diverged significantly within the UK. The HCPC has one 'Set of Standards of Conduct, Performance and Ethics' (HCPC, 2008), which apply to all of the regulated professions for which it has responsibility. This entails that the codes of practice in England that are required of social workers are different to those that are required in Northern Ireland (NISSC, 2004), Scotland (SSSC, 2004) and Wales (CGC/CCW, 2004).

Table 7.1   The requirements in the respective countries and The College of Social Work

Health & Care Professions Council (mandatory for registered social workers in England)[a]	Scottish Social Services Council (mandatory for registered social workers in Scotland)[b]	The College of Social Work (expected for College of Social Work members – applies in England only)[c]
1. You must act in the best interests of service users	1. Protect the rights and promote the interests of service users and carers	1. Protect the rights of, promote the interests of, and empower people who use social work services and those who care for and about them
2. You must respect the confidentiality of service users	2. Strive to establish and maintain the trust and confidence of service users and carers	2. Establish and maintain the trust and confidence of people who use social work services and their carers, promoting their independence while protecting them as far as possible from unwanted danger
3. You must keep high standards of personal conduct	3. Promote the independence of service users while protecting them as far as possible from danger or harm	3. Respect the rights of people who use social work services and their carers including their right to take reasonable risks, while seeking to ensure that their behaviour does not harm themselves or others
4. You must provide (to us and any other relevant regulators) any important information about your conduct and competence	4. Respect the rights of service users while seeking to ensure that their behaviour does not harm themselves or other people	4. Serve, and promote the well-being of, the whole community
5. You must keep your professional knowledge and skills up to date	5. Uphold public trust and confidence in social services	5. Promote social justice and display compassion and respect in my professional practice
6. You must act within the limits of your knowledge, skills and experience and, if necessary, refer the matter to another practitioner	6. Be accountable for the quality of their work and take responsibility for maintaining and improving their knowledge and skills	6. Uphold public trust and confidence in social work
7. You must communicate properly and effectively with service users and other practitioners		7. Be accountable for the quality of my work and take responsibility for maintaining and improving my knowledge and skills
8. You must effectively supervise tasks that you have asked other people to carry out		8. Behave in a respectful and collaborative way with other professionals and practitioners who share with me the duty to promote the well-being of people who use social work services and their carers
9. You must get informed consent to give treatment (except in an emergency)		9. Support the aims and objectives of The College of Social Work (TCSW)
10. You must keep accurate records		
11. You must deal fairly and safely with the risks of infection		
12. You must limit your work or stop practising if your performance or judgement is affected by your health		

(Continued)

Table 7.1 *(Continued)*

Health & Care Professions Council (mandatory for registered social workers in England)[a]	Scottish Social Services Council (mandatory for registered social workers in Scotland)[b]	The College of Social Work (expected for College of Social Work members – applies in England only)[c]
13. You must behave with honesty and integrity and make sure that your behaviour does not damage the public's confidence in you or your profession		
14. You must make sure that any advertising you do is accurate. This document sets out the standards of conduct, performance and ethics we expect from the health professionals we register. The standards also apply to people who are applying to become registered		

Notes:

[a] HCPC (2008) *Standards of Conduct, Performance and Ethics.* Available at: http://www.hpc-uk.org/assets/documents/10003B6EStandards ofconduct,performanceandethics.pdf

[b] SSSC (2004) *Codes of Practice for Social Service Workers and Employers.* Available at: http://www.sssc.uk.com/NR/rdonlyres/761AD208-BF96-4C71-8EFF-CD61092FB626/0/CodesofPractice21405.pdf (accessed 28 October 2008).

[c] TCSW (2013) *Code of Ethics for Membership of The College of Social Work.* Available at: https://www.tcsw.org.uk/uploadedFiles/TheCollege/Members_area/CodeofEthicsAug2013.pdf

When the codes of practice are compared across the four countries, it can be seen that there are significant differences in respect of those that apply in England. In Table 7.1 the major headings that describe the key components of the codes are given.

There are additional complications in the ethical frameworks landscape of the UK. The College of Social Work, established in 2012 by the Westminster government, is a charitable body charged with the responsibility of promoting and maintaining professional standards in social work. It is a membership organisation for social workers in England, but membership is not mandatory to practise professional social work. Similar bodies do not exist in the other countries of the UK; arguably the functions undertaken in England by the College are, to some extent, met by the regulatory bodies in those countries. In June 2013, the College of Social Work announced the publication of a Code of Ethics (TCSW, 2013). This bears a strong similarity to the codes of practice that are in force in Northern Ireland, Scotland and Wales. In addition, there are other codes of ethics that are concerned with particular activities within the domain of social work, notably the conduct of research (JUC SWEC, 2002) and practice education (NOPT, 2013). Thus for the social worker in the UK there are considerable complexities evident in the regulatory and ethical frameworks.

Seven tensions

In their day-to-day practice social workers are likely to be confronted by a number of challenges about how they ought to behave. While there may be an infinite number of detailed examples, there are clusters of 'professional tensions' that may require careful negotiation by social workers who need to be able to navigate their way through the moral dilemmas encountered within these groups of 'professional tensions'. Seven different types of 'professional tensions will be considered in turn: these represent the most important classes of professional tension that the practitioner is likely to encounter. A central first step in the successful resolution of any issue within one of these 'tensions' is to be able to recognise the particular class it belongs to, as this often gives an indication about possible strategies for resolution.

1. Professional boundaries

The term 'professional boundaries' has come to signify one of the most significant of these tensions; the notion of 'professional boundaries' contains the idea that there is a 'line' that divides behaviours that are acceptable and integral to social work practice and behaviours that are not acceptable in social interactions between social workers and the public. The term 'professional boundaries' is not normally used, although it could be, as demarcation of the boundary between an area of professional competence claimed by social workers, as opposed to an area claimed by other professions. The reach of the term 'professional boundaries' has usually been limited in professional discourse to refer to ethical issues within the domain of social work. For example, the International Federation of Social Workers, in its code of ethics (IFSW, 2012), stated that social workers must recognise *the boundaries between personal and professional life*, and should not abuse *their position for personal benefit or gain*.

While it may be relatively easy to accept this notion as an abstract principle, it may be rather harder to reach an agreed description of what falls either side of the 'line'. If indeed the boundary can be conceptualised as a simple 'line' that divides the acceptable from the unacceptable. Around the 'boundary line' there are likely to be difficult and taxing boundary issues that are contested: that is, what behaviours are acceptable in the personal domain, what behaviours are acceptable in the professional domain, and what if any is the overlap between the two domains. This can be illustrated diagrammatically, in Figure 7.1.

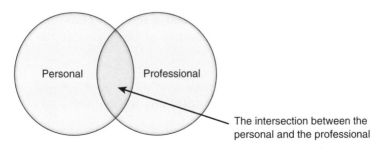

Figure 7.1   Personal and professional boundaries

This is less a matter of a simple division between what lies either side of a line than of which behaviours can be allocated to each segment and the size of the segments relative to each other. In particular, how large is the domain that overlaps the personal and the professional, if it exists at all? In their study, Doel et al. (2010) suggested that boundary issues may best be conceived as the interstices between four systems of required or expected behaviour: personal morality; professional codes; agency codes; and the consumerist expectation of the person using social work services. Given these complexities in the understanding of 'professional boundaries', there are different views about how hard and fast these boundaries may be. O'Leary et al. have argued that these boundaries are and should be 'permeable and dynamic' and that: *It is often the immediacy of boundary-setting decisions that perturbs practitioners* (2013: 146). However the notion of 'professional boundaries' is understood, different approaches have been adopted to the determination of what is acceptable and what is not in the conduct of the relationship between a social worker and a person who uses social work services. Two distinct approaches can be identified in the literature: these are considered in turn.

List model: taxonomy of unacceptable professional behaviours

One approach to determine what lies outside the 'boundaries' of professional social work practice is to ask how professional relationships differ from personal relationships with family members and friends or other kinds of social relationships and to draw up a list of unacceptable practices. This type of approach is grounded on the understanding that there can be a taxonomy – a list – of prohibited behaviours. This approach is most clearly articulated through the codes of ethics identified in the previous section. A major difficulty faced by any taxonomy is the extent to which it is accepted to be inclusive and comprehensive. Can a statement in a list prescribe for the practitioner whether a particular behaviour is acceptable on not? In some clear-cut cases consulting a taxonomy, for example a code of ethics, can provide clear guidance, in other more difficult examples of how to behave this may not be the case. More often that not it is the decision about how to apply the principle to a particular case that is the problem. The model described below may be of assistance in such cases.

Process model

A process model can provide a mechanism for the busy practitioner to help determine if a course of action is ethically acceptable. The GSCC, before its demise, published *Professional Boundaries: Guidance for Social Workers* (GSCC, 2012); in this document the GSCC outlined a series of tests to help identify if behaviours were likely to cross the boundary of being unacceptable professionally. These were:

- Would you be comfortable discussing all of your actions, and the rationale for those actions, in a supervision session with your manager?

- Would you be uncomfortable about a colleague or your manager observing your behaviour?

- If challenged, could you give an explanation as to how your actions are grounded in social work values?

- Do your actions comply with the relevant policies of your employer?

(GSCC, 2012: 7)

These are helpful questions for a busy practitioner to ask of him or herself, to determine if a proposed action is inside or outside of acceptable 'professional boundaries'. Two of these questions relate to the possibility of making the behaviours public; a further two to the justification that could be offered for the behaviours. Much rests on being able to justify the actions within the public arena. Hence, this approach can be summed up by asking 'How would others perceive my behaviour and could it be justified publicly?'

2. Dual relationships

In the US there is a well-established and long-standing literature about 'dual relationships'. The existence of a similar body of literature about such dual relationships has not been as strongly evident in other countries, for example in the UK. This literature specifies aspects of acceptable relationships between human service professionals, therapists and their clients or people that use their services. A dual relationship exists when, for example, a social worker becomes an employer, teacher, priest, sexual partner, etc., to someone with whom they currently work. Where it exists, this literature may provide an alternative way to determine the limits of acceptable boundaries, in some aspects of the interactions, between social workers and people that use social work services. A model of professional practice that incorporates ethical principles about 'dual relationships' would assert that such dual relationships will generally be found to be unacceptable because they have an impact on the nature of the professional social work relationship and compromise the ability of the social worker to act in the best professional interest of the person they are seeking to help, as other imperatives exist that derive from the secondary relationship – the non-social-work relationship. This was clearly stated by Kagle and Giebelhausen as long ago as 1994.

> *...dual relationships are potentially exploitative, crossing the boundaries of ethical practice, satisfying the practitioner's needs, and impairing his or her judgement.*

(Kagle and Giebelhausen, 1994: 213)

At first glance it may seem a straightforward matter that all 'dual relationships' should be regarded as unethical and therefore unacceptable for the reasons adduced by Kagle and Giebelhausen. However, professional social work practice is rarely simple. Professional behaviour is contextualised and highly nuanced through the realities of day-to-day practice. In many contexts, social workers and those that use social work may inhabit different, geographical, social and economic worlds yet live within the same urban conurbation. Their lives may only intersect through the professional dimension of social work practice. Where such structured separation between the social worker and the person using the services exists, it may be relatively easy to maintain a strict prohibition on 'dual relationships'. However, this structured separation of the lives of social workers from the lives of those that use services may not apply when community-based modules of delivery are chosen or required, for example in rural areas. Pugh (2007) identified several characteristics about rural communities which may lead to an implicit duality of relationships: an increased likelihood of contact through daily activities; the expectation that the social worker can be 'placed' within the social structure of the community; and a normative friendly style of professional relationships, which is qualitatively different from a more distant professional style. Hence, it would be unwise to make a prescriptive statement that all 'dual relationships' are ethically unacceptable as part of social work practice. While many may be unacceptable, there are situations in which they cannot be avoided. There can be similar discussions about how long after the conclusion of a professional social work relationship would it be acceptable to engage in another form of relationship with someone with whom the social worker had been working. Of course any such relationship would have to be legally acceptable. Despite these complexities, models of professional practice that include ethical principles about 'dual relationships', in which they are generally taken to be unacceptable, provide good guidance for ethical practice. Where 'dual relationships' do exist they should certainly be reviewed by social worker and supervisor.

3. Conflict of personal values and professional ethical requirements

The word 'value' or 'values' has a multitude of possible meanings, both within the domain of social work and beyond: this complexity was explored and illuminated in the seminal work of Timms (1983). Despite this complexity there is a consistent thread that has run through social work discourse for many years. This thread is grounded in the notion that the social worker may experience a conflict if his or her personal values are not aligned with those expected by the service user, promoted by their professional body, or required by their employer. A standard example, often used in the classroom, is as follows: how should a social worker, with an unshakable moral value that holds to the sanctity of life of the unborn child and who would under no circumstances countenance abortion, behave professionally when required to advise a woman, unexpectedly and unwillingly pregnant. The force behind this example is that the social worker cannot explore, with a clear conscience, the range of options open to a woman in these circumstances. So in this and similar situations, the social worker must either adopt a relativist view though which he or she rejects the idea of abortion for self or partner but will discuss the options available with the pregnant woman and, if necessary, assist her, should she choose to obtain an abortion. Or, if the social worker's views are universalist and strongly held, there is only one acceptable professional option and that is to arrange for another practitioner to provide the social work service for the pregnant woman, assuming that the social worker's employer will accept this solution. This is a powerful example; other instances where a social worker's values are out of alignment with professional requirements may be less compelling. In this example, the social worker's objection may be grounded in religious belief, or it may be humanist. There has been an increased interested in spirituality and faith-based social work in recent years (see e.g. Crisp, 2008; Tangenberg, 2005). There is potential for strongly held religious belief to conflict with secular professional requirements. Political allegiance provides another justification of strongly held values. For example, Baum (2010) found that Israeli social workers held strong views about their willingness to provide social work to Israeli settlers forced to evacuate from disputed areas: some 25 per cent (N = 108) were unwilling or guarded about offering social work help to this group.

4. Conflict of interest

In any professional walk of life a conflict of interest may arise. There is an item in all of these codes of practice and ethics, with the exception of England, that requires a social worker to declare a 'conflict of interest'. For example, item 2.6 of the NISCC code states a requirement of social workers to declare *issues that might create conflicts of interest and making sure that they do not influence your judgement or practice* (NISSC, 2004). One type of conflict of interest may arise when different members of the same family need social work help. Yet it may be impossible for one social worker to provide help to all members of the family as they may have conflicting interests. There is provision for this in most of the codes of practice in force in the UK. Where such conflicts exist it is the responsibility of the social worker to declare the difficulty and to seek ways that this can be managed, in all probability through the involvement of another social worker.

A second type of conflict of interest may arise where the interests of the social worker and the person seeking social work help are opposed. For example, where a student is on placement in an agency and his or her primary objective is to learn how to practise social work and to successfully complete the placement, then, consequently, there may be pressure for the student to demonstrate a measurable change in a short intervention period. However, the person using social work help may need a longer period of intervention. Such conflicts should be managed effectively through the supervisory processes.

One area of potential conflict of interest concerns the decision about which social worker in an agency works with a person needing help. In theory, barristers in England are supposed to provide legal representation for anyone that requests their assistance, provided it falls within the barrister's specialist area of legal knowledge. This so-called 'cab rank' principle operates where personal feelings about an individual or any breach of the law that they may have committed are irrelevant to the requirement for the professional lawyer to provide legal representation. So does the 'cab rank' principle apply in social work? There is no explicit statement in the codes of practice and ethics for England (HCPC, 2008),

Northern Ireland (NISSC, 2004), Scotland (SSSC, 2004) and Wales (CGC/CCW, 2004) that requires a social worker to provide social work services to all comers within his or her particular area of professional competence. If there were a conflict of interest about the provision of help to any individual then there would be an obligation for the social worker to make this explicit. There are, however, strong prescriptions against wrongful discrimination against various groups, which would in any case be unlawful.

5. Confidentiality and data protection

Historically, discussion in social work about data that refers to people that use services has been framed around the concept of 'confidentiality'. Clark has summarised the key arguments for the importance of confidentiality by drawing on the work of eight authors from a period of over 40 years, as follows:

- Lack of confidentiality violates the client's rights to protect his[2] reputation and keep his secrets, which defend privacy and autonomy.

- If the client cannot believe that what he says will not be passed on without his permission, truthful communication necessary to providing proper help will be inhibited.

- Failing to keep confidentiality may unfairly prejudice the client's interests because this could pass on to other parties information that they might use against the client.

- Where (as is usual) professional service is offered and accepted on the implicit or explicit promise of confidentiality, breaking confidence is straightforwardly a breach of promise or contract.

- The general welfare will be damaged if individuals are discouraged from seeking professional help through fear of unwarranted exposure.

These arguments for professional confidentiality are usually assumed to be broadly applicable to social work.

(Clark, 2000: 185–86)

Clark's summary of the arguments for confidentiality invites several questions. First, are these arguments still valid? *Prima facie*, the answer would appear be yes, although there are additional developments, unforeseen by Clark, that have added further dimensions to any consideration of confidentiality – more of that below. Second, are there any special or particular arguments about confidentiality that apply only to social work? Much as members of the profession may wish to be able to claim the special and unique nature of social work, the answer on this occasion is most probably no. The communication between social worker and the person using social worker services is not legally privileged in the same way as that between lawyer and client, or priest and penitent. Even if Clark has

---

[2]Gender specific language occurs in the original and has not been modified.

successfully enumerated the key justifications for the importance of confidentiality in social work, this listing does not make easy the day-to-day challenges of trying to make it work in the real world of professional practice.

Two important developments have occurred since Clark's summary in 2000 that impact on confidentiality in respect of social work practice in the UK. These developments are the implementation of the Data Protection Act (1998), and the growth of internet-based social work, including the use of social media. First, the Data Protection Act, *inter alia*, regulates who may have access to data, stipulates conditions for the granting of permission to access data and also sets standards for data storage. These components of the Act place *legal obligations*, rather than reliance upon practice codes or abstract principles, on social workers and the organisations for which they work about how to manage the information about people that use their services and to whom access is given to that information. Certainly, notions of what have traditionally been discussed under the banner of confidentiality now need to incorporate more fully consideration of issues about data protection.

Particularly over the past 10 years, there has been an exponential growth in the number of electronic communication methods that are available to professionals and public alike. This growth has been made possible through: high speed wireless connections to mobile phones that are capable of handling large amounts of data; the availability of Wi-Fi connections; the growth of social networking sites; and the availability of smart phones and tablets, which have enabled access to these services at all times and away from desk-based computers. These developments have enabled social workers to: communicate with people who use services via email and text; develop 'virtual' interventions at a distance; and have knowledge of, and access to, the 'online' lives, through social media, of people who use social work services. The possibilities for the creative use of social networks for benefit is enormous. They also have the potential to cause havoc and harm to an individual's social life. Reamer (2013), writing from a US perspective, has detailed some of the issues that are of concern for social workers about these developments, while Kimball and Kim (2013) note that the NASW code of ethics for social workers in the US does not address these issues. The same could also be said of the codes of ethics and practice used by social workers across the UK; while Steyaert and Gould (2009) have identified some of the risks associated with a 'digital divide' for the provision of social work between those that have access to the online or virtual world and those who do not.

6. Whistleblowing and unacceptable professional practice

Social workers are as likely as any other professional to observe poor or unacceptable practice by their colleagues or other professionals. All social workers are likely at some time or other to find themselves in the position where they observe that some form of organisational or professional practice is going or has gone wrong and is potentially damaging for people that use social work services. Social workers do not seem to be as fortunate as airline pilots who inhabit a world where a 'near miss' (that is, where something nearly went wrong) is something to examine as an educative tool for improvement – not that anyone wants any more near misses! At the heart of this approach is a 'no blame' culture. Rather the opposite seems to apply for social workers. As Rogowski has described, social workers in the UK inhabit a managerialist world where they have been held to expectations about the achievement of targets for the delivery of services and it appears that many social workers are required to spend an ever-increasing amount of time entering data into computers (Rogowski, 2012). The problem for anyone who observes unacceptable practice within an organisation is whether they can bring this to the attention of senior managers, who have the power and can act to deal with the problem, and whether they will be seen as promoting organisational goals or acting subversively. There are a number of examples where those that have 'blown the whistle' on poor practice have paid a high personal price that may include loss of employment. This possibility of the personal price that may be paid generates a tension between the drive to expose poor standards and improve service, and the risk of compromising the individual's professional career. This tension is not particular to social work.

7. Capacity, best interests and risk

Social workers have to deal with circumstances where an individual may pose a threat to themselves or to others. In many circumstances, when an individual is a threat to others, the police are likely to become involved, for example when children are in need of protection (safeguarding).[3] However, this is by no means always the case. Social workers may be charged with the responsibility to play a key role within a multi-disciplinary decision-making framework for the monitoring of risk, which entails the ability to calculate levels of anticipated risk. It is an extraordinarily difficult task to compute risk levels in a professional social work intervention. Social workers are not blessed with greater degrees of prescience than any other profession! Yet they are subject to 'moral luck', which implies that if a set of circumstances with a high or moderate level of risk turns out satisfactorily then no more will be said (see for example a debate that still has purchase in current social work practice: Hollis and Howe, 1987, 1990; Macdonald, 1990a, 1990b). If, on the other hand, there is an undesired outcome then the social worker will be seen to be accountable and will be held to blame – as has happened on many occasions in child protection. There is an ethical danger buried here for the social worker; in such contentious situations, where a career can be wrecked because of a negative outcome, social workers may be tempted to make decisions that protect their careers rather than the best interests of the child in question. For a current exploration of this issue of risk and accountability, see Pithouse et al. (2012), whose study reports on the attempts to reduce risk in child protection through the use of the computer-based Integrated Children's System (ICS), and Macdonald and Macdonald (2010) who argue for a intelligent approach to risk and its management. With regard to the protection of children,

---

[3]Current linguistic convention in England has adopted the inelegant term 'safeguarding' to refer to such situations. This term is not used in other countries, nor is it widely understood; hence more conventional and internationally understood terminology has been employed.

living in the community with a family, the key issue for social workers is to be able to recognise levels of risk and to initiate ways in which that risk can be managed in conjunction with other professionals.

The management of risk is not only confined to social work practice with children and families. Where social workers deal with adults (for example older people; those with learning disabilities; those who are mentally unwell, and so on) they may be confronted by a range of issues that derive from whether the person is able to make a decision for themselves about how to live their lives without endangering themselves or other people, that is, whether the person has 'capacity' The definition of 'capacity' and operational principles are to be found in the Mental Capacity Act (2005); this extremely important piece of legislation is grounded on five key principles:

1. Every adult has the right to make his or her own decisions and must be assumed to have capacity to make them unless it is proved otherwise.

2. A person must be given all practicable help before anyone treats them as not being able to make their own decisions.

3. Just because an individual makes what might be seen as an unwise decision, they should not be treated as lacking capacity to make that decision.

4. Anything done or any decision made on behalf of a person who lacks capacity must be done in their best interests.

5. Anything done for or on behalf of a person who lacks capacity should be the least restrictive of their basic rights and freedoms (Ministry of Justice, 2012).

The application of these key principles in day-to-day practice presents social workers with many ethical problems. For example, if an older person, living at home alone, with no relatives, is not providing adequate care for themselves and will not accept help from professional carers, at what point should the social worker intervene and what form should any intervention take. Similar problems arise for people with mental ill-health, where they may, on account of their illness, demonstrate a propensity to harm others. Where it is clear that an individual does not possess 'capacity' then the actions to be taken may be considerably easier to determine than in situations of ambiguity. In such situations social workers may experience quite an extreme sense of conflict between the right of the individual to pursue their life as they choose and the need to protect their best interests. Taylor (2007) has suggested that 'professional dissonance', a mechanism to hold the personal values about an action separately from the professional requirements, may be helpful in mental health practice and more generally across social work.

Accommodating moral challenges and tensions

Ethical tensions present social workers with many dilemmas in day-to-day professional practice. A temptation, in the hurly-burly of modern social work, is to ride roughshod over the finer ethical nuances in response to the pressure to resolve issues as speedily and cost-efficiently as possible. Such pressures should be resisted at all costs. Irrespective of the values held by an individual social worker, there are two major devices that can be used to reach an accommodation with the complex demands imposed by these moral challenges and tensions. The first of these devices is to pay attention to the process of decision-making. Key to this process is to engage in discussion about the ethical issue; in most instances this is most likely to be with the social worker's supervisor or a manager with professional responsibility in the field. Following such discussions, decisions taken are likely to assume an organisationally agreed position. Such shared decision-making processes are preferable both because they are likely to lead to an airing of the range of complexities embedded within the dilemma and because the social worker then has organisational backing for any action that is taken. This may not help the social worker employed as an independent practitioner and it may lead to additional tensions in situations where social workers are managed by managers with other professional backgrounds, who do not adhere to social work professional ethics. Nonetheless a consequence of such shared decision-making processes is that the decision taken should be one that can in principle be open to public scrutiny (although the details of the particular individual at the heart of the dilemma should not be revealed). It should be possible to justify the grounds for making a decision about how to resolve an ethical tension to members of the public and a court, if necessary. If this is not possible then it is most likely that the decision taken is flawed in some way.

The second device is to look to external reference points that confer additional legitimacy on the ways in which decisions are resolved. The most visible documents, that are international in reach, are the various declarations of human rights, most notably the Universal Declaration of Human Rights (United Nations, 1948). This declaration contains three broad sets of rights: political rights and freedoms; rights to a decent standard of living within the context of the level of resource available in a given country; and the rights to international frameworks across nations that promote peace and collaboration. These reference points, external to social work and to any particular society, provide a statement of the standards necessary to preserve human dignity and a decent life. The contribution of social work to the development of human rights has been investigated by Healy (2008), while Reichert (2006) has explored the direct application of human rights to social work through exercises. As is so often the case, the use of a 'human rights' based approach is promising in the abstract as a mechanism to engage with ethical issues and tensions, but the 'real-world' application is complex. For example, the application of human rights in social work leads immediately into the complex issue of universality and relativism (Healy, 2007). This issue has been at the heart of much discussion in social work – should individuals be treated according to common universal standards or should the individual's cultural, ethnic, religious (etc.) context provide a major determinant in how they are treated.

Conclusion

The regulation of social work through the registration of practitioners is designed to provide a mechanism that affords some protection for those that use social work. A key component of this protection is that only registered social workers are permitted to practise and that they are expected to conform to a set of ethical principles for the profession. These principles, found in 'codes of ethics' or 'codes of conduct', make explicit what is expected of social workers for the public and profession alike.

These ethical principles do not make ethical issues in social work magically disappear, nor are they intended to do so. Such ethical issues are an intrinsic part of professional social work and are a necessary concomitant of the landscape of a profession that both seeks to provide help to people and is required by law to protect some from themselves or others. Rather, the ethical principles provide guidance about how to respond to the complexities of day-to-day social work practice. These complexities will be there as long as there is a social work practice. We should not anticipate any tendency towards greater simplicity in social work practice, rather the reverse: our ever more complex world seems to generate new ethical tensions.

REFLECTIVE QUESTIONS

1. *Identify other ethical tensions than those discussed above, which are present in the day-to-day practice of social work; to what extent do their embedded complexities impinge on professional practice.*

2. *To what extent can social workers effectively manage their professional ethical concerns when working for large municipal organisations or large non-governmental organisations with their own distinct requirements for social work practice?*

3. *There has been a growth of direct payments to organisations by those that use services in recent years: to what extent does this approach impact on the ethical issues faced by social workers in their professional practice?*

4. *Ethical issues are often considered singly. Consider an example from practice that has involved a number of ethical issues – perhaps where there have been several family members. How is it possible to resolve these complexities?*

MMENDED
RTHER
ADING

Banks, S (2012) *Ethics and Values in Social Work* (4th edition). London: Palgrave Macmillan.

Beckett, C and Maynard, A (2013) *Values and Ethics in Social Work: An Introduction* (2nd edition). London: Sage.

Carey, M and Green, L (2013) *Practical Social Work Ethics: Complex Dilemmas Within Applied Social Care.* Farnham, Surrey: Ashgate.

Parrott, L (2010) *Values and Ethics in Social Work Practice* (2nd edition). Exeter: Learning Matters.

REFERENCES

AASW (2010) *Code of Ethics.* Canberra: Australian Association of Social Workers.

Baum, N (2010) Where Professional and Personal Values May Clash: Social Workers' Attitudes Towards Professional Involvement in the Evacuation of Israeli Settlers from Gaza and Northern Samaria. *European Journal of Social Work*, 13: 55–72.

CGC/CCW (2004) *Codes of Practice for Social Care Workers and Employers.* Available at: **www.ccwales.org.uk/the-codes-of-practice/** (accessed 30 August 2013).

Clark, CL (2000) *Social Work Ethics, Politics Principles and Practice.* Basingstoke: Palgrave.

Crisp, BR (2008) Social Work and Spirituality in a Secular Society. *Journal of Social Work*, 8: 363–75.

Doel, M, Allmark, P, Conway, P, et al. (2010) Professional Boundaries: Crossing a Line or Entering the Shadows? *British Journal of Social Work*, 40: 1866–89.

GSCC (2012) *Professional Boundaries: Guidance for Social Workers.* Available at: **www.scie-socialcareonline.org.uk/repository/fulltext/122181.pdf**

HCPC (2008) *Standards of Conduct, Performance and Ethics.* Available at: **www.hpc-uk.org/assets/documents/10003B6EStandardsofconduct,performanceandethics.pdf**

HCPC (2012) *Guidance on Conduct and Ethics for Students.* Available at: **www.hpc-uk.org/assets/documents/10002C16Guidanceonconductandethicsforstudents.pdf**

Healy, LM (2007) Universalism and Cultural Relativism in Social Work Ethics. *International Social Work*, 50: 11–26.

Healy, LM (2008) Exploring the History of Social Work as a Human Rights Profession. *International Social Work*, 51: 735–48.

Hollis, M and Howe, D (1987) Moral Risks in Social Work. *Journal of Applied Philosophy*, 4: 123–33.

Hollis, M and Howe, D (1990) Moral Risks in the Social Work Role: A Response to Macdonald. *British Journal of Social Work*, 20: 547–52.

IFSW (2012) *Statement of Ethical Principles.* Available at: **http://ifsw.org/policies/statement-of-ethical-principles/**

JUC SWEC (2002) *Code of Ethics for Social Work and Social Care Research.* Available at: **http://www.juc.ac.uk/swec-research-code.html**

Kagle, JD and Giebelhausen, PN (1994) Dual Relationships and Professional Boundaries. *Social Work*, 39: 213–20.

Kimball, E and Kim, J (2013) Virtual Boundaries: Ethical Considerations for Use of Social Media in Social Work. *Social Work*, 58: 185–88.

Macdonald, G (1990a) Allocating Blame in Social Work. *British Journal of Social Work*, 20: 525–46.

Macdonald, G (1990b) Moral Risks? A Reply to Hollis and Howe. *British Journal of Social Work*, 20: 553–56.

Macdonald, G and Macdonald, K (2010) Safeguarding: A Case for Intelligent Risk Management. *British Journal of Social Work*, 40: 1174–91.

Ministry of Justice (2012) *The Mental Capacity Act.*

NASW (2008) *Code of Ethics.* Available at: **www.naswdc.org/code.htm**

NISSC (2004) *Codes of Practice for Social Care Workers and Employers of Social Care Workers.* Available at: **www.niscc.info/content/uploads/downloads/registration/Codes_of_ Practice.pdf**

NOPT (2013) *Code of Practice for Practice Educators* Available at: **www.nopt.org/college-of- social-work-consultation/**

O'Leary, P, Tsui, M-S and Ruch, G (2013) The Boundaries of the Social Work Relationship Revisited: Towards a Connected, Inclusive and Dynamic Conceptualisation. *British Journal of Social Work*, 43: 135–53.

Pithouse, A, Broadhurst, K, Hall, C, et al. (2012) Trust, Risk and the (Mis)management of Contingency and Discretion Through New Information Technologies in Children's Services. *Journal of Social Work*, 12: 158–78.

Pugh, R (2007) Dual Relationships: Personal and Professional Boundaries in Rural Social Work. *British Journal of Social Work*, 37: 1405–23.

Reamer, FG (2013) Social Work in a Digital Age: Ethical and Risk Management Challenges. *Social Work*, 58: 163–72.

Reichert, E (2006) *Understanding Human Rights.* Thousand Oaks, CA: Sage.

Rogowski, S (2012) Social Work with Children and Families: Challenges and Possibilities in the Neo-liberal World. *British Journal of Social Work*, 42: 921–40.

SSSC (2004) *Codes of Practice for Social Service Workers and Employers.* Available at: **www.sssc.uk.com/NR/rdonlyres/761AD208-BF96-4C71-8EFF-CD61092FB626/0/ CodesofPractice21405.pdf** (accessed 30 August 2013).

Steyaert, J and Gould, N (2009) Social Work and the Changing Face of the Digital Divide. *British Journal of Social Work*, 39: 740–53.

Tangenberg, KM (2005) Faith-based Human Services Initiatives: Considerations for Social Work Practice and Theory. *Social Work*, 50: 197–206.

Taylor, MF (2007) Professional Dissonance: A Promising Concept for Clinical Social Work. *Smith College Studies in Social Work*, 77: 89–99.

TCSW (2013) *Code of Ethics for Membership of The College of Social Work.* Available at: **www.tcsw.org.uk/uploadedFiles/TheCollege/Members_area/CodeofEthicsAug2013.pdf** (accessed 30 August 2013).

Timms, N (1983) *Social Work Values: An Enquiry.* London: Routledge & Kegan Paul.

United Nations (1948) *The Universal Declaration of Human Rights.* New York: United Nations.

Chapter 8

Professionalism and practice-focused research

Roger Smith

Introduction: the place of research in social work

Social work as a discipline is an applied form of inquiry, obviously, in the sense that its central focus is practice; and it might seem equally obvious that the quality of practice in turn depends on an active engagement with research ('knowledge'), just as it is underpinned by the other two elements of the triad, 'skills' and 'values'. Thus, we might expect research activity to be readily recognised as a significant contributor to the pool of ideas and evidence informing and supporting practice; and we might also expect to see social work practitioners as active users and producers of research. Indeed, there has been much recent emphasis on the importance of 'evidence-based practice' in social work and other fields of state welfare, such as mental health and rehabilitation in criminal justice (Marsh and Fisher, 2005).

While the potential contribution of research to improvements in practice might have been acknowledged in principle, this does not always seem to be reflected in the day-to-day organisation and delivery of social work intervention. One possible explanation for this lies in the shortage of relevant skills and a lack of confidence amongst practitioners in knowing how to access, 'read', interpret and then apply the lessons of research, but there are certain to be other inhibiting factors as well. These may be predictable, such as lack of time, limited access to research findings, and organisational priorities and expectations. It is sometimes the case, too, that research findings themselves are not easy to assimilate, often being tentative and hedged with qualifications, or concluding not with answers, but with more questions. While these various constraints and limitations should be acknowledged and addressed, it remains the case that practitioners and their agencies should be well prepared, at the very least, to be able to find, evaluate and use research evidence effectively. It is of great importance, therefore, to 'be informed', and to retain an active orientation towards the continuing development of the knowledge base to inform one's own practice. Social work is not just applied common sense after all (Gammack, 1982).

The purpose of this chapter is to develop this argument further by exploring the underlying principles, skills and approaches which will help practitioners and others to approach social work research positively, at whatever stage, and to develop the capacity to identify what makes good (and bad) research, and how it can be applied effectively in variable and challenging contexts to inform and enhance the quality of practice. In brief, the aim is to suggest why it is so important to develop 'research-mindedness', and how to do so, both in the sense of contributing to improvements in practice and in helping to give substance to the core values underpinning social work itself.

Beginning with some reflections on the importance of 'research-mindedness', the chapter will then address both generic and specific questions on the nature of social work research – what are its applications, why we need it, how we can evaluate it, and how we can take a critical view of the messages it generates.

From this point, the chapter will go on to enumerate core research skills, to do with open-minded and systematic information gathering, coherent analytical approaches, interpretation of findings and critical reflection on the process and outcomes of the research activity. In covering this ground, it will also be useful to reflect on the commonalities between research and practice, notably in the kind of skills required and the manner in which they should be applied, as well as some of the common challenges, such as explicating and negotiating power relationships.

From this overview, the chapter will then go on to consider in more detail the distinctive features and value-base of practice-oriented research in social work. This, in turn, will help to demonstrate the particular strengths and potential contributions of research activity which is undertaken by practitioners (or intending practitioners) and which is, at the same time, properly user-centred.

Following on from this, it will also be important to set out some of the key issues concerning the practicalities of undertaking research 'professionally', including approaches to the organisation and management of investigations, and key ethical requirements, especially where service users are involved or affected (as they almost certainly will be).

Finally, the chapter will return to the question of the importance of research in and for social work, and its added value, as well as reflecting on the necessity of acquiring and retaining 'research-mindedness' over the course of a social work career, in terms of the pursuit of better outcomes for people who use services, and the promotion of the wider goal of achieving fair treatment and social justice.

Being 'research-minded'

The practical orientation of social work, combined with its aspirations to expert professional status, necessitate a readiness to inquire into the domain of activity which it encompasses. As we shall see, social work has already been the subject of extensive and varied investigation, and a significant body of evidence of potential value to practice is already in the public domain. It is therefore important to develop the capability to identify and access these sources, but also to be able to evaluate effectively the quality of what is produced, and gain a critical perspective on the findings that emerge, which may inevitably be complex, contradictory, 'unfinished' or partial (in both senses). It is the recognition of this point that has prompted the Social Work Reform Board to emphasise the significance of 'research-mindedness' in its own proposals:

> *The curriculum framework should provide opportunities for students to develop research mindedness, enhance their capacity for evidenced informed practice and prepare them to develop their own learning and curiosity. Teaching and learning about social work research clearly plays a significant and distinctive part in achieving these outcomes throughout their initial qualifying courses and throughout their career. The development of research literate students is key to promoting quality practice that can support change for children, families and vulnerable adults and lay the foundation for some future careers in academic social work.*

(Social Work Reform Board, 2011: 24)

A professional approach necessitates being open to new insights and knowledge as it is developed in the field of practice; but it also means not simply taking these at face value, or simply treating every emerging finding as superseding all that precedes it. Key elements of research-mindedness find direct parallels in the professional attributes associated with effective social work practitioners, such as: a rigorous approach to the process of inquiry; critical evaluation of the available evidence; the capacity to analyse complex material effectively; and the ability to organise such material into a considered and justifiable conclusion.

When evaluating the messages from research, while being receptive to the available evidence, we also need to have in mind a series of pertinent questions to be addressed to the findings with which we are presented, such as:

- Who commissioned this study? What is their agenda?

- Who carried out the research? What is their relationship to the commissioner?

- Are the methods used justifiable, clearly specified and soundly applied (as far as you can tell)?

- Are the findings properly documented? Are they consistent with the evidence from other related research?

- What messages can you take from the research? Are there any messages you can take from it which are not directly presented to you?

- In what ways might the evidence provided affect your thinking or practice?

- What important questions have not been considered/answered?

While it is important to evaluate research critically, and to be aware of its limitations, it is also important to value what it has to offer, even when its findings are not neat or conclusive, as tends to be the case.

Many of the questions outlined above apply to the conduct of research as well as its interpretation and use. Research awareness and research literacy are thus further enhanced through the process of designing and carrying out one's own investigative study, even in the light of the kind of constraints set out earlier. Carrying out a research project, however small scale or time limited, is not therefore just an end in itself, but it also, in turn, equips the researcher to better understand and adopt a critical perspective on practice-relevant findings.

What is (social work) research, then?

So, let us begin with the inevitable definitional questions: 'What is research?' And: 'What is social work research?'. Inevitably, for academic purposes, a definition of research must encompass a wide range of disciplines, with their very different objects of study, assumptions about the nature of reality and what counts as knowledge, and methods and tools of investigation, from philosophy to physics. Understandably, then, it is a challenge to arrive at an overarching definition which encompasses this breadth of perspectives without becoming unhelpfully vague and general. To be meaningful and useful, a definition of research must establish its distinctive characteristics, true for all disciplines, but which sets it apart from, say, journalism, or, indeed, the processes of critical inquiry, evaluation and assessment which are central to social work practice.

The *Oxford English Dictionary* definition seeks to achieve this as follows, defining research as *the systematic investigation into and study of materials and sources in order to establish facts and reach new conclusions*. This is helpful up to a point; it does seem important to recognise research as being 'systematic', that is, guided by rules of knowledge acquisition and the application of ideas (theory) which seek to gain an inclusive and comprehensive understanding of the object of study. In addition, though, the field of study and the research question need to be specified clearly and precisely – the central question must be 'researchable' (for example, 'Is social work effective?' seems like an important question but its scope is probably too wide to be directly answerable).

Not only must the question be clear and precise, but the methods of investigation and analysis must also be transparent and intelligible, capable of being reproduced by others and applied consistently. The application of these principles should, in turn, generate findings which are fully and precisely accounted for; but to justify its claims to be more than just knowledge-gathering, research must also be expected to generate ideas and theories, as well as material evidence. Research is uniquely characterised by its theoretical dimension, utilising, generating and/or testing concepts and new insights into the topic of inquiry. Findings must therefore be contextualised by explanations ('why' and 'how', as well as 'what'). Implicit in this characterisation is the assumption that the process of inquiry and discovery is intended to generate lessons for wider application, dissemination and use. In this sense, research activity may be distinguished from, say, a social work core assessment in child protection which may generate wider lessons and 'practice wisdom', but whose principal focus, rightly, is the well-being of the child or children concerned.

Research is also sometimes differentiated, and distinctions are made, between 'basic' and 'applied' forms of inquiry. Basic research is sometimes characterised as the means by which the building blocks of all other ('applied') research are constructed, establishing the core principles, ideas and fundamental 'truths' on which all subsequent investigations are based. It therefore tends to be seen as the source of essential theoretical principles and generalisable assumptions which hold good at all times.

Applied research, on the other hand, is depicted as being predominantly concerned with the situated investigation of processes and ideas in the 'real world'. Do the ideas developed in basic research 'work' in practice? Clearly, this form of research activity approximates more closely to the type of inquiry typically undertaken within social work, but this sometimes works to the disadvantage of the discipline. In the same way as practice is sometimes viewed as being based on ideas and approaches drawn from psychology, for instance, so too, social work research may be seen as essentially second-hand, relying on more established disciplines such as psychology and sociology for its core ideas and methods. Not only might applied research in social work be seen as limited because of its derivative qualities, but it may also be considered as limited in scope, essentially only being capable of localised application and giving rise to mid-range rather than grand theory.

While there might be a tendency to see social work research as principally an 'applied' form of inquiry, it would be unwise to consider that its value or quality is diminished by being grounded in 'real world' questions. This does not inevitably preclude research of this kind from opening up or addressing theoretical debates. If it were to become preoccupied purely with 'what works?', this would certainly diminish its ability to break new ground conceptually as well as in developing new forms of practice.

The domains of social work research

It seems self-evident that the quality of social work practice more or less depends on a sound grasp of the evidence relating to service users' circumstances and their experiences of interventions. How else would we be able to estimate need and make informed decisions about how to address it? What is the most effective response? And, when is it better not to respond, for fear of creating over-dependency or stigma? Critically informed and appropriate practice depends on answering this type of question, it would seem.

Developing this question, we might be able to identify a number of potential domains of inquiry in social work, each of which contributes to our understanding of what constitutes best practice. These could be typified in terms of: research for social work; research on/about social work; and research with social work. These effectively cover the issues of who we should be working with, what happens when we do, and what influences the conditions in which practice takes place.

1. Research *for* social work: In this category falls research which identifies, and attempts to account for, the circumstances of those who fall under the remit of social work intervention. Thus, for example, the changing nature and demography of ageing is a significant topic, and in this potential area of practice we might also be concerned to identify the incidence of specific conditions associated with getting older, such as dementia, or social isolation, while the expectations and needs (both subjectively and externally defined) and wishes of older people might all be areas of inquiry which help to identify the scope and potential requirements of social practice with this potential population of service users.

2. Research *on/about* social work: Under this heading are likely to be included investigations into the form, content and effects of social work interventions, from the perspectives of both service providers and those who use services. Thus, for example, the experiences and views of parents of children at risk of harm would be a legitimate area of investigation, while, equally, changes in the levels of safety and well-being amongst this group of children are a significant topic of interest to social work research.

3. Research *with* social work: Of equal importance is the task of establishing a sense of what constitute the 'conditions' for practice. That is to say, how practitioners experience and feel about their work, how they are supported and empowered to practise, and the processes by which they engage with and establish relationships with service users are all key questions which are capable of being addressed meaningfully through research. The subjects of appropriate training, professional development and effective supervision and management thus qualify as subject areas worthy of scrutiny, quite clearly.

As these brief summaries indicate, this suggests a very wide range of topics and potential research strategies relevant to social work, which in turn means that there is likely to be a considerable demand for work to be undertaken within the remit afforded by the discipline. There is also, therefore, an obvious question of capacity and, related to this, quality. How is it possible to generate the range and standards of research required to inform and improve social work practice in order to pursue the shared goal of achieving the best possible outcomes for people who use services, especially in times of financial stringency, as at present?

Over time there has been substantial investment in investigations of 'hot topics' in social work; for example, the Department of Health (1995, 2001) on several occasions during the 1980s and 1990s commissioned major programmes of inquiry into children's well-being and safeguarding services. These programmes of research were influential in emphasising the value of early preventive services, for example, although messages about the careful exercise of professional judgement in safeguarding cases were not always heeded quite so well. Other significant sources of funding from social work research include research councils (especially the Economic and Social Research Council) and charitable trusts, notably including the Joseph Rowntree Foundation. These have helped to provide a more independent source of evidence and ideas, and have often been useful in drawing attention to areas of need which have been unrecognised and unmet, such as the community care needs of disabled people from ethnic minorities (e.g. Vernon, 2002).

In the face of the accusation sometimes levelled at them of being uninterested in social work research, it is also of note that several consortia of provider organisations (statutory and voluntary) have themselves sponsored and coordinated research activity, often producing significant pointers towards 'good practice' (see Frost, 2005).

Beyond the institutional level, a great deal of social work research is carried out by qualifying students, practitioners and academic researchers, sometimes with and sometimes without the support of agencies and institutions. Indeed, this kind of research activity does afford the investigator a considerable degree of independence in deciding on types and method of inquiry; although at the same time, the experience of acting as a 'lone researcher' has its drawbacks in terms of frequently experienced limitations and constraints. Managing the scale of activity, gaining permissions, negotiating ethical procedures and simply finding time are all potential inhibiting factors, with the result that a great deal of small-scale but potentially highly useful research work is compromised from the start by what seem like insurmountable obstacles.

Developing skills, applying learning: the value of practice-focused research

As indicated, there are considerable overlaps between research and practice in social work; and it therefore seems that there may be much to be gained from developing 'research-mindedness' in preparation for practice or the enhancement of existing skills. As we have already noted, this might involve acquiring the capacity to read and evaluate existing research evidence critically, but it may also involve planning and carrying out one's own investigation.

Although there does seem to be some variation, depending on geography and agency setting, typically opportunities can be created for students (and practitioners) to undertake small-scale studies focusing on specific issues affecting service users. The findings and lessons learnt may be highly localised, but will nonetheless be of potential value in their specific context. In such cases the focus of the inquiry is likely to be the needs or aspirations of an identifiable group of service users (asylum seekers using a particular local resource, for example), the impact and experiences of a particular service (a support scheme for victims, possibly) or areas of unmet need (children with special educational needs, say), or unfair treatment (South Asian women affected by domestic violence, perhaps), which are capable of being investigated in 'close up'.

At the time of writing, I have just finished marking a series of research dissertations by practitioners undertaking agency-based studies as part of their post-qualifying learning, covering subjects as diverse as communication with young children, advocacy and practitioner well-being. In every case, the intention is to make use of their findings to influence and improve the service provided by the agency by offering practical and realistic recommendations for change.

Additional value can certainly be gained when the research in question can be used to validate, improve or change practice, or to draw attention to needs which are not being addressed effectively; that is, when it can be 'fed in' to organisational thinking, to enable service enhancements to be made. The study I undertook as a practitioner in juvenile diversion helped to 'validate' a number of aspects of practice at the time. With a sympathetic employer and a supportive external supervisor, I was able to carry out a detailed, mixed-methods study of the practices and outcomes of a 'sister' project which followed the same broad working principles (see Smith, 1987), but where I was not too close to the subject of inquiry. There is no doubt that organisational support and systematic supervision are important elements in facilitating practitioner research, but as in this case, the value for the agency of testing the validity of its approach to practice offers justification for this kind of limited investment.

So, where an agency may wish to gain an independent account of the value and effectiveness of its services for people with whom it works, the potential contribution of a small-scale research inquiry 'from outside' might well be substantial. Here, it would seem, there is a specific opportunity for practitioners/students in social work to combine skills development with meaningful contributions to practice knowledge and understanding of the service user perspective. While there are clearly practical challenges to be faced in organising and delivering an effective and valid piece of research, there are still good grounds for creating the space to undertake applied investigations of this kind.

Practice-focused research: bridging the divide

In addition to becoming attuned to research and appreciating its potential uses, those involved in social work practice may gain in other ways from undertaking applied research activity. For a start, research and practice share many common attributes, and it is arguable that the development and application of key research skills provides an additional opportunity to hone specific capabilities for social work practice. In this sense alone, then, engaging in research activity should not be seen as a diversion from the core task of learning how to 'do' social work, but as complementary to it. As well as being able to draw on the 'outputs' of research, intending and existing practitioners will benefit from understanding research processes from the inside.

Thus, for example, just as in practice, good research depends crucially on a process of systematic information gathering with a clear purpose in mind. The questions to be asked must be specific and answerable; the methods of inquiry used must be capable of producing sound evidence pertinent to these questions; the methods of gathering, recording and retrieving information must be robust, replicable and reliable. In support of this, the sources to be identified, the tools developed and quality control mechanisms to be applied must be designed to underpin the adequacy and credibility of the material gathered.

Furthermore, as in social work practice, the interview is a central feature of much social research. The organisation and content of a research interview have to be shaped by very similar considerations to those applying to practitioners undertaking assessments. In both cases, close attention needs to be paid to: location; timing; preparation; information-sharing; interviewer/interviewee characteristics and mutual expectations; context effect; specific communication issues; risks of harm or distress; ethical issues, such as vulnerability, disclosure and confidentiality; and 'what happens next?' This is not to suggest an exact equivalence between social work practice interviews and those carried out for research purposes, but rather to suggest that there is a very close alignment of the relevant professional skills. Undertaking subject-relevant research activity of this kind should, therefore, support the acquisition of relevant capabilities for practice; while, on the other hand, recognition of the extensive common ground between the two domains of inquiry may help those in, or preparing for, practice to feel considerably less apprehensive about undertaking research, as well as making sense of findings which they may be expected to assimilate into their own direct work.

It is not only in the acquisition and processing of information that there is considerable common ground between the worlds of practice and research. A similar case can be made for the requirement for sound analysis, interpretation, critical reflection and review. Although it is by no means the case that these skills are restricted to social work, their value in this field is particularly obvious. Thus, for example, it is reasonable to suggest that models of thematic analysis utilised often in qualitative research also offer significant lessons for the process of making sense of diverse and complex material gathered in the course of a safeguarding assessment in practice. Similarly, it is important for researchers and practitioners alike to develop the capacity to consider and account for their own place and influence in the process of interaction with research participants/ service users (Smith, 2004). The argument for a critically reflexive approach is now well made in the social work context (see e.g. Gould and Baldwin, 2004). What is the impact of our own actions, indeed our presence, as well as the formal nature of the relationships we have with those on the other side of the interaction? The argument for reflective skills as a key element of the social worker's toolkit is mirrored by the need for the researcher to 'factor in' the impact of their involvement and the way it shapes reactions and responses (the 'Hawthorne' effect; e.g. Coombs and Smith, 2003).

While there are clearly a number of areas of similarity between research and practice methods, there are also a number of key distinctions to be made between the practitioner role and that of the researcher (except possibly in some forms of participatory/action research). The nature of the relationship with participants/

service users is perhaps the most obvious of these; for instance, timescales are necessarily quite different (or they can be), with researchers having only limited involvement, whereas social work practitioners can expect to have a reasonably lengthy involvement with service users. The researcher is thus less 'engaged' and clearly does not have the same range of professional concerns and responsibilities. Even though they are accountable for their practice through their own ethical requirements, and arguably through a shared commitment to core social work values, researchers may have a greater degree of latitude to determine if and how to use information received in confidence. For practitioner-researchers, the distinction between aspects of their role may be difficult to sustain, in this and other respects; but it is obviously important to be clear with users/participants just which 'hat' one is wearing.

The researcher may, interestingly, be less 'unequal' with participants than is the case for practitioners, who may hold formal authority to act, or certainly be perceived as holding the 'power' to do so by service users (Smith, 2008), especially 'involuntary clients'. It might be argued, too, that research is geared in the main towards extracting findings and interpretations for wider use, while the practitioner is principally concerned with, and may be directly responsible for, the well-being and safety of the service user, thereby taking a more situated and task-oriented view. By the same token, the researcher is less bound by the need to find answers, and indeed applied research is often criticised (unreasonably) for not doing so; whereas, in the main, practitioners cannot leave challenging circumstances or personal crises unresolved.

Despite these distinctions, there remains a considerable skills overlap between practice and research in social work, especially in relation to information-gathering and analysis; and, equally significantly, research and practice in social work are able to draw on a common value-base. A shared commitment to the centrality of service user interests, to challenging disadvantage and oppression, while at the same time promoting social well-being, can and should reasonably be assumed. This, in turn, helps to point up some of the distinctive features of research in social work.

Initiating and undertaking practice-focused research

Despite its obvious benefits, for those involved in or intending to undertake practice-focused research there are likely to be significant challenges in planning and managing the process of inquiry. These arise from the predictable pressures of time, limited resources (often restricted to oneself), access problems (organisational gatekeeping, for example), permissions, time management, and the processes for eventual dissemination and use of findings.

In any research setting, but especially where such pressures apply, it is vital to maintain close control over the practicalities of the project; thus, breaking the overall task into manageable 'bite-size chunks' is almost certain to be a necessity. Indeed, at the risk of experiencing the frustration of 'not getting on with it', it will probably be productive in the long run to attend as far as possible to detailed preparation in advance. Davies (2007) suggests employing a 'timed road map' whereby the discrete elements of a research project are identified and timetabled as accurately as possible (Figure 8.1). In practice, some of these elements will be lengthy and continuous, such as the development of a detailed review of relevant literature, while others, such as securing ethical approval, will need to be undertaken at clearly specified points, in order to be able to proceed to subsequent stages.

Task	Sept	Oct	Nov	Dec	Jan	Feb	Mar	Apr	May	Jun	Jul	Aug
Literature Review	▓	▓	▓	▓	▓	▓	▓	▓	▓			
Develop project proposal		▓	▓									
Ethical approval process			▓	▓								
Data collection					▓	▓	▓					
Analysis							▓	▓				
Writing-up			▓						▓	▓	▓	
Dissemination												▓

Figure 8.1   Outline research project timetable

When teaching research design, I use the analogy of home decorating to illustrate that much of the groundwork of research consists of work which will subsequently remain invisible, but without which a good quality end product would not be possible. Thus, planning methods, gaining access, negotiating permissions and developing protocols may all involve substantial investment of time for no immediate return, but all enable the subsequent work to proceed on a sound basis with fewer chances of unexpected 'hold ups'. In fact, many of these tasks can be completed in parallel, along with other necessary initial steps, such as familiarisation with relevant research literature and other background material (policy documents, previous evaluations, operational procedures and guidance, for instance), and the development and testing of possible research 'tools' (interview schedules, or observational coding templates).

There may well be problems of gaining access or permissions from all those with a vested interest, including organisational heads, service users and practitioners. In

anticipation of this, it will probably be helpful to have alternative sites or partici-
pant groups in mind. In addition, for those practice-focused researchers who themselves are close to the intended field of inquiry, it will be important to establish a
clear distinction between different roles, whether with the organisation concerned,
colleagues or service users. Different rules of confidentiality or disclosure might
apply, and it is clearly important to establish explicit understandings about these.

Finding ways to accommodate less than perfect conditions for the conduct of
research is also likely to be a requirement for the organisation of practice-based
investigations. Managing the acquisition of data and ensuring that it remains
meaningful may well necessitate a creative approach to information gathering
and consideration of techniques such as 'triangulation' (Denzin, 1970) and the
development of different sources of usable material. While sample sizes may
need to be minimised, because of access difficulties or simply the limited availability of participants, making use of a range of data sources may well offer com-
pensatory gains (for instance, drawing on carers' as well as service users' insights
where these might be relevant). Increasingly, too, the potential for using the
internet and other electronic media provides additional options in terms of alternative data sources, and these may indeed be more in keeping with the preferred
modes of communication of research participants – while at the same time offering more certain safeguards in terms of anonymity and confidentiality. Research
in and around practice is almost certain to be shaped to some extent by 'the art
of the possible'; and this is only problematic where the credibility of findings or
messages from research becomes questionable.

Aside from the challenge of managing research which is directly engaged with
practice, ethical considerations are also likely to loom large. This is particularly
so for social work, given the need for researchers to remain grounded in the
core values of the profession, and also espoused by the academic discipline (see
Butler, 2002). Research in social work, as elsewhere, may well be based on motivations which stem from outside the immediate practice setting, whether from
the researcher's need to gain a qualification, the sponsor's interest in more effective practice or continued funding, or perhaps because the researcher is coming to the topic with a particular committed viewpoint. Such contextual factors
impose their own pressures and expectations and it is important to avoid making
unacceptable ethical compromises as a consequence. It is also important, clearly,
to avoid applying pressure on potential research subjects to participate; equally,
they should only be involved on the basis that they are fully informed about the
purposes and uses of the inquiry. It is particularly important to be clear about the
limited extent to which any of those involved, including the researcher, can control what happens with the material generated once it is 'out there' in the public domain. McLaughlin (2012: 70) draws attention to examples of unintended
and adverse consequences, sometimes over a considerable period of time, when
the findings of research become known and research subjects are identifiable and
may feel a 'sense of betrayal' (page 71).

The nature of the researcher–researched relationship is distinctive, too, as we
have already noted. While it is likely to be time-limited and more superficial than

the practitioner–service user relationship, it is still essentially bounded by the same underlying principles. We can expect that it will be user-centred and geared towards the promotion of well-being, the protection of those in vulnerable situations, empowerment and challenging discrimination. These principles apply in the sense both that they are underlying objectives and that they should underpin the research process itself.

Research in use: practice and principles

Of course, as it is an applied discipline, the endpoint of research in social work is the conversion of findings into subsequent use, generating new insights into the rights and needs of service users on the one hand, and providing signposts and tools for better practice, in their interests, on the other. Practice-focused research has to justify itself to commissioners and others, especially to people who use services, and it is therefore likely to be judged according to external as well as internal criteria of relevance and quality. While methodological concerns might focus initially on questions of 'validity' or 'plausibility', additional, equally important considerations of value and benefit also apply in this context.

For those engaged in social work research, it is thus helpful to think about the processes of dissemination and use from the start, and as part of a continuing dialogue with practice. It is legitimate, indeed, essential, to be concerned with 'impact' and what goes on beyond the end of a specific research 'project'. Considerations of use thereby become a central feature of the research process, linking in turn to those questions of values and principle which are rightly viewed as being fundamental to social work as it is practised.

Aside from those key ethical questions which apply to the conduct of a piece of research, others, too, need to be addressed: what considerations need to be given to the dissemination and promotion of messages from our inquiries, for example? And, what do we 'owe' participants, in terms of continuing involvement and promoting implementation? We must also be concerned with the question of what to do when findings emerge which are awkward and potentially challenging; for researchers who are close to the subject matter in other respects, or who are already involved with agencies which might come in for criticism, this can be testing. For research to retain its integrity, however, the possibility of challenge must be recognised; commissioners must be prepared for the possibility of 'bad news', and findings should be reported honestly and openly.

Conclusion: realising the value of practice-focused research

In this chapter I have sought to outline the attributes and potential contributions of 'practice-focused research', concentrating particularly on the place of those in and around practice in this endeavour. I have suggested that there is considerable potential for direct involvement in research activity to carry out the dual function of improving professionally relevant skills, while also offering insights which themselves may contribute directly to improvements in practice. Sometimes it might seem as if there is something of a schism between practice and research, with one stereotypically remaining essentially task-oriented and unwilling/unable to look up from the task in hand; while the other is caricatured as being preoccupied with self-serving, irrelevant or impractical investigations which rarely, if ever, produce meaningful or usable outputs. Whatever the substance of these stereotypes, the argument advanced here is that such depictions or beliefs are unhelpful and unnecessary, serving only to inhibit the potential for useful and productive dialogue.

Research can be seen to operate in a number of ways to enhance understanding and promote improvements in practice and outcomes for people who use services: research for practice, research in practice, and research as practice. That is to say, in the first instance research into key aspects of the social work domain can demonstrably act as a source of understanding of how to enhance services and interventions; in this case, the important attribute to be developed by practitioners is that of 'research awareness', the capacity to identify reliable sources, 'read' evidence critically, and apply the lessons from it to local settings and local needs. Research 'in' practice, as we have observed, provides an opportunity to develop key transferable skills, particularly in the sense of information gathering and synthesis; but it is also a potentially valuable resource in terms of generating important insights (usually small scale and localised) into aspects of practice and the service user experience. Research 'as' practice takes this further, and illustrates the potential for research activity in certain forms to act as the stimulus for collaborative working and direct engagement with service users and others in the process of change and service improvement.

> Social work is an evolving area of practice. It is important to use research to understand what works and there is rich evidence within the practice arena that should provide insight to complement and illuminate research.

> (Research in Practice for Adults Manifesto, **www.interactive.ripfa.org.
> uk/social-work-manifesto**)

Evidencing value is the responsibility of people doing practice as well as those undertaking research. Practice-focused research in social work promises a great deal in terms of its potential contribution to understanding need and promoting improvements in service provision. It depends, however, on a positive dialogue between practitioners and researchers and the acquisition of key skills ('research-mindedness') which enable those in practice to engage in, argue with and make sense of the processes and products of research itself.

REFLECTIVE QUESTIONS

1. *Research in social work rarely produces conclusive results? Is this a problem?*

2. *To what extent should social work research be user-led?*

3. *Is it ever legitimate to carry out research in your own practice setting? What safeguards do you need to put in place?*

4. *How can you retain your independence as a researcher?*

RECOMMENDED FURTHER READING

Butler, I (2002) A Code of Ethics for Social Work and Social Care Research. *British Journal of Social Work*, 32(2): 239–48.

Carey, M (2009) *The Social Work Dissertation*. Maidenhead: Open University Press.

Hardwick, L and Worsley, A (2011) *Doing Social Work Research*. London: Sage.

McLaughlin, H (2012) *Understanding Social Work Research* (2nd edition). London: Sage.

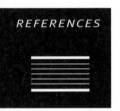

REFERENCES

Butler, I (2002) A Code of Ethics for Social Work and Social Care Research. *British Journal of Social Work*, 32(2): 239–48.

Coombs, SJ and Smith, ID (2003) The Hawthorne Effect: Is it a Help or Hindrance in Social Science Research? *Change: Transformations in Education*, 6(1): 97–111.

Davies, M (2007) *Doing a Successful Research Project*. Basingstoke: Palgrave Macmillan.

Denzin, N (1970) *The Research Act*. Chicago: Aldine.

Department of Health (1995) *Child Protection: Messages from Research*. London: The Stationery Office.

Department of Health (2001) *The Children Act Now: Messages from Research*. London: The Stationery Office.

Frost, N (2005) *Professionalism, Partnership and Joined-up Working*. Dartington: Research in Practice.

Gammack, G (1982) Social Work as Uncommon Sense. *British Journal of Social Work*, 12(1): 3–22.

Gould, N and Baldwin, M (eds) (2004) *Social Work, Critical Reflection and the Learning Organisation*. Aldershot: Ashgate.

Jordan, B and Travers, A (1998) The Informal Economy: A Case Study in Unrestrained Competition. *Social Policy & Administration*, 32(3): 292–306.

McLaughlin, H (2012) *Understanding Social Work Research* (2nd edition). London: Sage.

Marsh, P and Fisher, M (2005) *Developing the Evidence Base for Social Work and Social Care Practice*. London: SCIE.

Smith, R (1987) The Practice of Diversion. *Youth and Policy*, 19: 10–14.

Smith, R (2004) A Matter of Trust: Service Users and Researchers. *Qualitative Social Work*, 3(3): 335–46.

Smith, R (2008) *Social Work and Power.* Basingstoke: Palgrave Macmillan.

Smith, R (2010) *Doing Social Work Research.* Maidenhead: McGraw-Hill/Open University Press.

Social Work Reform Board (2011) *Final Report.* London: Social Work Reform Board.

Vernon, A. (2002) *User-defined Outcomes of Community Care for Asian Disabled People.* Bristol: Policy Press.

Chapter 9

Understanding continuing professional development

Patricia Higham

Introduction

Qualified social workers are expected to update and extend their knowledge, skills, and understanding for practice through a process of continuing professional development (CPD). Most social workers in the United Kingdom have thought of this process as 'PQ' – Post-Qualifying Social Work Education and Training, which comprises specific, regulated assessed modules or awards designated by the professional regulator to develop social workers according to employer requirements for practice. But social workers have to develop their practice within changing regulatory and professional environments.

England's strong regulation of PQ has been superseded by a greater emphasis on *professionalism*, where responsibility for professional development lies with the practitioner. The Professional Capabilities Framework (PCF) (The College of Social Work, 2013; Skills for Care, 2011), developed as part of social work reform in England, enables social work to be recognised as part of an international profession. The PCF applies to social workers in all roles and settings, and comprises nine domains expressed in practice levels ranging from application to qualifying courses to senior levels of practice. The first PCF domain is *professionalism*, which is expressed as a range of interdependent attributes: planning one's own continuing education; professional demeanour; managing personal and professional boundaries; using supervision; use of self; emotional resilience; ensuring personal well-being and safety while being an effective social worker; challenging poor practice; accountability line; and promoting and safeguarding social work's reputation. The other PCF domains are values and ethics; diversity; rights, justice and economic well-being; knowledge; critical reflection and analysis; intervention and skills; contexts and organisations; and professional leadership. Although developed specifically for England, the PCF has some relevance for social work practice in other UK countries.

This chapter will explore the changing landscapes of CPD/PQ, the reform of social work in England and relate this to the CPD/PQ frameworks in Northern Ireland,

Scotland and Wales. The chapter will focus on what the new CPD/PQ in England will look like, its relationship to social work reform, and its role in promoting higher levels of professionalism. First, the chapter will seek to draw lessons from social workers' past experience of PQ.

The history and context of PQ in the United Kingdom: the 1991 PQ Framework

Continuing education programmes for social workers in the United Kingdom were organised differently from programmes in, for example, the USA (NASW, 2002) and Australia (AASW, 2006). In contrast to 'continuing education' – a more prevalent term internationally – where a social worker selects learning activities from a range of content and learning methods – the United Kingdom developed highly regulated complex frameworks of post qualifying social work awards (PQ) based on assessment of practice competence. Until 1990–91, few academic programmes were designated for social work post-qualifying studies (Cutmore and Walton, 1997). In 1991 a UK-wide Post-Qualifying Award Framework (CCETSW, 1990) was introduced. Continuing professional development for social workers in the United Kingdom was channelled into a regulated award structure. The 1991 UK-wide Framework offered two levels of part-time regulated assessed awards, taking, on average, two to three years of part-time study to complete.

The social work regulator, the Central Council of Education and Training in Social Work (CCETSW), established 20 Post-Qualifying Consortia, comprising partnerships between regional employers and universities, to manage the 1991 UK-wide PQ Framework. Consortia accredited regional and local learning programmes for 'professional credits' leading to awards (GSCC website, 2006) that contained six requirements specific to the award level, which were built around the concept of practice competence. Requirements were assessed on a 'competent/not yet competent' basis, implying that eventually all candidates would demonstrate competence. Trained assessors used direct observation, self-reported accounts of practice, service user feedback, and managers' verification statements to assess practice. The 1991 PQ social work framework never achieved wide acceptance, unlike nursing's professional development framework which was linked to relevant academic awards.

The 2005 PQ Framework

From 1998, modernisation of the personal social services (DOH, 1998, 2000; DOH/SSI, 1998; Higham et al., 2001) introduced the first reform of social services and social work education that was intended to drive up standards. In 2001, the General Social Care Council (GSCC) took over the regulatory functions of the Central Council for Education and Training in Social Work (CCETSW) in England. The GSCC became responsible for setting up and maintaining a Social

Care Register on which social workers were registered (Brand et al., 1999; GSCC, 2002a). Scotland, Northern Ireland and Wales set up separate Care Councils and established their own country-specific requirements.

Closure of the 1991 UK-wide PQ Framework took place from 2006 to 2009, and it was then replaced from 2005 by four highly regulated country-specific PQ frameworks in England, Scotland, Wales and Northern Ireland. The country-specific awards comprised different levels of awards associated with practice specialisms. The awards were not linked officially to the later requirement that a qualified social worker must complete 15 days of 'PRTL' (Post Registration Teaching and Learning) over three years (GSCC website, 2009), although PQ study could contribute towards fulfilling the PRTL requirement. Professional credit was abandoned for academically accredited courses within higher education (although Northern Ireland retained some professionally accredited courses). The 2005 country-specific PQ frameworks in Scotland (SSSC, 2005: 30: P), Northern Ireland (NIPQETP, 2005: 4,14c) and England (GSCC, 2005: 4, 2, 19) continued to emphasise 'competence'. Wales adopted a different understanding (CCW, 2006: Appendix 1) – that PQ should develop *a model which promotes enhanced practice* and a *shift in assessment from behavioural competences to enhanced skills and knowledge.*

The 2005 English PQ Framework contained three kinds of Awards: a Post-Qualifying Award in Specialist Social Work; a Post-Qualifying Award in Higher Specialist Social Work; and a Post-Qualifying Award in Advanced Social Work. Five specialisms were introduced, with most offered at each level: mental health; adult social services; practice education; leadership and management; and children and young people, their families and carers. The 2005 PQ Framework in England (GSCC, 2005: 4, 2, 19) was based on GSCC requirements (including their Codes of Practice), National Occupational Standards, and Skills for Care/GSCC guidance on the assessment of practice in the workplace (GSCC, 2002b). The GSCC accredited universities to provide awards, with employers commissioning providers through regional planning networks (GSCC, 2005). Skills for Care England, in collaboration with the Children's Workforce Development Council, assumed responsibility for organising these regional planning networks. Strengths of the 2005 PQ Framework included its encouragement of workforce planning, its consistent quality assurance attained through an academic Award Framework, and its Specialist Awards linked to practice. Weaknesses of the 2005 PQ Framework included its complexity, employers' and practitioners' insufficient awareness of the Awards, a perceived lack of value placed on employer–university partnerships, and the regulator's failure to specify a national credit volume for attaining an award, thus unintentionally subverting the possibility of establishing a national standard. In different regions of England, social workers attained PQ Awards for different volumes of credit that required different amounts of time and effort to achieve the same award.

Lessons learned from the PQ frameworks

Notwithstanding its strengths, PQ's overall achievement fell short of making a significant difference to social workers' practice. Despite efforts and resources given to promoting PQ Awards, the effectiveness of PQ Award Frameworks remained open to some doubt. The 2005 PQ Framework, like the 1991 Framework, was insufficiently known and supported by employers and practitioners, who perceived the Awards as complex and difficult to understand. PQ study was said to be expensive, and some practitioners were unable to gain release from practice to undertake PQ. Without a recognised career framework, social workers may have perceived PQ Awards as of little value. Specifically, I argue that the GSCC's performance as a social work regulator was inadequate, with desultory attempts at standardisation that did not succeed in establishing a national standard (Higham, 2001). PQ was not linked to career progression, and the dominant concept of 'competence' did not encourage further practice development.

The PQ Consortium Wales – a successful PQ organisation

The PQ Consortium Wales achieved a good success record and, unusually, despite not being linked to academic standards and being tied officially to the concept of 'competence' with its competent/not competent assessment criteria, the Consortium assisted social workers to develop their practice beyond competence. The Consortium used a stable pool of well-trained assessors. Moderation and external examination processes safeguarded standards. Assessors developed informal benchmarking to promote high standards of practice, by drawing on a shared implicit vision of what a post-qualifying standard should be – for example the ability to apply substantial levels of critical reflective analysis to practice, increased self confidence and updated skills and knowledge, aspects that accord with the conceptualisations of Eraut (1994, 2006) and Benner (1984). The Consortium succeeded in uplifting candidates' practice because it was a country-wide Consortium (like Northern Ireland and Scotland) that promoted a consistent high standard of practice, and communicated effectively with its stakeholders to achieve consistent standards.

Disappointingly, like the 1991 PQ Framework, only a small minority of social workers completed the 1995 Framework Awards. Enrolments remained low (GSCC, 2006: 40). By mid-2009, only 2,490 of the 83,730 registered social workers in England had enrolled on PQ Awards (GSCC, 2010: 43) and some employers did not actively support their social workers to undertake PQ. By 2011, the GSCC reported a 34 per cent decrease in the number of social workers enrolling on a GSCC-approved PQ course (GSCC, 2011: 24). A significant detriment to the value placed on PQ was the absence of a national research-based evaluation of PQ outcomes and a failure to consider the many cumulative small-scale evaluations.

Lack of a national research-based evaluation of PQ outcomes

The social work regulator made no arrangements for a national evaluation of PQ's effectiveness. In the absence of significant research-based evidence, anecdotal reports suggested that not all employers were convinced that PQ made a difference to social work practice. Carpenter's paper for SCIE (2005) exposed a general lack of rigour in the level of evaluative research for evidencing outcomes of social work education, but arguably his monograph was published too late to influence views of PQ's effectiveness.

Despite the absence of a national evaluation, some small-scale programme evaluations, regional surveys and qualitative research examined the effectiveness of PQ study (Bourn and Bootle, 2005; Brown and Keen, 2004; Brown et al., 2008; Burchell, 1995; Clarke, 2001; Cooper and Rixon, 2001; Devine, 1995; Doel et al., 2006; Doyle and Kennedy, 2008; Hicks and Hennessy, 1996; Keys, 2005; Ogilvie-Whyte, 2006; Pollard et al., 2005; Postle et al., 2002; Reeves, 2003; Rowland, 2003, 2006; Rushton and Martyn, 1990; Skinner and Whyte, 2004). Higham (2011b) evaluated the outcomes for practice of PQ leadership and management modules, and found that the learning resulted in an increase in confidence, critical reflection and the ability to speak and challenge effectively within multi-professional teams, for example, with regard to commissioning decisions.

These studies reached similar conclusions, that PQ learning more often than not made a positive difference to practice by: improving candidates' knowledge and skills, and increasing their confidence; providing opportunities for professional development; enabling social workers to share issues and knowledge during PQ learning that helped to develop good practice; and encouraging critical reflection that social workers valued as an outcome and regarded as crucial for developing PQ practice. The different studies agreed that evaluating PQ outcomes is a difficult methodological task for which better approaches are needed.

The lessons learned from PQ indicate that CPD/PQ would be more attractive if it was linked to a career structure, was less expensive, more flexible and easier to understand, and if systematic evaluations of the effectiveness of its outcomes took place regularly.

Social work reform in England

The change of regulator and the move from PQ to CPD are part of a larger process of social work reform towards more professionalism. Perceptions that social work in England had failed to agree on a definition of its purpose, that its strong regulatory systems resulted in process-driven standardised approaches to practice, and that practice supervision occurred infrequently triggered reform in England. Major obstacles that kept social work in England from becoming a confident, effective profession included: a poor public image and understanding; education and training not ensuring a quality workforce; no agreed career structure; lack of practical resources including Information and Computer Technology; an overemphasis on process; supervision, reflection and analysis being squeezed out; and no single focus of responsibility for promoting the profession. Prompted by these concerns, and also by worries about the quality of social work practice, low morale, and the public outcry over the death of 17-month-old Peter Connelly, who died after prolonged abuse by his carers despite many previous contacts with police, health workers and social workers (Children England, 2012), the government organised a Social Work Task Force in 2009 to raise professional standards and establish a powerful voice for the profession.

The Social Work Task Force and CPD/PQ

The Department of Health and the Department for Children, Schools and Families set up the Social Work Task Force to examine the ways in which social work was being undertaken. Its members were drawn from local frontline services and senior leadership, research, the media, charities, service user organisations, unions and the British Association of Social Workers – an extensive range of stakeholders. The Task Force undertook a comprehensive review of frontline social work practice across adult and children's services. Its Final Report (DCSF, 2009) made 15 recommendations for reform, calling for, *inter alia*, a national framework for the continuing professional development of social workers. PQ was now to be subsumed within the broader concept of CPD. The recommended changes for CPD/PQ sat alongside other recommendations for a reformed system of initial social work training and education; clear, universal and binding standards for employers; a dedicated programme of training and support for managers of frontline social workers; a single, nationally recognised career structure; a new system for forecasting levels of demand for social workers; a new programme of action on public understanding of social work; and a single national reform programme.

The Social Work Reform Board's CPD/PQ recommendations

Subsequently the Task Force set up a Reform Board (DFE, 2012) to develop the recommendations for implementation, to monitor and report progress, and advise and influence stakeholders and the government. The Reform Board focused on developing policies in five key areas of reform that included developing principles that should underpin a Continuing Professional Development Framework. The new CPD principles aligned with another Reform Board priority to develop an overarching professional standards framework – the Professional Capabilities Framework for Social Workers in England. The Capabilities Framework set out, for the first time, consistent expectations of social workers at every point of their career to inform the design and implementation of education and training and a national career structure.

Capability: a broader concept than competence

The Professional Capabilities Framework helps social workers to develop their practice to levels beyond the limited standard of 'competence', which specified only an initial beginning level of practice. 'Competence' describes what individuals know or are able to do in terms of knowledge, skills and attitudes at a particular point. 'Capability' includes (but is not limited to) demonstrating competence to carry out an occupational role and the ability to develop further skills and knowledge to meet future demands. The Higher Education for Capability organisation explained capability (HEC, 1994) as a broader notion than 'competence' – concerned not just with current performance but also with growth and potential. 'Capability' brings together knowledge, skills, understanding, personal qualities and a capacity for autonomous learning (Stephenson, 1994). Stephenson (1998: 2) later defined 'capability' as: *an integration of knowledge, skills, personal qualities and understanding used appropriately and effectively – not just in familiar and highly focused specialist contexts but in response to new and changing circumstances.*

Benner (1984) adapted the Dreyfus and Dreyfus model of skills acquisition (1986), and located 'competence' on a progressive ladder that began with a 'novice' practitioner, and then progressed to 'advanced beginner', 'competence', 'proficiency', and 'expertise'. 'Competence' is reached at the conclusion of the social work qualification; 'proficiency' and 'expertise' can develop over time through practice experience, critical reflection and formal study. 'Competence' with its conceptual limitations to a single level of practice attainment arguably inhibited PQ practice, so its replacement by the Professional Capability Framework's different levels of capability provides a potentially more effective concept for CPD.

Eraut (1994) argued that 'competence' became a tool of governmental regulatory control over the professions (page 159), and that regarding a competent practitioner as *tolerably good but less than expert* (page 160) limits the concept of competence to the level of newly qualified practitioners and therefore fails to acknowledge practice development over time beyond the beginning level. Eraut (1994: 208–10; 2006: 5) prefers the concept of 'capability' which he explains as 'everything that a person can think or do', thus recognising that practitioners' capability extends beyond competence. This provides a good rationale for replacing 'competence' with the range of capability levels in the PCF that enhance social workers' professionalism.

Implications of the Munro recommendations for CPD/PQ

In 2010 following a general election, the government commissioned Professor Eileen Munro (London School of Economics) to recommend changes in systems for child protection in England, over which similar concerns had been expressed. Her Report (2011) complements the Reform Board recommendations. The Munro recommendations covered four areas: (1) valuing professional expertise; (2) sharing responsibility for early help; (3) developing social work expertise and supporting effective social work practice; and (4) strengthening accountabilities and creating a learning system. Munro wanted social workers to have more professional autonomy to exercise their professional judgement in complex situations. For this strategy to succeed, social workers must become well informed and confident in their ability to practise to the highest professional standards. The link to CPD and the capability strategies are clear.

The College of Social Work's support for CPD

The Reform Board recommended creating an independent College of Social Work in England, not as an educational institution or a regulator, but as the professional voice of social workers to represent and promote the social work profession. During 2011 the Reform Board passed responsibility to the College for, *inter alia*, implementing reforms related to continuing professional development and the Professional Capabilities Framework (PCF). The College identified a range of principles and actions for employers, social workers and educators that would promote the success of the new CPD policy (TCSW, 2012). (These principles make assumptions that social workers will continue to work within traditional local authority teams, and they make little reference to the increasing numbers of self-employed social workers.) The principles are:

- The CPD framework will align with relevant levels of the PCF and link to a career structure.

- Employers should support social workers to take professional responsibility for developing their skills to high professional levels, through undertaking learning and development activities beyond the standards required for re-registration.

- Annual appraisal cycles and supervision should identify, plan and monitor learning and development needs.

- Employers will be encouraged to develop learning opportunities in partnership with other employers and with universities.

- A wide range of learning and development activities, including time for critical reflection, learning from others and opportunities for access to research, as well as structured education and training, should be promoted.

Where does a Masters degree fit with the new CPD?

Specific provision for a Masters degree is notable by its absence. The Laming Progress Report on the protection of children (2009) initially recommended a practice based, practice focused Masters in Social Work Practice (MSWP) for social workers in children's services. The Task Force required that the proposed

Masters Degree should be made available to all social workers, including those in adult services. However, the Reform Board's CPD recommendations failed to propose a Masters degree as a specific new development, stating only that *there is an aspiration that social workers should have opportunities to achieve a relevant Masters' level award through modular programmes* (SWRB, 2011: Section 5, p. 9) and that higher education institutions are being encouraged to develop flexible programmes at Masters level in line with the PCF and other development needs identified in partnership with employers.

The different stages of a Masters Degree would lend themselves to gradual attainment of a Masters in the recognised steps of Post-Graduate Certificate, Post-Graduate Diploma and Masters stage. This progression suggests some compatibility with the Dreyfus/Benner practice stages of *novice*, *advanced beginner*, *competent*, *proficient* and *expert* (Benner, 1984; Dreyfus and Dreyfus, 1986). An example of how the stages and career structure might be aligned to a Masters degree is given below:

- **Competent to Proficient**: Social Worker – Post-Graduate Certificate = 60 M level credits (usually three 20-credit modules or four 15-credit modules);

- **Proficient**: Experienced Social Worker – Post-Graduate Diploma = 60 additional M level credits (usually three 20-credit modules or four 15-credit modules);

- **Proficient to Expert**: Advanced Practitioner /Practice Educator/Social Work Manager – Masters stage = 60 additional M level credits, usually based on a dissertation or project (usually a 20-credit research methods module and a 40-credit dissertation/project module, or a 15/45 credit split).

Change of regulator in England resulting in changed CPD requirements

The shift in England from strong regulation to professionalism, which began with the reform of social work in 2009, is affirmed by the change of social work regulator. In August 2012 the General Social Care Council, the social work regulator in England, closed and the Health and Care Professions Council (HCPC) became the social work regulator. HCPC's Standards of Proficiency (SOPs) for Social Workers in England (HCPC, 2012) refer explicitly in SOP 4 to requirements for professionalism: *Be able to practise as an autonomous professional, exercising their own professional judgement*. The change of regulator resulted in the demise of the Post-Qualifying Social Work Awards (PQ) and of the requirements for PRTL (Post Registration Training and Learning), with a new emphasis placed on continuing professional development (CPD). With the exception of Approved Mental Health Professional Training, HCPC will not regulate specific CPD courses.

HCPC regard CPD as a generic permissive concept which may (or may not) result in a specific award. Its concept of CPD will enable social workers to make broad choices of flexible learning for updating and developing skills and knowledge which may include programmes of academic learning leading to academic awards, or mean training days, reading a research report or taking part in discussion groups, thus echoing the Reform Board's CPD recommendations. This changes how social workers have traditionally conceptualised CPD as synonymous with PQ. CPD becomes the over-arching broad concept, within which specific awards and informal activities are located, and from which social workers can select what is meaningful to their own development.

HCPC's CPD requirements expect the professions they regulate to show that registrants have undertaken a range of planned learning activities throughout the two-year registration period, with critical reflection on that learning's impact on practice. Each time the registration period comes to an end, social workers will be required to summarise their CPD and its impact. In September 2014 the HCPC will ask a random sample of 2.5 per cent of social work registrants to provide more detailed evidence of their CPD, so it is important for registered social workers to keep a log of their learning. HCPC will recruit a panel of social workers as peer 'partners' to audit and scrutinise the CPD submissions.

Enhancing the quality of CPD/PQ

To enhance the quality of CPD learning opportunities, the College, in its role as a professional body, developed an *endorsement scheme*, so that education and training providers can demonstrate that their CPD learning programmes meet relevant criteria for practice development. The College also provides *Communities of Practice* – virtual meeting places – where professionals can come together to communicate, share resources, reflect and discuss matters that affect their practice. The College argues that engagement in professional debates can constitute CPD activity that helps social workers keep up to date with new policy and research. Another example of PQ enhancement is provision of an *online portfolio* for College members to use to plan and record their CPD activities.

CPD in Wales, Scotland and Northern Ireland

The changes in England – not only social work reform but also the new regulator – plant a footprint on the landscape of CPD/PQ in the other countries of the United Kingdom. HCPC has signed memoranda of understanding with the three Care Councils in Wales, Scotland and Northern Ireland. The changes in England resonate with CPD/PQ in the rest of the United Kingdom. In Wales, Scotland and Northern Ireland, the Care Councils continue to regulate social work. All three countries retain the expectation that social workers will complete requirements for PRTL (Post Registration Training and Learning).

- The Northern Ireland Social Care Council (NISCC) reviewed its Post-Qualifying Education and Training Framework in 2012, and the results of its consultation with stakeholders affirmed that the Framework, while needing some further development, continues to be fit for purpose. NISCC regulates three PQ awards: the Northern Ireland Specific Award; the Northern Ireland Specialist Award; and the Northern Ireland Leadership and Strategic Award. Candidates can complete accredited university courses to attain the Awards, or can take an Individual Assessment Route for PQ, based on practice activities.

- The Scottish Social Services Council (SSSC) developed a Continuous Learning Framework, which contains Personal Capabilities based on concepts of emotional intelligence, focusing on managing relationships and self management. The Continuous Learning Framework also contains organisational capabilities. The Council offers a Mental Health Officer Award and a qualification in Practice Learning.

- The Care Council for Wales (CCW) regulates Continuing Professional Education and Learning (CPEL) for social workers, and will feature a CPEL framework from 2013–14 with accredited university courses. The Care Council for Wales offers four programme levels: Consolidation for Newly Qualified Social Workers; Experienced Practitioners; Senior Practitioners; and Consultant Social Workers.

Three impediments to the success of CPD/PQ

The success of continuing professional development in all four countries depends on social workers' readiness to engage with CPD/PQ frameworks. However, their readiness may be hindered by the tradition of strong governmental regulation that diminishes social workers' professional autonomy. In England an unanswered question is whether social workers, their employers and social work education will respond positively to the new CPD framework, which moves away from specific regulated awards to an emphasis on social workers assuming professional responsibility for their own development. The Health and Care Professions Council is accustomed to working with health professions that have strong professional bodies and whose practitioners have embedded a sense of professionalism. HCPC registers professionals to undertake CPD but does not prescribe specific kinds of CPD learning. A recent anecdotal statement from a social work employer implied that the lightening of regulatory controls on PQ/CPD will mean that employers will ignore the expectation of supporting continuing professional development for social workers, and will not abide by the proposed employer standards. This is deeply worrying, if that attitude is typical.

A second possible impediment to the success of CPD/PQ in all the UK countries is the impact of the economic recession. CPD frameworks depend on gaining substantial acceptance and financial support from employers, practitioners and students. During a period of economic recession, when social work graduates and experienced social workers may experience difficulty in finding and retaining suitable employment, support for CPD could decline, thus threatening its take up and impact on practice.

The third impediment is that social workers may not be willing nor be sufficiently prepared to assume more responsibility for using critical reflection to develop their professional practice. Whether social workers can acquire more practice autonomy and exercise more professional judgement remains an open question. Much depends on how social work graduates construct their careers, whether they are able and willing to use critical reflection to improve their practice, and the extent to which they are supported by practice supervision. Undertaking a range of CPD activities will be ineffective unless social workers can make sense of what they have done, identify their learning, and apply this learning to practice to further develop their professionalism, as well as having the active interest and support of their employers.

Making CPD effective through critical analysis and reflective practice

Critical analysis and reflective practice are key factors that contribute to the future effectiveness of CPD/PQ. Reflection does not provide a magic formula to improve practice, but social workers can use reflection to identify key aspects of practice situations. Critical analysis is essential for developing practice capability. Fook and colleagues (Fook, 2002; Fook et al., 2000; Napier and Fook, 2000) studied how practitioners theorised and created knowledge, and came to the view that critical reflection is a 'self-researching' experience. Kolb, Schön, and Eraut have helped to illuminate the concepts of reflective practice.

Kolb's experiential learning model (Kolb and Fry, 1975), drawing on Lewin (1948) and Dewey's process of logical thinking (1938, 1997), moves from *concrete experience* to observation, *reflection* on the experience, *abstract concepts* formed following reflection, and then to *testing the concepts in new situations*. Kolb recommends using reflection to identify new practice meanings. 'Concrete experience' is not something that 'just happens' but should emerge from planned interventions that are critically analysed (Furlong, 2003) following the intervention. Kolb's model has the potential to help social workers to develop higher levels of practice capability.

Schön's model of reflective practice (1987, 1991) identified two types of reflection. The first of these is reflection-on-action (1987: ix), in which social workers consider actions of the past, and, over time, build thoughts and memories of remembered actions and formative events as part of their practice repertoire. The second kind of reflection is more difficult. 'Reflection-in-action' requires social workers to think on the spot and formulate ideas while practice takes place. This is a skill that can develop with experience. Eraut (1994) and Usher at al. (1997) doubted whether Schön's reflection-in-action could take place within fast-paced, changing practice situations. Eraut argued that Schön's concept of 'reflection' is not situated within social contexts, and, therefore, without critical analysis, it might lead unwittingly to unethical decisions.

Practice at advanced levels should demonstrate autonomy, original thinking, creativity, responsibility, problem solving in unfamiliar contexts, critical understanding of practice issues, and appropriate exercise of professional judgement. How can a social worker learn to evidence this advanced level of practice? Parton and O'Byrne's constructive social work (2000) is an appropriate theoretical model because it encourages social workers to share narratives that bring their inner resources to the fore. Discussing practice experiences in an action learning set can lead to awareness of different practice approaches. Constructive social work is a listening model that recognises uncertainties and promotes the 'art' of social work (England, 1986), in consonance with Keith-Lucas' 'art and science' of helping (1972).

Practitioners identify 'building blocks' for practice

Adult services social workers who attended the West Midlands Skills for Care Social Work Symposium on 1 March 2011 submitted detailed comments on social work reform (Higham, 2011c). Seventy practitioner delegates identified professional attributes that constitute significant 'building blocks' for achieving successful social work reform. These are particularly relevant for setting up the new CPD framework, and are applicable also to social workers in children's services. The building blocks included: taking responsibility; building confidence; being positive; gaining the ability to challenge; engaging with change; having access to relevant information and communication; clarifying the role(s) of social work; and advocating social work's contribution to the delivery of services. These building blocks enable social workers to engage with CPD, but also suggest a focus for selecting, planning and engaging in CPD.

Social workers said they needed to acquire more confidence – the same need that the Task Force identified in 2009. However, these social workers acknowledged their own responsibilities to update their knowledge and skills as professional practitioners. They said:

> *'I need to ensure I am proactive in getting involved in the social work change process.' 'A lot rests in the hands of social workers themselves.' 'Social workers have to be dynamic, highly charged and skilled.' 'It is important to recognise the voice and professionalism of the social worker.' 'We must empower social workers to use themselves as a resource that in turn empowers service users and citizens.' 'Social workers have responsibilities to engage with the changes proposed by the Reform Board and need to have the support to do this.' 'I need to be clearer about what I want/need from my managers.' 'I have a real sense that it is down to us locally to ensure we develop a dynamic, ongoing process.'*

They articulated a vision of what it means to be a professional:

> *'My own professionalism is down to me.' 'I have to take responsibility for being confident.' 'Social workers need to have their voices heard but not to rely on*

professional bodies to do it.' 'We have to take more responsibility for becoming assertive to protect the profession.'

(Higham, 2011c: 1–2)

Conclusions

Across the United Kingdom, CPD/PQ frameworks are modified from time to time so they remain fit for purpose – a sign of robustness and relevance to contemporary practice. The social work reforms and the new regulator are stipulated for England only, which raises the issue of how these changes might align with, or contrast with, regulation and enhancement of social work in other countries of the United Kingdom. The future may result in more divergence or possibly a ripple effect that could mean other countries considering some aspects of the new English CPD policy, to determine the possibility of some adaptation to their own national contexts, but those will be future decisions for the Care Councils. Similarly, England's CPD policy could benefit from considering CPD developments in the other UK countries.

In England, managers and practitioners in future will adopt a more streamlined, less regulated, and more economic approach to continuing professional development that offers more flexible choices. The risk is that this more flexible CPD will become a series of disjointed activities without coherence. Employers and universities could collaborate in developing CPD opportunities, including ways to link together elements of in-service training, day courses and relevant assessed academic awards within a CPD framework. CPD in England could include attaining a Masters degree, but because resourcing higher education modules is an issue, a co-funding strategy in which employers fund a module and the candidate self-funds another, a 'scholarship' system for selected candidates, and interest-free tax deductable study loans might enable social workers eventually to gain a CPD-relevant Masters degree. However, social workers would need to be self-motivated, with clear development goals for their own professionalism, and prepared to invest financially to attain a higher academic award.

The success of CPD/PQ strategies across the United Kingdom will depend on how much support is gained from government, employers, service users, carers and higher education, but crucially, from social workers themselves. CPD will succeed only if social workers take the initiative to learn about professional CPD/PQ requirements within their own country, and then plan accordingly, rather than waiting to be informed by their employers. They can access relevant information from the social work regulator website for their country. The College of Social Work website contains information on the Professional Capabilities Framework for England. CPD across the UK will succeed when social workers are able to undertake critical reflection on their CPD activities, and recognise the importance of doing this as part of their responsibility to develop their professionalism. Social workers are urged to engage with the CPD strategy of their own country.

REFLECTIVE QUESTION

1. *What practice and career priorities will inform your future CPD choices?*

2. *How confident are you about critically reflecting on your CPD activities and noting what you learned?*

3. *What kind of support would improve your CPD experiences?*

RECOMMENDED
FURTHER
READING

England

DCSF (Department of Health/Department of Children, Schools and Families) (2009) *Building a Safe, Confident Future: The Final Report of the Social Work Task Force. December 2009.* London: DCSF. DCSF-01114-2009.

DfE (Department for Education) (2012) *Building a Safe and Confident Future: Maintaining Momentum - Progress Report from the Social Work Reform Board.* London: DfE. DFE-00067-2012.

TCSW (The College of Social Work) Website: **www.tcsw.org.uk/**. The College website provides useful up-to-date information on the Professional Capabilities Framework and on enhancement support for Continuing Professional Development.

The Health and Care Professions Council Website: **www.hcpc-uk.org/**. The HCPC website explains the requirements for registration and re-registration of professional social workers, including the requirements for CPD. Useful guidance on what might constitute CPD activities is provided in the document *Your Guide to Our Standards for Continuing Professional Development.*

Northern Ireland

NISCC (Northern Ireland Social Care Council) Website: **www.niscc.info/**.The website contains information on continuing professional development requirements and expectations of social workers in Wales.

Scotland

SSSC (Scottish Social Services Council) Website: **www.sssc.uk.com/**.The website contains information on continuing professional development requirements for all social services workers in Scotland, including social workers, and specific expectations of social workers in Scotland.

Wales

CCW (Care Council for Wales) Website: **www.ccwales.org.uk/**.The website contains information on continuing professional development requirements and expectations of social workers in Wales.

UK-wide

BASW (British Association of Social Workers) Website: **www.basw.co.uk/**.The BASW website contains CPD information, including the BASW policy on CPD and policies on partnerships.

ERENCES

AASW (Australian Association of Social Workers) (2006) *Continuing Professional Education Policy*. Canberra: Australian Association of Social Workers.

Benner, P (1984) *From Novice to Expert*. London: Addison-Wesley.

Bourn, D and Bootle, K (2005) Evaluation of a Distance Learning, Postgraduate Advanced Award in Social Work Programme for Child and Family Social Work Supervisors and Mentors. *Social Work Education*, 24(3): 343–62.

Brand, D and Smith, G (1999) *Social Care Registration Project Consultation Paper on Proposals for a Draft Registration Scheme for the Social Care Workforce*. London: NISW.

Brown, K and Keen, S (2004) Post-Qualifying Awards in Social Work (Part 1): Necessary Evil or Panacea? *Social Work Education*, 23(1): 77–92.

Brown, K, McCloskey, C, Galpin, D, Keen, S and Immins, T (2008) Evaluating the Impact of Post Qualifying Social Work Education. *Social Work Education*, 27(8): 853–67.

Burchell, H (1995) A Useful Role for Competence Statements in Post-Compulsory Teacher Education? *Assessment and Evaluation in Higher Education*, 20(3): 251–9.

Carpenter, J (2005) *Evaluating Outcomes in Social Work Education Discussion Paper No. 1*. London: SCIE.

CCETSW (Central Council for Education and Training in Social Work) (1990) *Paper 31: The Requirements for Post Qualifying Education and Training in the Personal Social Services*. London: CCETSW.

CCW (Care Council for Wales) (2006) *Post Qualifying Learning and Development for Social Workers*. Report for Care Council. Appendix 1 March. CCW: Cardiff.

Children England (2012) Social Work Reform Briefing. Available at: **www.childrenengland.org. uk/upload/SOCIAL%20WORK%20REFORM%20BRIEFING.pdf** (accessed 15 February 2013).

Clarke, N (2001) The Impact of In-service Training Within Social Services. *British Journal of Social Work*, 31(5): 757–74.

Cooper, B and Rixon, A (2001) Integrating Post Qualification Study into the Workplace: The Candidates' Experience. *Social Work Education*, 20(6): 701–16.

Community Care (2011) What Makes a Professional? Available at: **www.communitycare. co.uk/articles/02/02/2011/116192/what-makes-a-professional.htm#sthash.dsHB0dDi. dpuf** (accessed 16 February 2013).

Cutmore, J and Walton, R (1997) An Evaluation of the Post Qualifying Framework. *Social Work Education*, 16(3): 74–96.

DCSF (Department of Health/Department of Children, Schools and Families) (2009) *Building a Safe, Confident Future: The Final Report of the Social Work Task Force. December 2009*. DCSF: London. DCSF-01114-2009.

Department for Education (DfE) 2012 *Building a Safe and Confident Future: Maintaining Momentum - Progress Report from the Social Work Reform Board*. London: DfE. DFE-00067-2012.

Devine, C (1995) *An Evaluation of Courses in Child Protection Studies at Dundee University 1989–1993*. Dundee: University of Dundee.

Dewey, J (1938) *Experience and Education*. New York: Collier Books.

Dewey, J (1997) *How We Think: A Restatement of the Relation of Reflective Thinking to the Educative Process* (revised edition). Mineola, Long Island: Dover Books. (Originally published 1910.)

Doel, M, Flynn, E and Nelson, P (2006) *Experiences of Post-qualifying Study in Social Work.* Capturing the Learning series. Sheffield: Practice Learning Taskforce/Centre for Health and Social Care Research, Sheffield Hallam University.

DOH (Department of Health) (1998) *Modernising Social Services.* London: Department of Health. Available at: **http://webarchive.nationalarchives.gov.uk/+/www.dh.gov.uk/en/Publicationsandstatistics/Publications/PublicationsPolicyAndGuidance/DH_4081593** (accessed 15 February 2013).

DOH (Department of Health) (2000) *A Quality Strategy for Social Care: Consultation.* London: The Stationery Office.

DOH/SSI (1998) *The Quality Protects Programme: Transforming Children's Services, LAC (98) 28.* London: The Stationery Office.

Doyle, C and Kennedy, S (2008) Children, Young People, Their Families and Carers. In Higham, P (ed.) *Post-qualifying Social Work.* London: Sage, pp. 49–62.

Dreyfus, HL and Dreyfus, SE (1986) *Mind over Machine: The Power of Human Intuition and Expertise in the Age of the Computer.* Oxford: Basil Blackwell.

England, H (1986) *Social Work as Art: Making Sense for Good Practice.* London: Routledge.

Eraut, M (1994) *Developing Professional Knowledge and Competence.* London: Routledge.

Eraut, M (2006) How Do We Represent Lifelong Professional Learning. Paper presented at EARLI SIG Professional Learning and Development Conference: Lifelong Learning of Professionals: Exploring Implications of a Transitional Labour Market. Heerlen, The Netherlands: Open University of the Netherlands.

Fook, J (2002) *Critical Theory and Practice.* London: Sage.

Fook, J, Ryan, M and Hawkins, L (2000) *Professional Expertise: Practice, Theory and Education for Working in Uncertainty.* London: Whiting & Birch.

Furlong, MA (2003) Self Determination and a Critical Perspective in Casework: Promoting a Balance between Independence and Autonomy. *Qualitative Social Work*, 2(2): 177–96.

GSCC (2000) *Post Qualifying Social Work Education and Training PQ Handbook,* London: GSCC.

GSCC (2002a) *Codes of Practice for Social Care Workers and Employers.* London: GSCC.

GSCC (2002b) *Guidance on the Assessment of Practice in the Workplace.* London: GSCC.

GSCC (2005) *Post-qualifying Framework for Social Work Education and Training.* London: GSCC.

GSCC (2006) *Annual Quality-assurance Report on Social Work Education and Training 2004–05.* London: GSCC.

GSCC (2010) *General Social Care Council Annual Report and Accounts 2009–10.* London: GSCC.

GSCC (2011) *General Social Care Council Annual Report and Accounts 2010–11.* London: GSCC.

GSCC Website (2006) *Post Qualifying Training,* **www.gscc.org.uk/Training+and+learning/Continuing+your+training/Post-qualifying+training/Post-qualifying+training+downloads.htm**. The GSCC website and all of its content has been archived for reference purposes only. To access an archive of the website please visit the National Archives: **www.nationalarchives.gov.uk**

GSCC Website (2009) *Post Registration Training and Learning.* The GSCC website and all of its content has been archived for reference purposes only. To access an archive of the website please visit the National Archives: **www.nationalarchives.gov.uk**

Health and Care Professions Council (HCPC) (2012) *Standards of Proficiency of Social Workers in England.* London: HCPC.

HEC (Higher Education for Capability) (1994) Capability Manifesto. *Capability,* 1: 1.

Hicks, C and Hennessy, D (1996) Applying Psychometric Principles to the Development of a Training Needs Analysis Questionnaire for Use with Health Visitors, District and Practice Nurses. *Journal of Research in Nursing,* 1(6): 442–54.

Higham, PE (2001) The Dilemma of Standardisation. Paper and presentation to GSCC PQ Assessors Standardisation Event, 27 November. London: GSCC.

Higham, PE (2009a) *Post-Qualifying Social Work Practice.* London: Sage.

Higham, PE (2009b) Evaluating PQ Outcomes: A Discussion Paper (unpublished), January (higham@eircom.net).

Higham, PE (2011a) 'Not a Regulator, but a Champion of Social Work': How the College of Social Work will Promote Social Workers. Continuing Professional Development (CPD). Presentation to Professors of Social Work Conference, May, Birmingham.

Higham, PE (2011b) 'We Help Build Social Workers' Capabilities beyond Initial Competence to Expertise'. Evaluation of a project to develop higher specialist expertise through master classes and post qualifying social work modules in practice education and leadership and management. Birmingham: Skills for Care West Midlands.

Higham, P (2011c) Building Blocks for Reform. Unpublished paper for West Midlands Skills for Care, Birmingham.

Higham, PE, with Sharp, M and Booth, C (2001) Changes in the Quality and Regulation of Social Work Education: Confronting the Dilemmas of Workforce Planning and Competing Qualifications Frameworks. *Social Work Education,* 20(2): 187–98.

Keith-Lucas, A (1972) *Giving and Taking Help.* Chapel Hill, NC: University of North Carolina Press.

Keys, M (2005) Child Protection Training for Primary Health Care Teams: Making a Difference? *Child Abuse Review,* 14(5): 331–46.

Kolb, D (1984) *Experiential Learning: Experience as the Source of Learning and Development.* London: Prentice-Hall.

Kolb, DA and Fry, R (1975) Towards an Applied Theory of Experiential Learning. In Cooper, CL (ed) *Theories of Group Processes.* New York: Wiley: 27–56.

Laming, Lord (2009) *The Protection of Children in England: A Progress Report.* London: The Stationery Office.

Lewin, K (1948) *Resolving Social Conflicts.* New York: Harper.

Munro, E (2011) *The Munro Review of Child Protection: Final Report – A Child-centred System.* London: DfE.

Napier, L and Fook, J (eds) (2000) *Breakthroughs in Practice: Theorising critical Moments in Social Work.* London: Whiting and Birch Ltd.

NASW (National Association of Social Workers) (2002) *Standards for Continuing Professional Education.* Available at: **www.socialworkers.org/practice/standards/cont_professional_ ed.asp#ce** (accessed 29 July 2009).

NIPQETP (Northern Ireland Post Qualifying Education & Training Partnership) (2005) *Draft Proposal for Development of NI Post Qualifying Framework. Consultation Document,* November. Belfast: NIPQETP.

Ogilvie-White, SA (2006) *Baselines: A Review of Evidence about the Impact of Education and Training in Child Care and Protection on Practice and Client Outcomes Evaluation and Evidence, Discussion Paper 2,* SIESWE. Dundee: University of Dundee.

Parton, N and O'Byrne, P (2000) *Constructive Social Work. Towards a New Practice.* Basingstoke: Macmillan.

Pollard, K, Miers, ME and Gilchrist, M (2005) Second Year Scepticism: Pre-qualifying Health and Social Care Students' Midpoint Self-assessments, Attitudes and Perceptions Concerning Interprofessional Learning and Working. *Journal of Interprofessional Care,* 19(3): 251–68.

Postle, K, Edwards, C, Moon, R, Rumsay, H and Thomas, T (2002) Continuing Professional Development after Qualification – Partnerships, Pitfalls and Potential. *Social Work Education,* 21(2): 157–69.

Reeves, S (2003) Commentary on R. Johnson: Exploring Students' Views of Interprofessional Education, *Journal of Interprofessional Care,* 17(1): 35–44.

Rowland, M (2003) Learning the Hard Way. *Community Care,* 30 October: 32–4.

Rowland, M (2006) Post Hoc Survey Evaluation: 2006 (unpublished survey). Birmingham: West Midlands Regional Post-Qualifying Consortium.

Rushton, A and Martyn, H (1990) Two Post-Qualifying Courses in Social Work: The Views of the Members and their Employers. *British Journal of Social Work,* 20(5): 445–68.

Schön, D (1987) *Educating the Reflective Practitioner.* San Francisco: Jossey-Bass.

Schön, D (1991) *The Reflective Practitioner: How Professionals Think in Action.* Aldershot: Ashgate.

Skills for Care (2011) *PCF Development Technical Group. Purpose, Development and Use of the Professional Capabilities Framework for Social Workers. PCF narrative. 31 August 2011.* Available at: **www.skillsforcare.org.uk/nmsruntime/saveasdialog. aspx?lID=11408&sID=2311** (accessed 15 February 2013).

Skinner, K and Whyte, B (2004) Going Beyond Training: Theory and Practice in Managing Learning, *Social Work Education,* 23(4): 365–81.

Social Work Reform Board (SWRB) (2010) *Building a Safe and Confident Future: One year On. Progress Report from the Social Work Reform Board December 2010.* Department of Education, **www.education.gov.uk/swrb**

Social Work Reform Board (SWRB) (2011) *Proposals for Implementing a Coherent and Effective National Framework for the Continuing Professional Development of Social Workers,* 26 May. Department of Education, **www.education.gov.uk/swrb**.

SSSC (Scottish Social Services Council) (2005) *Rules and Requirements for Specialist Training for Social Service Workers in Scotland,* December. Dundee: SSSC.

Stephenson, J (1994) *Capability and Competence: Are They the Same and Does it Matter?* Leeds: HEC/Leeds Metropolitan University.

Stephenson, J (1998) The Concept of Capability and its Importance in Higher Education. In Stephenson, J and Yorke, M (eds) *Capability and Quality in Higher Education*. London: Kogan Page.

TCSW (The College of Social Work) (2012) *The Future of Continuing Professional Development (CPD)*. Available at: **http://www.tcsw.org.uk/uploadedFiles/TheCollege/Media_centre/ The%20Future%20of%20Continuing%20Professional%20Development%20-%20 final%20paper%20for%20cpd%20AIG.PDF** (accessed 15 February 2013).

TCSW (The College of Social Work) (2013) *An Explanation of the Professional Capabilities Framework (PCF)*. TCSW website: **www.collegeofsocialwork.org/pcf.aspx** (accessed 15 February 2013).

Usher, R, Bryant, I and Johnson, R (1997) *Adult Education and the Postmodern Challenge*. London: Routledge.

Chapter 10

Understanding and using supervision in social work

Marion Bogo

Introduction

A substantial body of practice literature about professional development of social workers through supervision has emerged over the past century. The focus is twofold: field education or practice learning for students and supervision of staff. In contrast the empirical literature to support concepts and principles is more limited. In this chapter concepts and principles for staff supervision are identified, drawing on selections from the conceptual, empirical and practice literature, largely developed in North America and the United Kingdom. The aim is to illuminate the essential features for an integrated approach to staff supervision that can be used in contemporary practice settings.

Supervision in social work: definitions

Historically in social work, supervision developed in relation to an agency's mandate. Agencies were entrusted by society, government or benefactors to deliver a particular type of service to the community. Social workers were hired to implement programmes in relation to that mandate and supervisors held the function of ensuring service was delivered effectively. Even in these early days social work leaders recognised that a professional model of social work supervision entailed not only attending to management or administrative functions regarding the organisation, performance and oversight of work, but also to the professional development of staff. Since the effectiveness of service depends to a considerable extent on the competence of the social worker, activities that increase the professional ability of staff are pivotal to implementing the agency mandate. Social work scholarship and research, as well as the experience of social work leaders, appears to draw the same conclusion: a professional supervision model that includes attention to educational and supportive functions which increase social workers' capability is more likely to achieve agency goals than a predominantly managerial supervision approach.

Since students in the newly formed schools of social work in the early part of the twentieth century engaged in learning not only in academic courses but also in community agencies, the term (student) supervision was also used in reference to field work (in North America) or practice learning (in the United Kingdom). In the mid-1950s the Council on Social Work Education was established in the United States and educational terminology was introduced when referring to field work (Raskin et al., 2008). Currently practice learning and field education or field instruction are the preferred terms in the scholarly and empirical literature despite the persistent everyday use of the term supervision when referring to students. In the literature of related fields such as psychology and medicine, clinical supervision appears to be used to refer to the education of students, interns and residents.

In social work, however, two distinct bodies of knowledge and research have developed over the past half-century, with one addressing the supervision of staff in agencies and the other focused on the education of social work students in the field practicum (Bogo, 2010; Bogo and McKnight, 2005). The empirical literature in education of students in the field has developed with concepts, models and techniques to ensure the primacy of the student role as learner (see e.g., Bogo, 2010; Doel, 2010). While there are some useful similarities in concepts, principles and practices, considering this literature separately provides clarity and focus, recognising important differences in context and purpose between supervision of staff and field education/practice learning for students. Accordingly, this chapter focuses only on staff supervision and aims to identify concepts and principles based on selections from the extant conceptual, empirical and practice literature largely developed in North America and the United Kingdom. With the goal of achieving the best outcomes for service users, the Social Work Reform Board in England recognised the pivotal role played by supervision and developed standards for organisational performance, monitoring and review of the way employers have provided supervision (SWRB, 2012). It appears that many of the components of supervision supported in the literature are included in the standards.

An examination of definitions and functions of supervision in social work over many years finds continuing themes of importance stressed by those considered leaders in conceptualising this central professional activity (Kadushin, 1976; Kadushin and Harkness, 2002; Morrison, 2005; Shulman, 2010). These themes relate to the organisational context and the administrative function, the worker's professional development and the educational function, the worker's well-being and morale and the supportive function, and the crucial nature of the supervisor and supervisee relationship.

Organisation context and the administrative function

Regarding the organisational context, the first principle of supervision is that it is a method to ensure that the organisation's mandate is achieved and that clients benefit from service. Accountability is not only used to refer to the efficient use of resources. Two important contemporary themes in social work are relevant to considering accountability: (1) examining whether the services we offer are leading to improved outcomes for service users; and (2) organisational cultures that emphasise not only *doing* but also the importance of reflection, critical thinking and learning from situations that are not successful in the interests of continuous learning that improves service. Supervisors are expected to provide leadership in both these areas.

The literature identifies a list of tasks that include induction of new workers into the organisation through recruitment and orientation, work management through assignment and review of work (Kadushin and Harkness, 2002), and assisting social workers to implement agency policy and procedures and work within the structure of the agency (Shulman, 2010). Evaluation of the quality of the worker's performance is an important aspect of the administrative function and affects decisions about the supervisee's career advancement and salary increases (Gibelman and Schervish, 1997). Morrison (2005) highlights the framework derived from statutory responsibilities and legal requirements, including the importance of clarity about authority (the worker's, the supervisor's, the agency's) and the related need for a regular review of work, plans and recording.

The supervisor is located at the interface between front-line workers and managers and can facilitate the flow of information between these groups. The role is more than a conduit; consistent with social work perspectives, supervisors play crucial mediating and brokerage functions affecting organisational culture and change. For example, a study of supervision of social workers in the United Kingdom found it assisted them with the dissonance they experienced between professional values and the tasks required of them in mental health settings (Taylor and Bentley, 2005). Similarly, in mental health settings in the United States, Australia, and the United Kingdom studies found practitioners perceived clinical supervision as increasing job satisfaction (Schroffel, 1999; Strong et al., 2003) and, along with team support, as protective against stress and burnout (Lloyd et al., 2002). In a study of group supervision Pittman (2009) found that when workers perceived the supervisor as skilful in facilitating mutual aid between group members, workers also perceived organisational support for their practice. These studies lead to a compelling conclusion: good supervisors can affect the way workers experience the organisation.

Supervisors play a key role in introducing and gaining acceptance of new agency policies and procedures. For example, in Ontario, Canada, a provincial initiative changed the approach to child protection from a dominant focus on risk assessment to one of collaboration, empowerment and strengths-based work with families. In a study of supervisors' experiences in this transformation of child welfare practice, participants noted that they often felt as if they were walking a tightrope as the 'harbingers of change'. Front-line staff had strong reactions to the new policy and felt it put *...unrealistic demands on them to protect children, use new approaches ... with limited resources.* Supervisors used the expression 'don't shoot the messenger' to express that they felt caught in the middle (Bogo and Dill, 2008: 146).

Supervisors who can work both 'up and down' the organisation's hierarchy communicate the purpose and essence of new policies, process staff's reactions to them, are open to listening to concerns, and willing to convey issues to managers and advocate for staff when appropriate, rather than dismiss or avoid problematic issues. Clearly the culture of the organisation will affect supervisors' perceptions of how risky or how welcome are messages about difficulties in implementing new programmes.

Related to supervisors' ability to function at the interface between staff and senior management is their recognition that front-line workers are often in the best position to identify changes in clients' situations and challenges to service delivery. Workers can glean this information from their daily encounters with service users and community members and, anecdotally on a case-by-case basis, are likely to share this with their supervisor. The astute supervisor is in a unique position to listen to workers' individual stories and recognise themes and trends that emerge across a number of situations. Supervisors can play a crucial role in collating and presenting this information, putting issues on the agenda for attention by agency managers and service directors as well as for other agencies in their service network. This process involves the supervisor in the role of advocate – for needed change in community programmes, in agency processes that will better meet the needs of service users, and in organisational arrangements to facilitate and support the professional practice of the staff. Morrison (2005) refers to these activities as part of a supervisor's mediation function.

As social work has increasingly developed an evidence-base for practice, agencies must find ways to re-evaluate their policies and programmes and introduce approaches based on emerging new knowledge. New systems for collecting data to provide information about the outcomes for service users are part of this focus. In addition, there is the need for leaders who identify new evidence-informed practices that might be adapted for their organisation. Clearly supervisors must be part of these efforts. They are in a unique position to focus on outcomes for service users and to identify approaches that are not producing desired results. With colleagues, they can search for evidence about approaches that might be more effective for the agency and work out arrangements for developing expertise of staff in these approaches.

The focus in the discussion thus far has been on the supervisor's role in the organisation as a representative of the administration. It is important to remember that the supervisor and front-line worker are also members of the organisation, and their practice and experience will reflect its dynamics and climate. This observation receives considerable support in work in child protection. For example, in interviews with child welfare supervisors they identified the crucial nature of local managers' leadership to create an organisational culture that supports clinical excellence on a daily basis through promoting continuous professional learning for front-line workers, supervisors and managers (Dill and Bogo, 2009).

These sentiments are echoed in two national reports – one in England (Munro, 2011) and one in the United States (Social Work Policy Institute, 2011). Of interest is the similarity in these reviews based on the opinions of experts, experiences of staff and review of empirical studies. Organisational barriers to effective help for families are identified and include organisational climates that emphasise administrative functions in supervision, such as oversight of adherence to regulations, to the detriment of valuing time for educational and clinical supervision such as developing the ability to conceptualise practice, examine dynamics and engage in critical thinking, and develop improved clinical practice competence. The US report concludes:

> *The growing body of evidence supports the important role of supervision as a linchpin for creating a sustainable workforce, an organizational culture based on continuous learning and evidence-informed practice and improved outcomes for children and families.*

> (Social Work Policy Institute, 2011: 15)

In Munro's (2011) comprehensive analysis of the child protection system in England she highlights the importance of organisational context and the need for *a learning system that constantly seeks to improve the quality of help that vulnerable children and families receive* (page 105). Arguing for a systems change, active leaders are needed who will identify and manage required changes in the interests of improving performance and service, with the full support of the entire organisation and moving *from a command-and-control culture encouraging compliance to a learning and adapting culture* (pages 106–7).

While these observations emanate from the field of child protection it is very likely that they are universal across publicly funded settings in which social workers practise. The essential point is that supervision is not a two-person system; it occurs within the context of the organisation and is powerfully affected by the values, perspectives and practices in that environment.

Social workers' professional development and the educational function

The second dominant theme in the literature is the notion that client outcomes are related to supervisees' ability to provide effective service. Hence supervisors focus on workers' practice and the continuing development of professional competence, proficiency and expertise. The links between supervision, worker performance and client outcome are difficult to study and the empirical literature in social work and related fields of psychology and psychotherapy do not yet provide evidence to support this claim. Hence we cannot yet say definitively that supervision makes a difference for service users. Reviews of the research literature document issues and challenges. For example, a comprehensive review of the literature on supervision in publicly funded services in the United States for people with mental health and substance use issues found the majority of articles descriptive or conceptual, with empirical studies that were largely exploratory, and only a small number focused on the association between supervision and client outcomes (Hoge et al., 2011). Where outcomes were examined, study methods were not robust, relying largely on self-reports of workers and agency directors. The reviewers found a small number of studies that demonstrated client improvement when multi-disciplinary staff were trained and supervised on specific treatment approaches such as Trauma Focused Cognitive-Behavioural Therapy (Lau et al., 2004) or Multisystemic Therapy (Henggeler et al., 2002). Another review examined 30 years of studies of psychotherapy supervision and client outcome, pointing out significant methodological problems in the designs of most studies (Watkins, 2011). This author noted only three studies that begin to show how supervision and outcomes can be studied, highlighting the work of Bambling et al. (2006). In this well-executed study experienced psychology and social worker practitioners and supervisors used a supervision manual in the treatment of patients with major depression. While supervision positively affected the working alliance, client retention in treatment and a reduction in symptoms, the researchers were not able to determine whether these outcomes were the result of supervision or of a specific type of pre-treatment session. This session focused on alliance building and the authors suggest the strong alliance may have inflated the results.

Despite the scant evidence base related to client outcome, there is considerable evidence about the positive effect of supervision on staff, particularly the educational function. This includes direct teaching about all aspects of social work such as practice with the client, the team, the professional environment, and the relevant political and social systems (American Board of Examiners in Clinical Social Work, 2004). Morrison (2005) lists a wide range of approaches used in workers' development including coaching, mentoring and encouraging reflective practice.

An extensive meta-analysis was conducted by Mor Barak and colleagues (Mor Barak et al., 2009) of 27 studies of supervision in child welfare, social work and mental health. This review found associations between supervision that workers experienced as positive and worker outcomes such as increased job satisfaction, organisational commitment, retention, job performance and psychological well-being. Supervision, however, is not necessarily either positive or benign. The review also found that detrimental outcomes occur when supervision is experienced as negative. These outcomes related to intention to leave, turnover, job stress, burnout and negative psychological well-being such as depression and anxiety.

The meta-analysis identified three dimensions of supervision: providing task assistance; social and emotional support; and supervisory interpersonal interaction. The first dimension encompasses the educational function and activities discussed in the supervision practice literature such as providing educational activities, tangible advice, knowledge, coaching, skills, and solutions for clinicians' practice. This dimension, task assistance, had the strongest link to beneficial worker outcomes (Mor Barak et al., 2009).

This finding is similar to a study of professional staff from a number of disciplines in mental health and addictions fields where supervisors were not necessarily from the same profession as the practitioners.

> *Almost universally participants agreed that the key elements of valued supervisors are their clinical expertise and ability to provide new and relevant practice knowledge in a respectful and safe process.*

> (Bogo et al., 2011: 133)

Conceptualising practice and promoting workers' capability and competence

When considering the educational function it is important for the supervisor to have an explicit understanding of the nature of effective or competent practice that frames the goals of promoting the worker's knowledge and practice. The supervisor can work collaboratively with the worker to use a shared view of competence as the framework to assess the worker's learning needs, to provide specific assistance, and to develop a unique educational plan for continuing professional development. In the past decade social work and related health and human service professions have increasingly conceptualised the preparation of students in pre-qualification programmes and social workers in continued professional development in terms of achievement of competence, capability or ability. While there is some controversy about the meaning of these terms in the literature, they are frequently used interchangeably and essentially refer to a number of features. See Taylor and Bogo (2013) for a discussion of the difference in terminology with respect to the Performance Capability Framework in England.

The term competence will be used in this chapter based on the theoretical and empirical work conducted in Toronto, Canada (Bogo, 2010; Bogo et al., 2006; Regehr et al., 2012). It will be apparent from the following discussion that it is synonymous with the term 'capability' in the new framework. The move away from the use of the term 'competence' in the UK reflects concerns that some interpretations of competence neglected broader, holistic approaches. However, from a series of studies an *holistic* competence model is proposed that consists of two interrelated dimensions (Bogo, 2010). One dimension is referred to as meta-competence and captures higher order, overarching qualities and abilities of a conceptual, interpersonal and personal/professional nature. The second dimension refers to procedural competence or observable skills, carried out through complex practice behaviours. The latter are more usually associated with traditional or functional models of competence.

Meta-competencies appear related to individuals' ability to use discrete behaviours in a purposeful, integrated and professional manner. The term is used in the related fields of management (Fleming, 1991; Hall, 1986), medicine (Harden et al., 1999; Talbot, 2004), professional psychology (Weinert, 2001) and refers to mental agility and creativity (Reynolds and Snell, 1988), problem solving and analytic

Social Work Practice Competence
ORGANISATION CONTEXT

Skills	Self-regulation Emotions, reflection self-awareness
Complex Practice Behaviour	
Knowledge Generic and specialist Theoretical and empirical	**Judgement** Assumptions, critical thinking, decision making

PROFESSIONAL CONTEXT – VALUES

Figure 10.1   Competence in social work

capacities (Cheetham and Chivers, 1996, 1998), interpersonal communication, self-awareness and self-development (Hatcher and Lassiter, 2007; Talbot, 2004). Harden and colleagues (Harden et al., 1999) suggest that meta-competencies such as the ability to integrate theory, ethics and emotional intelligence into clinical reasoning and judgement, operate through the performance of basic competencies. Weinert (2001) suggests that the development of meta-competencies depends on self-awareness, self-reflection and self-assessment.

Figure 10.1 depicts this holistic competence model and highlights generic dimensions, all of which are interrelated and applied flexibly given the uniqueness of the practice situation, and within contemporary social work stances that value collaboration, empowerment and anti-oppressive practices. Supervisors in particular fields can use this model to articulate the way in which generic elements are expressed in the specific setting, for example in practice with elderly clients in assisted living residences, in family therapy with adolescents in out-patient settings, in child protection, in discharge planning in medical or psychiatric hospitals, and so on.

Competence is seen in the practitioners' performance of complex practice behaviours. Hence in any competence model the focus is initially on what the practitioner is actually *doing* in practice. Behaviour with clients and others relevant to the practice situation represents the worker's integration of a number of dimensions and is enacted through the use of skills or techniques through the various phases of the helping process – engagement and relationship building, assessment and intervention, and termination and evaluation.

In carrying out these complex behaviours practitioners must locate their practice within their profession, mindful of the values and ethics that lead one to act with integrity. As discussed above, practice is significantly influenced by the organisation, in particular the mandate, administrative regulations and expectations of the agency. The supervisor and worker will be cognisant of the worker's understanding of and ability to use professional and organisational factors effectively in the interests of service users. Particular gaps in knowledge or professional ethics may require focus and attention. For example, Doel et al. (2010) studied the source of worker guidance regarding professional boundaries and found the great majority of their sample relied on their own perspectives of what was or was not appropriate, rather than research findings, professional codes, or agency policies.

Framed by their organisational context, the practitioner draws upon generic and specialist knowledge to understand the situations confronted, to engage in critical thinking and to bring judgement to bear on the decisions they must make. Focusing on the left side of Figure 10.1, supervisors and workers will examine whether the practitioner has the needed specialist knowledge and skill to practise effectively in the setting. Since social work education by its very nature prepares graduates with generic knowledge and skill, unless the new worker was assigned to a similar setting for practice learning, it is very likely there will be gaps in foundation knowledge about the population served and in specific intervention models. With the growing emphasis in social work on evidence-based practice, some workers will need to learn approaches that have shown positive outcomes for the client population served. A continuing professional development plan will need to be established for each worker which identifies the focus for supervision. If the supervisor does not possess the content expertise needed by the worker for the best intervention in a specific case, arrangements could be made for time-limited focused supervision with someone who does. Specialised training workshops or courses to attain formal knowledge can also be part of the professional development plan for the worker.

New research on the transfer of learning of evidence-based treatments to actual practice, however, finds that while such workshops improve attitudes, knowledge and confidence, attendees do not gain and maintain sufficient practice skill (Martino, 2010). Supervision approaches that explicitly focus on identified knowledge, attitudes and values, and performance skills are proposed instead (Falender and Shafranske, 2007). Reviews of studies in counselling psychology and addictions find that practitioners' use of, maintenance of, and competence in, complex therapeutic procedures learned in workshops can be enhanced through supervisor feedback to supervisees in their daily practice (Herschell et al., 2010). Again, if the current supervisor does not have this expertise, time-limited focused supervision on a new approach can supplement the usual supervision. If the approach is to become part of the agency's usual practice, it is important for the supervisor to become expert in the approach as well.

Regarding the right side of Figure 10.1, supervisors and workers will focus on the practitioner's subjective experiences, the way they think and feel in relation to their functioning in a professional capacity. Theorising and research on decision making in professional work has largely regarded reasoning as a cognitive or rational process. Contributions from neuroscience research, however, highlight the relationship between cognitive processes and the role of emotion in affecting what we focus on, remember, how we make decisions and problem solve

(MacNaughton and LeBlanc, 2012). Input from the subcortical (emotional) areas of the brain strongly affects the higher cortical (cognitive) neural structures (Damasio, 1994). Recognising that emotion and cognition are not separate in the brain provides an expanded understanding of how emotional and social information is processed, with important implications for practice and supervision.

It is important to acknowledge that emotional experiences will powerfully affect assumptions that operate in the way assessments and resulting decisions are made in practice. Munro (2011) also draws on neuropsychology and highlights that *emotional responses occur automatically and outside conscious awareness ... in response to perceptions, integrating a wide range of data to produce a judgment in a relatively effortless way* (p. 90). This insight is similar to our understanding of tacit or implicit knowledge that operates below the surface and influences professional practice (Schön, 1987). Supervision can assist workers to identify the feelings and thoughts that underpin their practice, to critically examine practice data in light of one's feelings, and help workers *draw out their reasoning so that it can be reviewed* (Munro, 2011: 90).

Supervisory processes and the supervisor's competence as an educator

Given the previous discussion of competence, it appears important for supervision to consist of the following three interrelated processes: observation of practice; reflective discussion; and providing feedback, modelling, and coaching. First, there must be opportunities for the worker and the supervisor to review the practitioner's actual practice. A competency-based approach emphasises what the worker is able to *do*; hence the worker's enactment of complex practice behaviours in interaction with service users provides the foundation for all input from the supervisor. If practice is not observed how can supervisors have meaningfully reflective dialogues about practice – they must spend time trying to 'figure out' what might actually have transpired to elicit the responses on the part of the worker or service user that are presented as challenging? Also, how can supervisors give feedback on skills if they have not seen the skills in action?

Supervision, however, usually involves the worker presenting the clients' situation in verbal and/or written form. The earlier discussion of neuroscience pointed out that our emotional reactions powerfully affect our cognitive understanding and recall of our experiences. Therefore, one can assume that distortion is a normal part of everyday life and will affect our review and discussion of a practice situation. Hence, it is important for supervisors to regularly observe workers' practice. The time for such review must be used judiciously given current resource constraints. Always with client consent, and based on the worker's stage of development and length of time working with the supervisor, observation opportunities will vary. Occasionally an entire interview can be observed or selected segments can be recorded, reviewed, and then observed together. Many settings have one-way mirrors and supervisors and team peers can observe sessions.

The second process involves reflection. Both Kolb's experiential learning model (Kolb, 1984) and Schön's views on continuing learning for professional practice (Schön, 1987) underscore the importance of reviewing and thinking through a practice experience and learning from it. Reflective dialogues in supervision can attend to the various components of competence presented above. The practice situation and interventions can be linked to various explanatory and intervention theories, to evidence-based approaches, to ethical guides, and to empirical knowledge about the population and issue. Explicit articulation of underlying concepts can promote generalisation and transfer to other practice situations. In supervision attention can also be paid to the way practitioners' subjective reactions and assumptions are affecting critical thinking, reasoning, judgements and decisions about the situation and the way to proceed. Munro (2011) notes the importance of supervision for reviewing how workers reason and the importance of critical challenge by others to identify and correct biases.

The importance of staying current with new and effective approaches to practice has been underscored above. In reflective discussions supervisors who are conversant with the literature can motivate workers to examine how emerging new knowledge can improve their practice and assist service users. Research findings are examined in light of clinical and ethical issues relevant to the uniqueness of the particular practice situation. Evidence-based practice provides additional information to use in decision making and planning (Gambrill, 2006).

The third educational process entails providing feedback, modelling and coaching. A number of reviews of studies of supervision in social work (Bogo and McKnight, 2005) and psychology (Ellis, 2010; Milne et al., 2008) offer support for the importance of providing corrective feedback. This finding is supported by tenets of social learning theory, as well as reviews and meta-analysis of studies in psychology on effective methods of teaching helping skills (Hill and Lent, 2006). Supervisors need to be highly conversant with the dynamics in the practice situation and workers' practice to provide specific, informed, focused suggestions about how one could proceed differently. When feedback is linked to the conceptual and knowledge base underpinning practice, workers are assisted to integrate theory and practice and to transfer new learning to similar situations. Modelling may involve supervisors accompanying workers or having workers observe the supervisors' practice. The educational function rests on the supervisors' knowledge and skill as an expert practitioner. In addition, they must be able to teach that practice expertise and to develop workers' ability to integrate new knowledge into the worker's own personal-professional use of self.

Workers' well-being and morale and the supportive function

Another theme in the supervision literature is the importance of providing support for the social worker. This function involves helping the worker handle stress, through providing encouragement, reassurance and appropriate autonomy

(Kadushin and Harkness, 2002). The focus is on enhancing staff morale and the job satisfaction of social workers. Morrison (2005) points out that workers need a safe climate to examine the impact of practice on them, and a place to express their own feelings. Supervisors are expected to be aware of the *overall health and emotional functioning of the worker, especially with regard to the effects of stress* (Morrison, 2005: 45). In such activities supervisors need to maintain a professional boundary between, on one hand, supporting workers through providing a space and a place to examine and explore feelings, and, on the other hand, avoiding quasi-therapeutic explorations and instead clarifying when personal therapy is evidently called for.

The supportive function receives empirical support in Mor Barak's (2009) analysis and follows the educational dimension in importance. It is the second dimension in the analysis and defined as that of supervisors providing social and emotional support that is concerned with addressing workers' emotional needs and job-related stress.

Earlier in this chapter contributions from neuroscience were noted, specifically that emotion and cognition are linked and affect our functioning in everyday life and in our professional roles. This research reinforces social work's long-standing recognition of the importance of self-awareness and expands this concept to recognise that practitioners can become emotionally dysregulated as a result of the professional work in which they engage. Specifically, emotional reactions to practice situations encountered can leave one feeling anxious, upset or distressed, to the extent that one begins to have difficulty thinking and acting, demonstrating reactions of fight, flight or freeze. In this case the subcortical areas of the brain are so overwhelmed by emotions that the higher cortical neural structures are affected, making thinking and taking action more challenging (Gray et al., 2002; Lewis and Todd, 2007). These states may arise as a result of the worker's unique psychological issues, previous traumatic experiences, or feeling incompetent to deal with the situation at hand (Bogo et al., 2012).

Of importance for supervision is to assist workers in recognising and managing these states so that they can engage with service users in an intentional and purposeful manner. This includes paying some attention to workers' use of self; the way in which their unspoken assumptions, beliefs, values, schemas and rules can operate out of awareness but powerfully affect the way in which they work with others (Reupert, 2009). It also suggests the importance of assisting workers in recognising their internal states, developing a mindful approach to their own internal state as well as that of the service user or colleague, and finding ways to stay calm and grounded. A strong theme in the literature is that supervisory processes that assist workers with self-awareness and emotional regulation must be professionally focused and not cross boundaries into quasi-therapeutic processes.

The administrative and educational dimensions of supervision discussed thus far should theoretically provide the context and content for interactions that attend to the worker's emotions and subjective reactions to the work in a way that provides effective, and hence supportive, approaches. This function then becomes integrated in the supervisors' activities and offered through the working relationship with the supervisee. These comments are relevant for social workers receiving supervision from a social worker. There are, however, many settings where social workers are receiving supervision in multi-professional teams from individuals in disciplines other than their own, such as in health, mental health and addictions.

The empirical literature regarding this shift is scant; however, in an investigation of the experiences of a range of professionals in a mental health and addictions setting two important findings emerged (Bogo et al., 2011). One was that, especially for experienced practitioners, supervisors' ability to offer expertise through educating and supervising staff to master effective interventions for the population served and to support staff in their professional practice was important. The second key finding was that all staff expressed a need for support of their professional self-identity through opportunities to interact with their profession-specific community in the setting, and to discuss issues, values and new developments from their unique perspective. Particularly where there is only one social worker on a team, professional meetings are important to provide such professional support. Consistent with notions about professional development over one's career and related needs in supervision, new graduates strongly expressed the desire to connect to their primary profession since now, beyond the beginning stage of development, they identified their needs for reinforcement of generic social work knowledge in their specialised practice setting, mentorship and career guidance.

The supervisor and supervisee relationship

The final theme that recurs in the literature is the importance of a particular type of supervisor and supervisee relationship; one that provides a parallel for many of the qualities desired in the worker and client collaborative relationship (Shulman, 2010). This emphasis on the relationship reflects the belief that learning, growth and professional performance are affected by the context in which they occur. Empirical evidence for this belief is found in Mor Barak's (2009) analysis and identification of the third dimension of supervision which is concerned with the nature of the supervisory interaction and the workers' perceptions of the supervisory relationship and their satisfaction with it.

The following characteristics were gleaned from a review of studies of characteristics social workers value in supervisors: that they are available; provide support and encourage professional growth; serve as a professional role model; communicate in a mutual and interactive supervisory style; are knowledgeable about tasks and skills and can relate these techniques to theory; hold practice perspectives and expectations about service delivery similar to the supervisee's; and delegate responsibility to supervisees who can do the task (Bogo and McKnight, 2005). These characteristics reflect a mutual respectful relationship where supervisees can count on supervisors to be helpful with their professional work.

Morrison (2005) points out the necessity for empathic, emotionally attuned supervisors who convey to supervisees that their sessions are collaborative and offer a secure space for discussion. In such a context workers may gain trust over time to be open about concerns and 'mistakes' and such a relationship context will lead to more initiative, creativity and risk-taking. Shulman (2010) has also noted that, similar to a helping relationship in practice, the supervisory relationship is based on rapport, trust and caring. Supervisees learn about the type of relationship valued by clients through experiencing these qualities in supervision and through modelling after the supervisor. In this respect, the dynamics and skills parallel the worker and client relationship. The difference, however, is that supervision is *focused on helping staff members carry out their work-related tasks* (Shulman, 2010: 14) rather than on the psycho-social issues of the supervisee.

There can be tension in carrying out the diverse aspects of the supervisory relationship given the authority ascribed by the agency to the supervisor. Shulman's (2010) guidelines for contracting at the beginning of the relationship and revisiting and reviewing these issues over time are helpful. He recommends supervisors initiate discussion of a number of issues in a specific and direct manner so that important topics do not go underground or are left to vague speculation. Supervisors are encouraged to share their sense of the purpose of supervision and to describe their role in fairly concrete ways, with examples. Supervisors should also discuss the mutual obligations and expectations regarding the authority of the supervisor. These issues should be addressed in a way that encourages and seeks input from the supervisee about her expectations, perceptions and needs. In this way both members of the dyad learn about each other's area of expertise, what can usefully be raised for attention, what are the limits surrounding confidentiality and decision making, and where there is room for negotiation and change.

Training for supervisory roles

There is growing recognition in many fields that supervision is an advanced practice competence and requires special training, knowledge and skills. Milne and colleagues, working in psychology in England (Milne et al., 2011), reviewed studies of supervisor training and found some support for the effectiveness of training supervisors using feedback, role play and modelling through live and video-recorded demonstrations. Studies also reported the use of traditional educational methods such as the use of guided reading, verbal instruction and discussion. Frequently, experienced workers are appointed as supervisors due to their competence as workers. It should not, however, be assumed that good practitioners will automatically be good supervisors. Clearly there is a need to develop new supervisors' competence in the various dimensions of the role as well as in managing the accompanying tensions.

Concluding thoughts

At the beginning of this chapter it was noted that two distinct bodies of knowledge and research regarding the education of students and supervision of staff developed over the past half century. Given the emphasis on improving practice learning, it is likely that most social workers experienced a form of instruction as a student that included and balanced attention to administrative/managerial, educational and supportive functions within the context of a collaborative relationship. Now in the role of social worker or supervisor, that experience may serve as a role model or standard. However, the context of pressured work environments and the demands for accountability may make it challenging for supervisors to offer best practices.

In addition, the fundamental purpose of staff supervision differs from that of student instruction: in the former the agency employs a professional to provide services to users, and in the later the student is the user, expecting the university and agency to provide an effective education. Nevertheless, many of the processes reviewed in this chapter are used effectively in student practice learning in the field and, in fact, may have been initiated in that realm. The challenge for the staff supervisor remains one of balance – ensuring that social workers' expertise is enhanced through educational approaches in supervision that attend to the workers' unique professional development stage and needs, while discharging their responsibilities in administration. Supervision time is too precious to spend on reporting; rather it should involve a stimulating interchange that develops workers' expertise, raises important educational, professional and service issues for supervisors to act upon, and ultimately provides better services for the community.

Despite the lack of strong research evidence that supervision positively affects client outcomes, it has endured as a central process in social work. The research, however, does support positive outcomes for staff and for organisations. In contemporary high-demand work environments this may be sufficient reason for its continued importance. Indeed, The Social Work Reform Board supports this position, and in the Standards for Employers and Supervision Framework (2012) identifies key principles which all employers should put in place. The principles expect employers to:

- *make sure that social workers can do their jobs safely and have the tools and resources they need to practice [sic] effectively and confidently to assess risks and take action to minimise and prevent them;*

- *ensure that social workers have regular and appropriate supervision;*

- *provide opportunities for Continuing Professional Development, as well as access to research and practice guidance* (Social Work Reform Board, 2012: 31)

Also, the importance of reflective and clinically focused supervision is a theme which features throughout Munro's (2011) review of the child protection system in England.

The view of supervision presented in this chapter is one that is holistic and aims to integrate the related functions of administration, education and support. Each of these factors can be seen as influencing the others, and, it is believed, that when operating in concert they provide enhanced working environments. Such environments can energise social workers to, actively and creatively, continuously pursue new knowledge to assist service users and to improve the circumstances of persons in their communities. While the nature and quality of the relationship between the supervisor and supervisee is of extreme importance in affecting workers' perceptions, supervision is more than a two-person system. Supervision is seen in the context of the organisation, both reflecting and contributing to the organisational culture, and in turn affecting the nature of practice and the service provided.

The Standards expect employers to develop a *clear framework for undertaking effective supervision, with identification of key elements as well [as] frequency and environment* (Social Work Reform Board, 2012: 32). Hopefully the concepts and practices presented in this chapter will prove useful as organisations, employers and social workers continue to develop their knowledge and skill to positively affect service users and their communities.

REFLECTIVE QUESTIONS

1. *What are some of your fundamental beliefs about the nature of competent social work practice? What are the key 'ingredients' you want to develop and see in your staff's performance?*

2. *What are some of your fundamental beliefs about how people learn? What is the role of feelings, thinking and acting in learning?*

3. *Given your thoughts on the above, what are the key components of your model of supervision?*

4. *How does the context in which you work affect your model (e.g., the regulations and mandate in the agency, the way power and authority are enacted, the nature of the team)?*

RECOMMENDED FURTHER READING

Carpenter J, Webb, C, Bostock, L and Coomber, C (2012) *SCIE Research Briefing 43: Effective Supervision in Social Work and Social Care.* SCIE, England. Available at: **www.scie.org.uk/publications/briefings/briefing43/**

Kadushin, A and Harkness, D (2002) *Supervision in Social Work* (4th edition). New York, NY: Columbia University Press.

Milne, D, Aylott, H, Fitzpatrick, H and Ellis, MV (2008) How Does Clinical Supervision Work? Using a 'Best Evidence Synthesis' Approach to Construct a Basic Model of Supervision. *The Clinical Supervisor*, 27(2): 170–90.

Mor Barak, ME, Travis, DJ, Pyun, H and Xie, B (2009) The Impact of Supervision on Worker Outcomes: A Meta-analysis. *Social Service Review*, 83(1): 3–32.

Shulman, L (2010) *Interactional Supervision* (3rd edition). Washington, DC: NASW Press.

REFERENCES

American Board of Examiners in Clinical Social Work (2004) Clinical Supervision: A Practice Specialty of Clinical Social Work. A position statement of the American Board of Examiners in Clinical Social Work.

Bambling, M, King, R, Raue, P, Schweitzer, R and Lambert, W (2006) Clinical Supervision: Its Influence on Client-rated Working Alliance and Client Symptom Reduction in the Brief Treatment of Major Depression. *Psychotherapy Research*, 16: 317–31.

Bogo, M (2010) *Achieving Competence in Social Work through Field Education.* Toronto, Ontario: University of Toronto Press.

Bogo, M and Dill, K (2008) Walking the Tightrope: Using Power and Authority in Child Welfare Supervision. *Child Welfare*, 87(6): 141–57.

Bogo, M and McKnight, K (2005) Clinical Supervision in Social Work: A Review of the Research Literature. *The Clinical Supervisor*, 24(1/2): 49–67.

Bogo, M, Katz, E, Regehr, C, Logie, C, Mylopoulos, M and Tufford, L (2012) Toward Understanding Meta-competence: An Analysis of Students' Reflections on their Simulated Interviews. *Social Work Education.* 32(2): 259–73 doi: 10.1080/02615479.2012.738662.

Bogo, M, Paterson, J, Tufford, L and King, R (2011) Interprofessional Clinical Supervision in Mental Health and Addiction: Toward Identifying Common Elements. *The Clinical Supervisor Journal*, 30(1): 124–40.

Bogo, M, Regehr, C, Woodford, M, Hughes, J, Power, R and Regehr, G (2006) Beyond Competencies: Field Instructors' Descriptions of Student Performance. *Journal of Social Work Education*, 42(3): 579–93.

Cheetham, G and Chivers, G (1996) Towards a Holistic Model of Professional Competence. *Journal of European Industrial Training*, 20(5): 20–30.

Cheetham, G and Chivers, G (1998) The Reflective (and Competent) Practitioner: A Model of Professional Competence which Seeks to Harmonise the Reflective Practitioner and Competence-based Approaches. *Journal of European Industrial Training*, 22(7): 267–76.

Damasio, AR (1994) *Descartes' Error: Emotion, Reason and the Human Brain.* New York: Avon.

Dill, K and Bogo, M (2009) Moving Beyond the Administrative: Supervisors' Perspectives on Clinical Supervision in Child Welfare. *Journal of Public Child Welfare*, 3(1): 87–109.

Doel, M (2010) *Social Work Placements: A Traveller's Guide.* Abingdon: Routledge.

Doel, M, Allmark, P, Conway, P, Cowburn, M, Flynn, M, Nelson, P and Tod, A (2010) Professional Boundaries: Crossing a Line or Entering the Shadows? *The British Journal of Social Work*, 40(6): 1866–89.

Ellis, MV (2010) Bridging the Science and Practice of Clinical Supervision: Some Discoveries, Some Misconceptions. *The Clinical Supervisor*, 29(1): 95–116.

Falender, CA and Shafranske, EP (2007) Competency in Competency-based Supervision Practice: Construct and Application. *Professional Psychology: Research and Practice*, 38(3): 232–40.

Fleming, D (1991) The Concept of Meta-competence. *Competence and Assessment*, 16: 9–12.

Gambrill, E (2006) *Social Work Practice: A Critical Thinker's Guide* (2nd edition). Oxford: Oxford University Press.

Gibelman, M and Schervish, PH (1997) Supervision in Social Work: Characteristics and Trends in a Changing Environment. *The Clinical Supervisor*, 16(2): 1–15.

Gray, JR, Braver, TS and Raichle, ME (2002) Integration of Emotion and Cognition in the Lateral Prefrontal Cortex. *Proceedings of the Natural Academy of Sciences*, 99(6): 4115–20.

Hall, DT (1986) *Career Development in Organisations*. San Francisco, CA: Jossey-Bass.

Harden, RM, Crosby, JR, Davis, MH and Friedman, M (1999) AMEE Guide No. 14: Outcome-based Education: Part 5 – From Competency to Meta-competency: A Model for Specification of Learning Outcomes. *Medical Teacher*, 21(6): 546–52.

Hatcher, RL and Lassiter, KD (2007) Initial Training in Professional Psychology: The Practicum Competencies Outline. *Training and Education in Professional Psychology*, 1(1): 49–63.

Henggeler, SW, Schoenwald, SK, Liao, JG, Letourneau, EJ and Edwards, DL (2002) Transporting Efficacious Treatments to Field Settings: The Link between Supervisory Practices and Therapist Fidelity in MST Programs. *Journal of Clinical Child and Adolescent Psychology*, 31(2): 155–67.

Herschell, AD, Kolko, DJ, Baumann, BI and Davis, AC (2010) The Role of Therapist Training in the Implementation of Psychosocial Treatments: A Review and Critique with Recommendations. *Clinical Psychology Review*, 30(4): 448–68.

Hill, CE and Lent, RW (2006) A Narrative and Meta-analytic Review of Helping Skills Training: Time to Revive a Dormant Area of Inquiry. *Psychotherapy: Theory, Research, Practice, Training*, 43(2): 154–72.

Hoge, MA, Migdole, S, Farkas, MS, Ponce, AN and Hunnicutt, C (2011) Supervision in Public Sector Behavioral Health: A Review. *The Clinical Supervisor*, 30(2): 183–203.

Kadushin, A (1976) *Supervision in Social Work*. New York, NY: Columbia University Press.

Kadushin, A and Harkness, D (2002) *Supervision in Social Work* (4th edition). New York, NY: Columbia University Press.

Kolb, DA (1984) *Experiential Learning: Experiencing as the Source of Learning and Development*. New Jersey: Prentice-Hall.

Lau, M, Dubord, GM and Parikh, SV (2004) Design and Feasibility of a New Cognitive-behavioural Course using a Longitudinal Interactive Format. *The Canadian Journal of Psychiatry*, 49(10): 696–700.

Lewis, M and Todd, R (2007) The Self-regulating Brain: Cortical-subcortical Feedback and the Development of Intelligent Action. *Cognitive Development*, 22(4): 406–30.

Lloyd, C, King, R and Chenoweth, L (2002) Social Work, Stress and Burnout: A Review. *Journal of Mental Health*, 11(3): 255–65.

MacNaughton, N and LeBlanc, V (2012) Perturbations: The Central Role of Emotional Competence in Medical Training. In Hodges, BD and Lingard, L (eds) *The Question of Competence: Reconsidering Medical Education in the Twenty-first Century*. Ithaca, NY: ILR Press, pp. 70–96.

Martino, S (2010) Strategies for Training Counselors in Evidence-based Treatments. *Addiction Science & Clinical Practice*, 5 (December): 30–40.

Milne, D, Aylott, H, Fitzpatrick, H and Ellis, MV (2008) How Does Clinical Supervision Work? Using a 'Best Evidence Synthesis' Approach to Construct a Basic Model of Supervision. *The Clinical Supervisor*, 27(2): 170–90.

Milne, DL, Sheikh, AI, Pattison, S and Wilkinson, A (2011) Evidence-based Training for Clinical Supervisors: A Systematic Review of 11 Controlled Studies. *The Clinical Supervisor*, 30(1): 53–71.

Mor Barak, ME, Travis, DJ, Pyun, H and Xie, B (2009) The Impact of Supervision on Worker Outcomes: A Meta-analysis. *Social Service Review*, 83(1): 3–32.

Morrison, T (2005) *Staff Supervision in Social Care*. Brighton: Pavilion.

Munro, E (2011) *The Munro Review of Child Protection: Final Report*. United Kingdom: Department of Education. Available at: **www.education.gov.uk/publications**

Pittman, JH (2009) The Role and Impact of Group Supervision for Social Work Practitioners. PhD, University of Maryland, Baltimore, MD, Health Sciences and Human Services Library.

Raskin, M, Wayne, J and Bogo, M (2008) Revisiting Field Education Standards. *Journal of Social Work Education*, 44(2): 173–87.

Regehr, C, Bogo, M, Donovan, K, Anstice, S and Kim, A (2012) Identifying Student Competencies in Macro Practice: Articulating the Practice Wisdom of Field Instructors. *Journal of Social Work Education*, 48(2): 307–19.

Reupert, A (2009) Students' Use of Self: Teaching Implications. *Social Work Education*, 28(7): 765–77.

Reynolds, M and Snell, R (1988) *Contribution to Development of Management Competence*. Sheffield: Manpower Services Commission.

Schön, D. (1987) *Educating the Reflective Practitioner*. San Francisco: Jossey-Bass.

Schroffel, A (1999) How Does Clinical Supervision Affect Job Satisfaction? *The Clinical Supervisor*, 18(2): 91–105.

Shulman, L. (2010) *Interactional Supervision* (3rd edition). Washington, DC: NASW Press.

Social Work Policy Institute (2011) *Supervision: The Safety Net for Front-line Child Welfare Practice*. Washington, DC: National Association of Social Workers.

Social Work Reform Board (SWRB) (2012) *Building a Safe and Confident Future: Maintaining Momentum*. Available at: **www.gov.uk/government/uploads/system/uploads/attachment_data/file/175947/SWRB_progress_report_-_June_2012.pdf**

Strong, J, Kavanagh, D, Wilson, J, Spence, SH, Worrall, L and Crow, N (2003) Supervision Practice for Allied Health Professionals within a Large Mental Health Service: Exploring the Phenomenon. *The Clinical Supervisor*, 22(1): 191–210.

Talbot, M (2004) Monkey See, Monkey Do: A Critique of the Competency Model in Graduate Medical Education. *Medical Education*, 38(6): 587–592.

Taylor, MF and Bentley, KJ (2005) Professional Dissonance: Colliding Values and Job Tasks in Mental Health Practice. *Community Mental Health Journal*, 41(4): 469–81.

Taylor, I and Bogo, M (2013) Perfect Opportunity ~ Perfect Storm?: Raising the Standards of Social Work Education in England. *The British Journal of Social Work*. doi: 10.1093/bjsw/bct077.

Watkins, CEJ (2011) Does Psychotherapy Supervision Contribute to Patient Outcomes? Considering Thirty Years of Research. *The Clinical Supervisor*, 30(2): 235–56.

Weinert, FE (2001) Concept of Competence: A Conceptual Clarification. In Rychen, DS and Salganik, LH (eds) *Defining and Selecting Key Competencies*. Seattle WA: Hogrefe & Huber: 45–66.

Chapter 11
Working with the media

Ray Jones

Introduction

This chapter reflects on how the media has related to and depicted social work. This has not generally been a positive experience for social work or social workers. However, because the print, radio and television media comments and commentaries have impact, and now social media and the internet more generally should be added as having influence, there is a role and requirement for social workers to engage with the media and to seek to have the contribution and realities of social work recognised. Based on the author's experience of media contacts and contributions, the chapter shares some learning on how to seek to work proactively as well as reactively with the media.

Working with the media, and seeking to inform public opinion and perspectives, may be difficult but it is even more important a task when public services, and social work in particular, are criticised and castigated by a largely right-wing print press in support of a political agenda which uses the excuse of austerity to demonise those who are disadvantaged and increasingly in difficulty and made further deprived, and even destitute, by the self-preserving policies of the powerful.

Social workers know from professional experience the pain and shame inflicted on children, families and disabled and older people by cuts in public services and in the welfare state. But too many of the public-at-large have isolated and inoculated themselves from knowing about the distress for increasing numbers in marginalised communities. There is a story to be told, and social workers should be contributors to this story-telling about the difficult lives of others and about the contribution social work can in part make to enhance the well-being of those who are stranded and whose life chances are strangled by increasing inequality and poverty.

Media portrayals of social work and social workers

There is a strong evidence-informed view that social workers have for a long time had a bad press (see e.g., Galilee, 2006; Glasgow University Media Group, 1976). For some parts of the media this might be seen as a part of a political agenda.

For the *Daily Mail*, *Mail on Sunday* and the *Sun* attacking social workers with stories that are either misinformed, deliberately inaccurate or unbalanced is a part of a broader agenda which castigates the public sector and sees public services as a self-serving cost to everyone and to the economy. And when the story is about social work the script usually either describes social workers as powerfully intrusive, imposing and inept or as weak, witless, wacky and wicked. Here are two media headlines, and in both stories the press comment is critical of social workers:

> *Woman, 34, suing social services for not taking her into care ... claiming her mother beat, starved and neglected her.*

> (Hoyle, 2012)

> *State child snatchers: As social workers hand back a child they falsely claim was abused, an investigation exposes one of the great scandals of our age.*

> (Booker, 2011)

But the quotes above show something more than social workers being attacked for apparently being too ready to act and not being active enough. They also show either an ignorance or deliberate misrepresentation of the (limited) powers of social workers and that decisions about removing children from parents are made by courts not social workers.

The same damned-if-you-do and damned-if-you-don't dilemma is also reflected in the media coverage and comment about adoption, with the last two articles quoted below written by the same journalist:

> *The human misery of adoption delays is laid bare.*

> (Bennett, 2011)

> *Why we couldn't adopt in Britain: Three of these couples adopted from abroad and the reasons they were rejected in British agencies will leave you in despair.*

> (Lawrence and Stocks, 2011)

> *'I was stolen from my mother': the deeply disturbing truth about adoption.*

> (Lawrence, 2010)

While all public services get a bad press within the mass selling tabloids, there is a pecking order, a hierarchy, of professional status and vulnerability to press hostility, with councils and their social workers at the forefront of the targeting, which even allows the alleged failings or omissions of others to be used as a means of targeting social workers, as in this example:

> *A mother whose daughters suffered nappy burns had her children taken into care because social services wrongly thought she had scalded her deliberately.*

> (Narain, 2012)

But below the first paragraph of this story in the *Daily Mail* it becomes clear that it was not social services who had wrongly thought the little girl had been deliberately harmed. Instead it was when the mother took her daughter to hospital that doctors examined her and *they called the police and [the mother] was arrested on suspicion of abusing the little girl by scalding her with hot water*. What did the social workers do? They kept the children within the family by placing them with their paternal grandmother.

A similar press report with a *Daily Mail* headline which read *Nurse who killed two sons was 'let down by social services who failed to spot warning signs of severe post-natal depression'* was misleading and wrong. The rest of the report being about health visitors not social workers – who did not know the family – missing signs of severe depression (Pemberton, 2011), although the headline was later changed, following a challenge, with 'social services' replaced by 'NHS workers' (Levy, 2011).

But there is a danger that social workers get over-sensitised to the bad press they receive. Firstly, hardly anyone in any walk of life gets a good press. Bad news is apparently the best news. Secondly, those who are continuously exposed to bad news may get somewhat inured to it. To some extent it may lose its impact. And thirdly, the purveyors of the bad news are contaminated themselves and are not respected or trusted. For example, an Ipsos MORI survey of public trust in different occupations (which did not specifically include social work) found that the most trusted occupations were all in the public service sector – doctors (89%), teachers (86%), professors (77%) and judges (75%) – and the least trusted were government ministers (19%), politicians generally (18%), and least trusted of all at 17 per cent were journalists (Ipsos MORI, 2011).

The impact of negative media reporting, however, cannot be ignored, either for its personal impact on individuals who are targeted in the coverage or for the service overall. When the tabloid telling of the 'Baby P story', about the death of 17-month-old Peter Connelly, was at its zenith in 2009 a survey undertaken for the Local Government Association found that 42 per cent of people questioned stated that their opinions of social workers had worsened since the reporting about 'Baby P's' death (Marsh 2009; *Metro* 2009). This reflected people's perceived opinions of social workers. However, to get a more reliable take on the impact of the reporting would have required a before and after survey to see if the views of respondents had actually changed.

The telling of the 'Baby P story' was exceptional. Between November 2008 when the story was breaking and a year later in November 2009 it was found that there were 2,832 reports and comment pieces in the United Kingdom's national newspapers referring to 'Baby P', that is an average of almost eight reports every day for a year. The *Sun* alone, which with Rebekah Brooks as its editor majored on the 'Baby P story' and with its self-proclaimed 'campaign for justice' demanding the sackings of social workers and their managers, had 848 articles in the year referring to 'Baby P', an average of 2.3 stories every day (Elsey, 2010).

The 'Baby P story' may have been exceptional in its virulence but the press-directed vilification of social workers when a child dies is not unique, even if it is unpredictable. It ignores the fact that the child protection services in England and Wales are comparatively successful in protecting children contrasted with other countries (Pritchard and Williams, 2010). But with about 70 children dying each year as a consequence of abuse or neglect it is hit-and-miss whether the death of any one child will attract any, or any sustained, media attention. However, when the media do focus on a death it is the social workers who are placed under scrutiny and this is a media tradition which has a 40-year history going back to 1973 and the inquiry into the death of Maria Colwell (Butler and Drakeford, 2011).

The denigrating and demoralising nature and impact of social work's negative media coverage has been noted both in the past (see e.g, Aldridge, 1994; Ayre, 2001; Franklin, 1999) and more recently by Munro who commented on *the sustained nature of the negative media images of social work that have been commonplace* (Munro, 2011b: 122) and by the Social Work Task Force:

> *Social workers have spelled out to the Task Force how deeply concerned they are by the way their profession is reported in the media ... They have expressed their anger at how social workers often appear singled out for the blame in the aftermath of the tragedy of a child's death.*

(Social Work Task Force, 2010: 48)

There has also been a consequence of the media coverage for individual social workers and for trends in decision-making and, therefore, for children and families. For example, care applications for children to the courts increased by 39.7 per cent in 2009–2010, the first full year after the 'Baby P' story was first told in November 2008, and even within a month of the *Sun* and others demanding the sackings of social workers and managers in Haringey there was an increase in England from 496 care proceedings applications in October 2008 to 592 in November and 719 in December (CAFCASS, 2012).

It is not, however, only child abuse and child deaths which attract sporadic sustained media interest, although it is the deaths of children rather than, for example, disabled adults which are more likely to gain media attention. In the 1990s, for example, it was social workers' involvement with young people involved in anti-social behaviour which became a frequent focus for the media. There were a cluster of stories about the 'Ratboy' (*The Independent*, 1993), a story which was resurrected and referred to again 20 years later when he was imprisoned for burglary (Kennedy, 2013), and about the 'Costa Kid' (Gordon et al., 1993), where for more than six months there was national and international media reporting that social workers and a social services director (the current author!) had funded a 14-year-old boy who was heavily involved in petty crime to spend two weeks in Spain staying with his grandmother who lived there (she was one of the few positive relationships and influences for the boy).

But these are still media stories about young people, and the parallel press interest at the time of the 'Baby P story' was about two brothers in Edlington, Doncaster who seriously assaulted two other boys and where social workers took the blame for not having taken action earlier in relation to the brothers (Doncaster Local Safeguarding Children Board, 2009).

But when there is a tragic and terrifying death of a disabled adult, as with Steven Hoskins, a man with a learning disability killed by young people and an older man in Cornwall (Cornwall Adult Protection Committee, 2007), it usually does not capture the media's sustained interest – and therefore does not capture the public's interest – in the way the death of a child does. However, the exposé in 2011 by an undercover BBC *Panorama* reporter of the collective abuse of people with a learning disability at Winterbourne View private hospital (South Gloucestershire Safeguarding Adults Board, 2012) is a recent example of media coverage of adult abuse in institutions, not dissimilar to the exposure of abuse of people with a learning disability at Ely Hospital in Cardiff in the 1960s (Butler and Drakeford, 2003).

Social workers fight back

Social workers, and agencies, authorities and associations who employ social workers or have sought to speak on behalf of social workers, have tried to influence the media portrayal and the public perception of social work and social workers. Guidance has been produced about working with the media (Local Government Association, 2010; Unison, 2011). This has often focused on actions to get good news stories covered in the local press and beyond with guidance on press releases and invitations to the media to meet social workers and to see them at work, with advice about 'day in the life' features, case studies from service users who are willing to speak to the media, and award ceremonies for social workers. The guides also provide information about how to respond to the media at a time of crisis. Pre-empting requests for information at a time of crisis, and to inform journalists more generally, briefing packs about social work have been prepared for journalists (*Community Care*, 2009; The College of Social Work, 2012), and the British Association of Social Workers has a guide on public speaking (BASW, 2011).

More dramatically and proactively, a few organisations employing social workers have worked with the media to allow the realities and complexities of social work to be presented to the public. For example, Bristol City Council allowed the BBC (BBC, 2004) to film social workers at work and a six-part weekly series was produced and broadcast on BBC 1 television in November and December 2004. A professional advisor to the series commented that:

> Hopefully the programmes will open up an area of debate and discussion based on the real working lives of child care social workers. The programmes are intended to be a remedy to the florid or weak representations of social workers occasionally found on TV soaps like The Bill or EastEnders. The series should also challenge other popular stereotypes of social workers

> (Fraser, 2004)

175

The series provided a powerful portrayal of the care and commitment of social workers, and also showed the difficulties and distress of those the social workers were seeking to assist. Social workers and their agencies have been criticised for being reticent about engaging with the media (Lombard, 2009; Maier, 2009; Munro, 2011a), but the experience of Bristol's social workers, the council and the director of children's services must have been generally positive as between 2009 and 2011 they were again willing to participate in a BBC 'fly on the wall' three-part series about social work which was broadcast early in 2012 (Hudson, 2012), and which was commented upon favourably in the progress report of the Social Work Reform Board (2012: 11). The confidence of Bristol City Council and its social workers to allow social work in action to be filmed is rare but not unique as Coventry City Council has also allowed filming over six months for a BBC *Panorama* Special called 'Kids in Care' (BBC, 2010), with positive comments about the programmes (Brody, 2010; Mangan, 2010), and then again in 2011 allowed the BBC to film for a programme about children, families, social workers and adoption.

Individual social workers have also engaged with the media to promote an understanding of social work, the key contribution it can make, and also about the difficulties faced by social workers. For example, at the time that there was considerable media coverage and comment about social work when the 'Baby P' story was prominently featured in the media, several social workers gave accounts of the realities of the daily professional lives of social workers (Anonymous, 2008; Ferguson, 2008; Jones, 2008; McKitterick, 2008), and one social worker became a frequent media commentator, a go-to person for the print press, radio and television (Taylor, 2009). Joanna Nicolas contacted the BBC after hearing a misleading report on Radio Four's *Today* programme stating that social workers had taken a baby from a mother at birth, with no reference to the fact that this was a decision made by a court. She is now often contacted to speak about the realities of social work.

Reasons to be engaged with the media

But why should social workers engage with the media? Firstly, it may not be optional. When the media determine that a story will be reported social workers may be a part of the story even if this is not their wish or intention. One response is not to contribute to the story, and this may be a sensible decision if it is likely that the story is negative, and even distorted, but will be short lived and the social worker or agency decide not to add to or feed the story. This may avoid prolonging or extending the coverage but it leaves the social worker's account left untold.

The second option, therefore, is to respond to the story which is emerging. This is an opportunity to have the voice of the social worker or the agency heard, but this is still likely to be a marginal voice and an afterthought towards the end of the story-telling which has already been structured by the reporter. It may give the media the opportunity to claim fairness in that they sought and included the view of the social worker or agency, but three or four sentences towards the end of a press report which is many paragraphs long, and may even be spread over pages, is hardly satisfactory balance. But even when minimised and marginal, those few comments may at least provide some corrective or add some complexity for the readers or viewers who are then challenged to think for themselves about what may be lying behind the story which is being told.

The comments from agencies, however, often appear defensive and uninformative. Firstly, the comments may carry little credibility if credited to a faceless and nameless 'council spokesman' or 'press officer'. This reinforces the image of an impersonal, unaccountable and uncaring bureaucracy, which may be how the agency is already being presented in the story.

Secondly, restricted by confidentiality and a commitment to protect information about clients or others, the response may be no more than it is not possible to comment because of confidentiality or continuing court proceedings. But even then, it is often possible to give in general terms an account of the types of issues and considerations which should be informing social work and agency decisions without referring to a specific incident or case. This requires, however, that someone who is professionally well informed about policy and practice is willing to be in contact with the media, and this is hindered when the agency's protocols and procedures are that media inquiries should only be dealt with by the press or communications team or officers. They are often not confident or competent to discuss in general terms practice or policy issues. They are then likely to be seen as stone-walling and obstructive. Sometimes it may be that the most appropriate means of getting the media briefed about the general policy and practice issues relevant to a specific story is to get someone who has experience and expertise but who is independent of the agency to give a background briefing to the media.

But when stories are likely to emerge, there is the possibility of engaging with reporters early to seek to inform them about the embryonic story, to give a background briefing about practice and policy issues, to explain about complexity and the reality of decision-making, and to shape understanding and story lines. For example, when a serious case review is to be published, briefing the media rather than waiting for the media reaction and then responding is likely to be a more constructive strategy, and if the serious case review is predicted to be high profile, attracting much media attention, working with the media on a general background understanding of issues prior to publication may also be sensible. Too often, however, there is preparation of how to respond to the media at the point of publication but little preparation of the media.

This suggests the value of building relationships over time with journalists working in print, radio and television. These relationships can never be totally trusting and open. A journalist's role is to report and to story-tell. They have editors and producers who will determine the editorial line to be taken within a story. The journalists should also quite rightly retain their independence and not be compromised through close relationships with others. But building a relationship of mutual respect if not total trust is more likely to lead to social worker and agency views and voices being reported and reported with fairness.

Media engagement should not be limited, however, to individual cases or responding to media coverage of crisis or of dramatic events. There is also the opportunity through the media to inform the public at large about the work of social workers and the realities of this work. This takes confidence and commitment both from agencies and from social workers. It does mean being exposed to critical comment as well as positive perceptions. Overall, however, the likely picture for the public is of good, caring and committed people doing difficult and distressing, and sometimes traumatic and threatening, work. Unlike the simplified and partial story lines in the press, or the distorted presentation in the tabloids and the soaps (*Community Care*, 2012), the complexity of what social workers do, and the crucial importance of their work, gets illustrated and told. It may not make for comfortable reading, hearing or viewing, but is often engrossing as social workers are a part of 'human interest stories' which capture attention and emotion.

And it is not only an opportunity for social workers to talk about their work. It also allows the public to be informed about and confronted with the reality of the lives of people who are often marginalised, stigmatised and unheard – the so-called scroungers and shirkers and the fiddlers and frauds – but who experience devastating deprivation, disadvantage and distress, and whose lives are full of pain and sorrow. The public memory is likely to be of their own shock and horror when faced with the terrible lives lived by so many of those whom social workers are seeking to assist or protect. The virtue of social work itself is then valued.

Media realities

But the media does not exist to publicise and promote social work. Its role should be to report and to inform, albeit too often it may focus on its own vested interest of increasing sales and audiences with titillation and exaggeration as a means to a commercial end. It also too often both shapes and panders to the prejudices of others as a means of creating and cornering its market. So there should be a realism about what the media can and will do. There are, however, some media realities which when acknowledged and remembered are likely to assist the media to give more constructive coverage.

Firstly, reporters today are likely to be generalists rather than subject specialists. As noted by Dean (2012), the days of specialist social services, health, housing or industrial relations reporters and correspondents are largely long gone. Although some broadsheet newspapers and some regional and national radio and television news programmes still have specialist reporters, reducing financial costs and losses has meant reducing dedicated subject specialists. The consequence is that the reporter leading on a story may have little background knowledge of the context for the story. The danger here is that the story when told is ill-informed and inaccurate. The opportunity is to brief the reporter on background policy and practice issues which may be relevant in understanding the story.

Secondly, the media moves at pace. News is only news for a short time. It has to be reported quickly. Speed is necessary to meet deadlines for the next print run or news bulletin or to avoid being left behind by online coverage. It is not, therefore, usually sensible and acceptable to inform a reporter that they will get a response tomorrow or later in the week. There may be occasions when this is feasible, but often the story will have been told in a news bulletin later that day or in that evening's or tomorrow morning's paper. This means being willing to put oneself out to engage with the media within the timescales and with the urgency with which they are working.

But the fact that news is news for only a short time has another angle. Continuing stories need new storylines. News needs novelty. A big story reported day after day and week after week is a story which journalists have to continuously fuel and feed. There is then the opportunity to engage in the shaping of continuing stories by contributing new perspectives and information and by offering new voices and faces. Even when a story starts off as simplistic and may be inaccurate its continuation allows complexity and accuracy to be injected.

Thirdly, different media have different markets and different biases. For example, it is well to understand and be aware that when asked to comment on at least some talk radio stations you will be interjecting in a programme which is argumentative and opinionated and where points scoring is a major part of the process. It may then be sensible to recognise that the presenter is always going to win the argument. They structure the interview, often leave little space for the interviewee to contribute, are harassing and usually have the last word. The best that can be hoped for is that the three or four sound bite points to be made are delivered and, if possible, repeated and reinforced. Seeking to engage in the debate is a lost cause when there is no control over how the debate is being managed and manoeuvred.

Ten tips and techniques

In agreeing or seeking to work with the media there are some general points and practices which may, therefore, be helpful.

Point 1: be briefed about the media with which you are engaging. An interview on BBC Radio 4 is different from one on BBC Radio 5. Radio 4 news interviews tend to be more professionally focused and restricted whereas Radio 5 interviews are often more conversational in style and may become more wide ranging. And the time allowed for an interview on a radio or television news programme is likely to be much less than the time given by a feature programme such as BBC Radio 4's *Woman's Hour* or *You and Yours*.

Point 2: reach out to the media as well as waiting and being responsive. The media has a lot of space and time to cover, especially with the advent of 24-hour news channels, talk radio and web-based news coverage. Local radio and local papers, in particular, are often responsive to contacts about local stories, or local angles on national and international stories, and even programmes such as BBC Radio 4's *File on Four* or Channel 4's *Dispatches* are always having to think about and plan for future programmes. Feeding them suggestions and information may capture an interest and an opportunity for a story to be shaped and told.

Point 3: keep it simple. Although it is important that the public understand the complexity of the work of social workers, and that the media should report this complexity, it is unlikely that anyone will be able to remember more than three or four key points from an interview or a report.

Point 4: be prepared. Determine in advance what are the three or four key points to be made. Write them down and, unless on television, use them as a check list during the interview.

Point 5: be determined. In an interview it is important to answer questions asked but also to use questions asked as an opportunity to deliver the key points to be made ... 'I partly agree with what you are saying but it is also important to recognise that ...'.

Point 6: is it better to agree to a pre-recorded interview than a live interview? This may not be an option, but the reality of a live interview is that the requirement is to respond there and then to whatever is asked or said and this can sometimes take an interview into areas and angles which were not anticipated. A pre-recorded interview allows the opportunity to pause and to do again a part of the interview if not confident or happy with the first response or the direction of the interview. However, a live interview is often more within the interviewee's control as it cannot be edited before its first broadcast and therefore what is broadcast is what the interviewee said in full and in the way and in the context in which the interviewee said it.

Point 7: it is impressions as well as words that count. Be composed rather than agitated and panicky, sit calmly rather than fidgeting, controlling the adrenalin but being aware of what is happening, and remember emotional intelligence as well as intellectual intelligence. Seek to engage with the interviewer, but always have in mind the bigger audience beyond the interviewer. And interviews are more about points-making than points-scoring. The interviewee with credibility in a Jeremy Paxman interview on BBC's *Newsnight* is often the interviewee who makes their points but does not get drawn into a head-to-head confrontation. The panellist who has impact is usually not the one who says the most and talks over and interrupts others, but the one who calmly says want they want to say with clarity and remains composed and modest.

Point 8: impressions are not only about words and behaviours. They are also about dress and presentation. Less important when being interviewed by a press reporter or for a radio interview, but for television being smart and formally dressed is – with few exceptions – likely to give an impression of gravitas, reliability and being informed. It is the same when appearing on television as when attending court.

Point 9: the task is to communicate and convince, not to show off. Avoid big words and jargon. Jargon and being seen as clever is not likely to be engaging. In no more than a few minutes or a few lines the aim is to capture the audience's interest and then their understanding and then their agreement with whatever is being communicated. Make it less understandable or make it hard work for the audience and the likelihood is that they will actually or metaphorically switch off. It may be helpful to keep in mind a relative or friend and to be thinking how would I be communicating and talking with them about this issue rather than thinking this is a time to impress as I am on the radio or television or in tomorrow's newspaper.

Point 10: know that you will be disappointed. No interview will go quite as intended or hoped. It is hardly ever possible to deliver all of the three or four planned points and to reinforce the points to make sure they are heard or read. The overall shaping of the interview or what is reported will not be as you wanted. The impression created will not have been as confident or coherent as intended. But some points are likely to have been landed and some information provided. This is often as good as it gets and it is still a success and worthwhile.

The internet and social media

Getting the voices of social workers heard is now, however, easier, even if the mainstream print, radio and television media may not be interested in the realities and achievements of social work. No longer do the big media magnates have control of what is published and what is broadcast. Communication across communities has been enfranchised by the world wide web, by search engines such as Google, by Twitter and by blogging, and by internet social media such as Facebook. As noted by Jukes:

> The electrification of the word has liberated text. Words can be copied and disseminated at virtually no cost, at the click of a mouse. They can be retrieved, searched and analysed just as rapidly. Constructed out of code, the digital domain makes sound, word, image all legible, editable and rewritable. Every day, billions of thoughts and conversations, formerly lost to the ether, are now recorded in text messages, chat boxes, emails, blog comments, tweets and Facebook updates. Now that a quarter of the world's population is online means that nearly two billion people are commenting, arguing, laughing, fighting, debating in searchable, retrievable text; never have we been so literary, never have we read so much and written our history so comprehensively.

(Jukes, 2012: 273)

This presents a tremendous opportunity for social workers to have their voices heard. From time to time I have written pieces published in the *Guardian* (and other newspapers). I am disappointed when what I submit does not get into the print pages but only appears online. I am wrong. I am told that the online readership is much larger than the readership of the print pages.

Here is one example of the impact and the immediacy of social media. At the National Adult and Children's Services conference in October 2012 there was a two-way exchange via Twitter. Ermintrude2 – a lively and well-informed champion for social work who is a regular blogger – challenged Paul Burstow – the former adult social care minister in the coalition government – about what was described as 'the very real concerns of a practitioner on the frontline of social work'. The Ermintrude–Burstow exchanges were seen by a much wider Twitter audience and it was commented that *[i]t's a welcome break from a political system that often sees MPs and ministers hear more concerns from think tanks than frontline workers* (McNicoll, 2012). The comment by McNicoll, a *Community Care* journalist, was itself in a blog on the *Community Care* website.

There are other social worker bloggers who tell it like it is both for themselves and for their service users, but there are always risks and limits in what can be written, especially if an employee and identities become known. This may be what happened with fightingmonsters.wordpress.com as when the site was searched in December 2012 the approved mental health social worker who blogged and twittered as 'fighting monsters' noted that the site was quickly having to be closed down.

So the internet and social media provide an opportunity for social workers to bypass traditional media and to have their voices heard, but this risks getting into confrontations with employers if criticising the agency or of being identified and open to abuse or threat by others. The dangers of sharing personal information through social media are recognised for children. There are also dangers for adults, including social workers. Guidance about using social media, and its dangers and risks, has been provided by BASW (2012).

Concluding comments

Representing and championing one's profession is a part of every professional's role and responsibility. It is partly achieved by working and behaving well and having credibility and generating trust and respect. It is an everyday task.

But there is also a role in explaining and promoting one's profession which is wider and more general than just being an exemplary practitioner or manager of professionals. It involves speaking for the profession, explaining what it does and why, and responding to criticism and castigation. This does not mean defending poor or inappropriate practice and behaviours. Indeed, this should be challenged and exposed.

Working with the media provides an opportunity to promote an understanding of the positive contribution social work makes in the lives of people and communities, often at a time of personal crisis, of psychosocial transition or interpersonal and community conflict (Jones, 2012a). The media in all its forms influences public awareness and understanding. It creates as much as it responds to agendas and public interest. It shapes the public values context in which social workers work. It is a vehicle for communication and influence. Choosing not to engage with the media does not leave a vacuum. Instead it leaves a media script which may be uninformed and distorted but which will still be told.

Individual social workers as employees of social care organisations may be more exposed when making comment in the media on social work issues and are likely to be seen as representing, or at least as speaking from the experience of working within, their current organisation, and this may place them in conflict with their employers. This is not so likely for independent social workers who are self-employed, or for social workers in academic posts where their comments are about social work and not about their education or research institutions.

This is why being a part of a collective organisation championing social work and social workers may make it more acceptable and feasible for social workers to provide the media with comment and information. They are then doing it on behalf of the collective organisation and not as an employee of any organisation. The British Association of Social Workers and the College of Social Work both encourage and assist their social work members to speak on behalf of social work. Trade unions play a similar role, albeit one where the focus is more on promoting the (employment) interests of their members rather than primarily promoting the profession of social work.

Engaging with the media may seem, and be, fraught and frightening. If the only time there is media contact is when responding to another story where the script already written is that social workers got it 'wrong', the nature of the contact is likely to be reactive, seen as defensive and with social work on the back foot. This in part is inevitable, but it is still an opportunity to inform and to shape stories and understanding (Jones, 2012b).

However, social workers should be proactive as well as reactive in informing about and promoting the profession of social work. As noted above, social workers and their leaders in Bristol and Coventry have done this – and each has done it more than once. They have received public praise for the work they do every day as shown through the media coverage and also professional applause for their commitment in being champions for social work. Being a representative, advocate and champion for social work is a part of the professional social worker's role.

REFLECTIVE QUESTIONS

1. *Is it important for social workers to actively seek to engage with the media? If so, why?*

2. *On reflection, how would you note and describe different media styles and behaviours, and how would you take these into account in any contact with different parts of the media?*

3. *Collective organisations of social workers can provide strength and security when engaging with the media. How could you be active within these collective organisations locally as well as possibly nationally?*

RECOMMENDED FURTHER READING

Dean, M (2012) *Democracy Under Attack: How the Media Distort Policy and Politics*. Bristol: Policy Press.

Jones, R (2012) Child Protection, Social Work and the Media: Doing As Well As Being Done To. *Research, Policy and Practice*, 29(2): 83–94.

Local Government Association (2010) *Giving Social Work a Voice: How to Improve Social Workers' Relationship with the Media*. London: Local Government Association.

Unison (2011) *Media and Social Work: A Unison Survival Guide*. London: Unison.

REFERENCES

Aldridge, M (1994) *Making Social Work News*. London: Routledge.

Anonymous (2008) Only a Matter of Time. *Guardian Society*, 26 November, 1–2.

Ayre, P (2001) Child Protection and the Media: Lessons from the Last Three Decades. *British Journal of Social Work*, 31(6): 887–901.

BASW (2011) *Public Speaking Guidance*. Available at: **www.basw.co.uk/resource/?id=1333**

BASW (2012) *How to deal with Social Media: A Social Work Union Guide*. Available at: **www.basw.co.uk/resource/?id=782**

BBC (2004) *Someone To Watch Over Me*. London: BBC.

BBC (2010) Kids in Care, *Panorama*, BBC 1, 14 October.

Bennett, R (2011) The Human Misery of Adoption Delays is Laid Bare. *The Times*, 12 December, 14.

Booker, C (2011) State Child Snatchers: As Social Workers Hand Back a Child They Falsely Claim was Abused, an Investigation Exposes one of the Great Scandals of Our Age. Available at: **www.dailymail.co.uk/news/article-2027272/South-Gloucestershire-social-workers-hand-child-falsely-claim-abused.html**

Brody, S (2010) Panorama. Kids in Care – a Review, *Community Care*, 6 October. Available at: **www.communitycare.co.uk/blogs/childrens-services-blog/2010/10/panorama-kids-in-care-a-review**

Butler, I and Drakeford, M (2003) *Scandal, Social Policy and Social Welfare*. Bristol: Policy Press.

Butler, I and Drakeford, M (2011) *Social Work on Trial: The Colwell Inquiry and the State of Welfare*. Bristol: Policy Press.

CAFCASS (2012) *Three Weeks in November … Three Years On … CAFCASS Care Application Study 2012*. London: CAFCASS.

Community Care (2009) *A Journalist's Guide to Social Work*. Sutton: Community Care.

Community Care (2012) Fury Over Eastenders' 'Misleading' Social Work Storyline. Available at: **www.communitycare.co.uk/articles/09/10/2012/118586/fury-over-eastenders-misleading-social-work-storyline.htm**

Cornwall Adult Protection Committee (2007) *The Murder of Steven Hoskin: A Serious Case Review: Executive Summary*. Truro: Cornwall County Council.

Dean, M (2012) *Democracy Under Attack: How the Media Distort Policy and Politics*. Bristol: Policy Press.

Doncaster Local Safeguarding Children Board (2009) *Serious Case Review: 'J' Children*, 29 March. Department of Education.

Elsey, S (2010) *Media Coverage of Child Deaths in the United Kingdom: The Impact of Baby P: A Case for Influence?* Edinburgh: Centre for Learning in Child Protection.

Ferguson, H (2008) To Protect Children We Must First Protect Social Workers. *The Guardian*, 13 November, 32.

Franklin, B (1999) (ed.) *Social Policy, the Media and Misrepresentation*. London: Routledge.

Fraser, S (2004) Give Social Workers a Second Chance. *Society Guardian*, 10 November. Available at: **www.theguardian.com/society/2004/nov/10/childrensservices.politics1**

Galilee, J (2006) Literature Review on Media Representations of Social Work and Social Workers. In *21st Century Social Work Review*. Edinburgh: Scottish Executive.

Glasgow University Media Group (1976) *More Bad News*. London: Routledge and Kegan Paul.

Gordon, A, Holliday, R and Barton, F (1993) Spanish Holiday for a Criminal Aged 14. *Mail on Sunday*, 22 August, 3.

Hoyle, A (2012) Woman, 34, Suing Social Services for Not Taking Her Into Care … Claiming her Mother Beat, Starved and Neglected Her. *Daily Mail*, 15 June. Available at: **www.dailymail.co.uk/news/article-2160042/Woman-34-suing-social-services-taking-care--claiming-mother-beat-starved-neglected-her.html**

Hudson, A (2012) Risk and Trust in the Media Spotlight, 9 May. London: College of Social Work.

Ipsos MORI (2011) *Trust in Professions 2011*. Available at: **www.ipsos-mori.com/Assets/Docs/Polls/Veracity2011.pdf**

Jones, R (2012a) The Best of Times, the Worst of Times: Social Work and its Moment. *British Journal of Social Work*. Advance access, published 8 October, doi: 10.1093/bjsw/bcs157.

Jones, R (2012b) Child Protection, Social Work and the Media: Doing As Well As Being Done To. *Research, Policy and Practice*, 29(2): 83–94.

Jones, S (a pseudonym) (2008) 'He Blocked the Door and Pulled a Knife'. *The Times*, 13 November, 8.

Jukes, P (2012) *The Fall of the House of Murdoch: Fourteen Days that Ended a Media Dynasty*. London: Unbound.

Kennedy, R (2013) Rat Boy's Back to his Old Tricks … and Now Back Behind Bars. Available at: **www.chroniclelive.co.uk/news/north-east-news/newcastles-infamous-child-terror-anthony-5816307**

Lawrence, J (2010) 'I was Stolen from my Mother': The Deeply Disturbing Truth about Forced Adoption. Available at: **www.dailymail.co.uk/femail/article-1308117/I-stolen-mother-The-deeply-disturbing-truth-forced-adoption.html**

Lawrence, J and Stocks, J (2011) Why We Couldn't Adopt in Britain: Three of These Couples Adopted from Abroad and the Reasons They were Rejected by British Agencies will Leave You in Despair. Available at: **www.dailymail.co.uk/femail/article-2062031**

Levy, A (2011) Nurse Who Killed Two Sons was 'Let Down by NHS Workers who Failed to Spot Warning Signs' of Severe Post-Natal Depression. Available at: **www.dailymail.co.uk/news/article-2021204**.

Local Government Association (2010) *Giving Social Work a Voice: How to Improve Social Workers' Relationship with the Media.* London: Local Government Association.

Lombard, D (2009) Com Care Tries – and Fails – to Charm Council Press Officers. *Community Care*, 7 September. Available at: **www.communitycare.co.uk/blogs/social-work-media/2009/9**

Maier, E (2009) Ten Reasons Why Social Workers Must Speak to the Media. *Community Care*, 22 April. Available at: **www.communitycare.co.uk/blogs/social-work-media/2009/4**.

Mangan, L (2010) Panorama Showed How the Absence of a Mother Leaves a Void that is Filled with Misery. *The Guardian*, 6 October, 25.

Marsh, A (2009) Public Trust in Social Workers Down Since Baby P, 25 March. Available at: **www.localgov.co.uk/index.cfm?method=news.detail&id=76825**

McKitterick, B (2008) Being Constantly Suspicious is Part of the Territory. *The Times*, 13 November, 2–3.

McNicoll, A (2012) Social Worker's Twitter Spat with Ex-minister Shows Power of the Social Media. Available at: **www.communitycare.co.uk/bl;ogs/mental-health/2012/10/social-workers-twitter-spat-wi/.**

Metro (2009) Baby P Death Hits Social Work Trust. *Metro*, 25 March. Available at: **www.metro.co.uk/news/596126-baby-p-death-hits-social-work-trust**

Munro, E (2011a) *The Munro Review of Child Protection. Interim Report: The Child's Journey.* London: Department for Education.

Munro, E (2011b) *The Munro Review of Child Protection. Final Report: A Child-centred System*, Cm 89062, Department for Education. The Stationery Office: Norwich.

Narain, J (2012) Mother whose Children were Taken Away for Eight Months ... Because of Nappy Burns. *Daily Mail*, 18 July, 9.

Pemberton, C (2011) Social Workers Blamed for Health Visitors' Mistakes. Available at: **www.communitycare.co.uk/blogs/childrens-services-blog/2011/08/social-workers-blamed-for-health-visitors-mistakes/**

Pritchard, C and Williams, R (2010) Comparing Possible 'Child-Abuse-Related-Deaths' in England and Wales with the Major Developed Countries 1974–2006: Signs of Progress. *British Journal of Social Work*, 40(6): 1700–18.

Social Work Reform Board (2012) *Building a Safe and Confident Future: Maintaining Momentum: Progress Report from the Social Work Reform Board.* London: Department for Education.

Social Work Task Force (2010) *Building a Safe and Confident Future – The Final Report of the Social Work Task Force.* London: Department for Education.

South Gloucestershire Safeguarding Adults Board (2012) *Winterbourne View Hospital: A Serious Case Review.* Available at: **www.southglos.gov.uk/wv/report**

Taylor, A (2009) 'I'm Happy to Talk to the Press': Independent Social Worker Joanna Nicolas Has Become Something of a Media Consultant. *Community Care*, 16 July, 18.

The College of Social Work (2012) *Fact Files*. Available at: **www.tcsw.org.uk/media-centre/fact-file-guides-for-journalists/?terms=facts%20files**

The Independent (1993) Profile: How Ratboy Made His Name: A 14-year-old Becomes a Byword for Trouble. Available at: **www.independent.co.uk/voices/profile-how-ratboy-made-his-name-a-14yearold-becomes-a-byword-for-trouble-1509508.html**

Unison (2011) *Media and Social Work: A Unison Survival Guide*. London: Unison.

Chapter 12

Fifty years of professional regulation in social work education

Graham Ixer

Introduction

The role of regulation in England has attracted considerable political debate in the context of public policy over the previous decade, ranging from the high-profile issues which have emerged within the financial sector through to health and social care. In some cases the decision-making process has been driven by value for money considerations, including public spending cuts; in others it has been a response to perceived deficits in the quality of the respective workforce performance under scrutiny. In some cases there has been no clear evidence base for the decisions made by government.

However, whatever the merits or otherwise of the case, the change in the current regulatory landscape for social workers is likely to bring a period of instability. The social work regulator, the General Social Care Council (GSCC), was abolished in 2012 and its functions transferred to other organisations, which was neither planned nor evidenced based. This change provides a unique point to reflect and review the history of the regulation of social work education, now 50 years old. While on one level this chapter provides an account of key elements of its history, it also looks behind the chronology in order to identify the perennial challenges which bedevil this task in every policy arena. Through this process various issues will be identified, all of which are of relevance to the current 'state of social work education' in England, which, of course, represents the workshop in which professional social work is forged.

There appears to be widespread consensus across the sector of the link between 'good social work practice' and high-quality training (Brown et al., 2008; Dickens, 2011: 31). This is something that the Social Work Task Force claimed in their first report (DCSF, 2010a). In examining the events over the past 50 years, few developments can be seen as really unexpected or entirely new, and simultaneously a process of constant change has devalued many achievements because of the ... nce to learn from the past. Social work change is ultimately driven by polit-... ology rather than professional need or empirical evidence, which for the profession of social work is its major weakness. This article is mainly based on examining all the press releases, news and key reports published by CCETSW and the GSCC from 1972 to 2012. It describes the key events as part of an important story never been told in totality and then analyses the emerging issues.

1962 – the beginning

The formal regulation of social work education can be traced back to 1962 in the Council for Training in Social Work (CTSW), which formally approved training courses, although unregulated training courses had existed much earlier. In 1970 the CTSW was renamed the Central Council for Education and Training in Social Work (CCETSW) and was put on to a statutory footing. CCETSW was the statutory UK body responsible for promoting, approving and quality assuring the training of social work and social care in the personal social services (University of Warwick, 2012). However, CCETSW ceased to exist from 30 September 2001 when its functions transferred to the General Social Care Council in England and to newly established care councils in the other parts of the UK. In 2012, in England, these functions transferred again, but this time to a multi-professional regulator, the Health Professions Council (renamed Health and Care Professions Council, 1 August 2012), although the Care Councils in Northern Ireland, Scotland and Wales remain unchanged.

1970–1979 – origins of key developments

The key focus for CCETSW was the objective to increase the size of the workforce, because of new developments within the wider welfare state and the need for more trained professionals. The emphasis was on expanding social work numbers by training more people who would both join and remain in the profession (CCETSW, 1972). There was a need to create opportunities for staff development and to begin to professionalise the industry (CCETSW, 1973a). A new in-service scheme was launched for residential social workers along with a whole range of short courses that CCETSW approved (CCETSW, 1973b). The year1973 was an important one for social work as it was during this year that for the first time the profession acknowledged the need for, and subsequently developed the first ever, codification of values of social work in the UK. Unlike many other professions of its time, social work recognised that its remit was not solely determined by skills and knowledge acquisition but had a value base which could be defined and underpin service delivery and the training of social workers (CCETSW, 1973c).

The development of values

Values were not seen as something static but as dynamic and posing a challenge to match 'what we believe' with 'what we know' and 'what we do.' In 1976 Paper 13 was published as a key milestone in challenging the misunderstanding of values. It sought to bring about a healthy debate in exposing prejudice and discrimination in a more open way (CCETSW, 1976).

CCETSW never shirked the difficult conversations and pronounced the need for 'more ethnic minority groups in social work' (CCETSW, 1979a: 1). This recruitment dimension was to recur as an ever-growing feature in the subsequent life of the organisation (CCETSW, 1984). CCETSW was synonymous with values, anti-discrimination and anti-racist social work. CCETSW saw racism as the major challenge to the profession, but as it confronted the political establishment it began to make enemies (CCETSW, 1987). The dichotomy for CCETSW was how it could persuade government that the anti-racist 'time bomb' should and could be defused and that this was a cause worth pursuing because values are deeply political and contested. Much later, in 1987, CCETSW set up a specialist group to advise on the subject of how to manage the challenge of racism. The 'Black Perspectives Committee' was established. As well as CCETSW's need to develop its own organisation to become more racially and culturally sensitive to changing society, it had to engage more robustly in policy and resource availability (Christodoulou, 1988). Explicit values became the cornerstone of CCETSW's identity and the majority of its stakeholders saw CCETSW as leaving a helpful legacy when it was finally abolished in 2001. During the 1980s it backed its uncompromising rhetoric on anti-discriminatory practice with action and published key guidance, *One Small Step Towards Racial Justice* (CCETSW, 1991a), to support new requirements on values in the unified qualification, the Diploma in Social Work – Paper 30 (CCETSW, 1989).

During those early days CCETSW recognised the importance of ensuring consistent standards and began the process to recognise centres for advanced studies (CCETSW, 1974a). Its drive for quality and competence was being felt across the training continuum because for the first time CCETSW recognised the need for curriculum guidance and published key material to support the new emerging curriculum for those working in day centres (CCETSW, 1974b), with disability and the community (CCETSW, 1974c) and in juvenile courts (CCETSW, 1974d).

Development of practice skills

Recognition of the role played by residential staff was increasing and in March 1975 Paper 9.1 was published to pilot a new form of training called the Certificate in Social Services (CSS). This was specifically designed for enabling people in residential work to 'train on the job'. Many years later teacher training introduced a similar scheme called 'Teach First' (University of Manchester, 2010) as a fast-track entry for graduates into the profession, and now in children's social work, replicating the same philosophy, two similar initiatives have been set up, namely 'Step up to Social Work' and 'FrontLine' (MacAlister, 2013) – schemes which provide 'on the job' training. In this period the practice curriculum was first recognised as an important and essential element of social work skills training and in 1976 offered the first ever short course for practice teachers (CCETSW, 1977a). This recognised the important role of the teacher and assessor of practice. The CSS also recognised the important role of partnership between the university and employer that would bring together a combination of analytical and practice-based skills training.

It was not until 1991 that, as a result of a social work scandal in a residential children's home, a government-led review by Sir William Utting introduced a new initiative to provide specialist skills for residential workers who had been neglected in favour of field social workers (DoH, 1991). The Residential Child Care initiative was a specific pathway on 'DipSW' that helped to redress the balance of practice skills between generic social work and specialised residential care. The initiative was very successful in that it provided specialist skills but ran out of money and ceased a few years later. The debate on generic versus specialist training surfaced later in 2009 when government again questioned the relevance of generic training in its review of social work education (DCSF, 2010a).

Finding good quality placements has always been an issue for education providers. The first co-ordinated response to placement pressure emerged in wider research on the diverse ways for managing practice resources. The placement deficit posed continuing challenges and was reported in the placement crisis of 1992 (CCETSW, 1992a). This stated that only 56 per cent of placements were then in the statutory sector compared to 70 per cent in 1989, although this figure has remained stable ever since (GSCC, 2012a). The concept of the 'student unit' was introduced as a way of supporting students in placement (CCETSW, 1975). Despite the placement problems, these were good days for social work education and for the first and only time a Secretary of State for Health, David Ennals, visited an education institution as part of what was being seen as political support for social work (CCETSW, 1977b).

As CSS training expanded in the 1970s the practice placement agenda took on a new dimension as it looked at the contribution of probation placements (CCETSW, 1978a). This followed a number of training initiatives including direct training for those working in secure units (CCETSW, 1978b). Throughout the history of social work education finding good placements has always been problematic (GSCC, 2010). Even a government-sponsored initiative had no real lasting effect; for example, in 1992 the government funded 65 practice teachers (Government's Practice Placement Initiative) to help the most badly off areas of England and Wales to develop new placements (CCETSW, 1992b). The initiative was lost when the money ceased. Other initiatives have come and gone, such as the Practice Placement Initiative (PPI), a grant to fund joint training of practice teaching across social work and nursing, and the Practice Learning Taskforce which sought to increase the supply and quality of placements (Practice Learning Taskforce, 2003).

In 1979 a new CCETSW study was published that for the first time looked at how students were being assessed in practice and recognised the role of the 'independent practice assessor'. It argued for a more systematic assessment of student competence (CCETSW, 1979b). This led much later to CCETSW setting up its own scheme of quality assurance by having a list of external assessors who worked in unison with the university-appointed external examiner. There was and still is much debate about the role of theory and practice. CCETSW argued that theory cannot be separated from practice as it was an integral part of learning (CCETSW, 1977c). The role of the external assessor was in part a recognition of this. It is unclear from the evidence whether the assessors were mainly academics or practitioners which might have determined their specific focus.

Evolution of social work as a specialist profession

The embryology of regulated Post-Qualifying (PQ) training started its roots in Paper 17.1 as part of new guidelines in 1977 recognising that to be an effective social worker, qualifying training was not sufficient (CCETSW, 1977b, see Higham, Chapter 9 in this volume). It seems ironic that it took another 35 years for this concept to be fully accepted by government when it finally agreed to a new assisted and supported year in employment (ASYE) in 2012. Further, the idea of ASYE is a contested area of knowledge and now being implemented outside of regulatory control, which is unlikely to deliver the period of 'consolidation' that PQ provided. However, despite the delay to PQ there had been constant recognition of the need for it. For example, a lead article by Marilyn Pietroni at the Tavistock Institute titled 'Right or Privilege' argued that *Social workers with basic level qualifications should not be expected to handle complex cases such as child abuse without further supervision and specialist training* (Pietroni, 1991: 4).

Paper 17.1 was an important milestone as it started a new career framework for social workers acknowledging that once trained, one was not the finished professional. Continuous professional development was essential to safe and effective practice. The first 'nationally approved' PQ programme was established in 1981 (CCETSW, 1981). PQ always struggled to establish itself despite the first ever PQ framework being implemented in 1991 and a revised new framework in 2005. Government appeared to only become interested in training as a reaction to major disasters such as the Orkney Inquiry into child abuse, when Lord Clyde argued for more PQ opportunities for social workers facing challenging times in children's social work (CCETSW, 1994). Other examples of government perniciousness are not rare. Following the Victoria Climbié inquiry into a child death, a government-led initiative attempted to have every social work trained in specialist child care (DoH, 2003a). Also, the 'Baby Peter' inquiry into Haringey's social services in 2009 began a government-led programme to develop new standards for qualifying in children's social work. This was part of 'raising the quality of the profession' (CWDC, 2010b).

These initiatives appear to come and go in cycles following public outcries for action, and therefore continuingly fail to provide sustained improvement. When in 2008 the government began to abandon 'PQ' training for 'Newly Qualified Social Work' standards, there was neither a proper rationale nor evidence of need, as with many other initiatives driven by political ideology. It was no surprise when the new NQSW standards (CDWC, 2010a) replicated what was known as 'PQ1', the first part of PQ. The evaluation of the NQSW pilot demonstrated similar outcomes to PQ in that worker confidence had increased (Bates et al., 2010; DoE, 2012), leaving one to wonder why improving what already exists was so bad that we had to change it!

1980–1990: the embryology of a three-year degree

New student assessment of practice placements was published in 1980 together with new regulations for the Certificate in Social Services (CSS) (CCETSW, 1980). However, while the sector recognised the growing demand for CSS and the need to give greater scrutiny to the assessed outcomes of students, such professional training appeared isolated from the continuum of training. Social work training started at qualifying level in either CQSW or CSS. The introduction of the Preliminary Certificate in Social Services was seen as a part way towards qualification, which led much later to an expansion in the access to professional training routes through further education colleges and open college networks. This addressed the equalities agenda of widening participation where many potentially excellent social workers saw themselves excluded because they had neither employer sponsorship nor the necessary academic profile to meet entry requirements. The crude measurement of degree classification for fast-track graduate programmes appears to be the current choice for assessing potential intellectual capability under the banner of 'raising standards' (see 'Frontline', MacAlister, 2013).

CCETSW began to unify all its awards, and viewed knowledge, skills and values as an integrated capability. It was during this period that on 18 December 1985 it first announced its mandate for a three-year qualification (CCETSW, 1985). However, the government agreed to only two years and the Diploma in Social Work was born in 1989 being the single qualification for social work. Those with the Home Office Letter of Recognition, Preliminary Certificate in Social Care, Certificate of Qualification in Social Work and/or Certificate in Social Services were automatically recognised.

1990–2000 – a period of government change and fragmentation

In 1992 a new health and social care occupational standards council was set up. This led in 2000 to the creation of the Sector Skills Council for social care and the first ever national occupational standards that underpinned all training. The agenda of raising standards and greater scrutiny developed momentum. It was felt that social workers should only be assessed by accredited practice teachers although this ambition was never fully implemented due to the issue of placement demand (CCETSW, 1995a). Standards remained high on the social work agenda. However, while DipSW seemed to have a good future, the Home Office unexpectedly announced it was abandoning the DipSW in probation in favour of locally led criminal justice training within the 'NVQ' framework which remains today (CCETSW, 1995b).

By the early 1990s CCETSW became clear on the professional pathways available to social workers by introducing the 'Training Continuum' (CCETSW, 1991b).

The continuum started at level 1 in the national vocational qualifications framework through DipSW (level 4) through to the Advanced Award (level 5) in the PQ framework. Shared credit was awarded across the continuum enabling other professions to access qualifications and gain credit from other training where relevant. Employers saw the 'Training Continuum' as a flexible progression pathway that was nationally recognised by awards.

In 1993 the Warner Inquiry proposed a new specialist childcare diploma. CCETSW rejected this as not being the answer to competent generic social work at entry level. The debate about specialist versus generic training continues today. However, the government did manage to achieve specialist standards in a new PQ childcare award in 1998 and dispersed substantial funding to local authorities to train all childcare social workers. Much later the PQ childcare award was abandoned for alternative training, outside the national qualification framework, which was led by the Children's Workforce Development Council (see Bates et al., 2010).

A year earlier, in 1992, a sector-led initiative aimed to set up a social work workforce regulator similar to that in place for health. The proposal suggested CCETSW be replaced with a new General Social Services Council with additional powers to register the entire social care sector (CCETSW, 1992a). Originally supporting this, CCETSW voiced serious concerns about how any single body could realistically register an entire sector such as social care (CCETSW, 1992b).

Despite CCETSW's success and achievements, a government debate on whether it should continue or be replaced with a distinct social work regulator emerged again in 1996. CCETSW was dismayed that despite a 10-year campaign from employers and others, government continued to reject the idea of a regulated workforce and decided in favour of a small standards body as a result of a key consultation – *The Obligations to Care* (CCETSW, 1997b). However, as CCETSW welcomed its new chief executive, Jennifer Bernard, there was a change of government in May 1997 and it was announced that CCETSW was to be replaced by a small body taking on new functions to register social workers. This saw the birth of four new regulators as devolution drove the agenda for national rather than UK regulation. The initial plan for the General Social Care Council (GSCC) was to register the entire workforce but this was too costly, although the other three UK care councils did go ahead. Moreover, this did little to address the public protection issues of unqualified and unsupervised care professionals working with vulnerable people, which has recently proved to be a dangerous mistake (see the Winterbourne investigation into abuse [Care Quality Commission, 2011]).

The birth of service user involvement

The end of 1997 saw a landmark in the history of service user involvement in social work education (CCETSW, 1997a). A CCETSW and DH sponsored conference saw the launch of controversial research by Professor Phyllida Parsloe (Bristol) and research fellow Paul Swift. Their proposition was to involve service users for the first time in the assessment of social work students. The success of service user involvement by CCETSW continued with its successor body the GSCC who saw service user involvement 'at the heart of everything we do' (Smith, 2002). Not only did the GSCC involve service users in developing policy such as the first ever codes of practice but also as lay inspectors in the regulation of social work education. This was initially a controversial move but proved successful as reflected in the GSCC learning report (GSCC, 2012a).

Social care reform – from 'nothing' to 'too much'?

As CCETSW prepared to close and transfer its functions to four new care councils an additional new body was born. As part of a workforce strategy social care was to have its first ever Sector Skills Council, called the Training Organisation for Personal Social Services (TOPSS). The devolved agenda for splitting workforce regulation and development was at the heart of the new government (CCETSW, 1998). This meant that the TOPSS functions were split among the four UK countries. Apart from England these functions transferred into the new regulatory bodies, whereas in England it remained a separate body. However, the workforce landscape was now very confusing, going from one UK body to seven. Children and adults policy was split in England creating two new bodies – Skills for Care (adults) and Children's Workforce Development Council (children), together with the GSCC. Taking the other three countries into account, this meant the UK Sector Skills Council for social care was split between five bodies. However, because one body was required to hold the UK licence, the government created another body for this purpose called Skills for Care and Development. This meant that in 2001 the UK now had seven different bodies, a confusing mix for the sector, entailing massive duplication and ambiguity among each other's lead roles.

It is difficult to evaluate the cost of these bodies and their value for money, which is probably why the government announced changes in 2010 which saw the closure of two of its bodies, the GSCC and CWDC (DoH, 2010a). Moreover, social work saw its dedicated workforce regulator, the GSCC, being taken over by a health regulator – the Health Professions Council. It cost many millions of pounds to set these bodies up and more to close them down, something journalists were beginning to question (McClenogan, 2012).

2000–2012 – a government rather than a profession led approach to rebuilding social work

The GSCC continued the work of CCETSW. In November 2002, the GSCC began looking at changing the PQ framework, which was finally completed in February 2005 when the quality assurance responsibility of training was shifted to the training providers. In September 2003 the first qualifying degree programme started (GSCC, 2003a), moving from a diploma to a degree in qualifying training. The GSCC also made its mark in regulation and launched the first ever qualification for regulators of social care with the Regulatory Care Standards Award being offered at Anglia Polytechnic University (GSCC, 2003b). By May of 2003 the government offered £3,000 a year in bursaries to students to offset the increase in tuition fees to help increase the number of social workers coming into the profession (GSCC, 2003c). There was a sudden increase in student recruitment (+33%) the following year (GSCC, 2003d).

With a new social work degree starting in 2003 and a new PQ framework in 2005 one would assume a time of consolidation was needed. That was not to be, as government and the sector continued to influence what and how social work was being delivered. Because the GSCC was not an independent body it had limited powers and, moreover, did not own the standards it regulated against. The standards were owned by government and out of date. By 2009 there was an increased focus on social work education. A government Children's Select Committee was damming of the poor quality of training for social workers (DCSF, 2010b). However, the government's own research on the social work degree gave a positive report on how it met all expectations (SCWRU, 2008). Later that year the government set up a social work task force. This specifically reviewed all aspects of social work and developed into the Social Work Reform Board (SWRB) (DCSF, 2009). In its first report the task force supported the GSCC in having greater powers to enhance the quality of training. However, the decision to close GSCC and transfer its functions meant this was never realised (DCSF, 2010a).

In 2012 the SWRB set up the first ever college of social work, which took on many of the functions from the GSCC that did not transfer to the HPC. In addition, at a time of flux and change for the sector the government also announced a Law Commission review of regulation in an attempt to be more consistent across the regulatory landscape (Law Commission, 2012) but this came too late to affect the closure of the GSCC.

In summary, these events reflect a long and important history of social work regulation from 1962 to 2012. Its impact on the sector and those students, whom regulation serves, can at be best be described as holding the profession accountable to its values, and, at its worst, regulation can be seen as a passive recipient of political ideology rather than professional need.

Critique of the regulatory impact

In the absence of robust research it is difficult to measure the value of regulation in relation to its impact. The key outcomes from this review can be seen in the areas of CPD and the values of social work.

Social work values have been an integral part of the profession since 1973. However, despite this centrality, the discourses on social work values are problematic. Values are deeply political and ideological, which is part of the problem.

Thompson argues that values are a key expression of ourselves in practice and cannot be separated from it (Thompson, 2005). The rhetoric of values has caused confusion and misunderstanding about its purpose. CCETSW took up the vanguard of the 'black perspectives' as a direct challenge to the politically dominated culture of that time to ensure black students were treated more fairly (Penketh, 2000: 52). Social work values are an expression of our beliefs – in the humanity of fairness, rights and equality, although this was seen at the time as 'political correctness gone mad' (Pinker, 1995).

Despite the pressure to water down the teaching of values, social work has learnt a new language, successfully steering a careful path between rights and responsibilities from the radical anti-racist approach of the 1980s (Ferguson, 2009). In 2002 the GSCC developed the first national codes of practice for social care workers. These were in essence enshrined values of ethical practice. They presented a more acceptable face to values. This compromise means that values have survived, albeit through a manifestation of practice that is more passive and less active. Values have been discussed here only in a UK context although its recognised values transcend cultures (see Lena Dominelli's work on international social work for a wider discussion [2010a and 2010b]).

Although the social work profession claims it has only recently established a clear CPD pathway with the publication of the 'Professional Capabilities Framework for Social Workers' (College of Social Work, 2012), CPD has been well established in social work for many decades. CCETSW's national PQ framework established a progression route beyond qualifying level from 1991, although PQ-level awards started much earlier. An award-based training was originally managed through local consortia, which were more flexible in recognising learning, applying credit and finally giving a PQ award. This covered all forms of certified and uncertified professional learning. Also there is some evidence that those completing PQ awards made a positive impact on their practice (Keen et al., 2013).

The creation of PQ awards through two PQ frameworks has helped provide social workers with a vehicle to go beyond their consolidation of practice. However, one has to question the government's failure to empower the Social Work Task Force to implement its vision for a 'Licence to Practice' year linked to registration. The Assessed and Supported Year in Employment (ASYE), now managed by employers rather than through independent regulation, missed a wonderful opportunity. This would have put social work on the same regulatory footing as doctors. Moreover, integrating the existing PQ standards into a fully regulated ASYE scheme would have helped to develop practitioners in a more progressive way, not to mention saving money. Instead the profession has allowed itself to abandon well-established PQ standards for new standards similar in nature but outside an independent quality assurance system and reliant on employers rather than an independent body. It is impossible to measure the cost of these changes in funding and disruption. The profession now has to start again, like it did in 1991, bedding down a new CPD system and hoping over the next decade that the sector rises to the challenge.

As social workers struggle for professional identity during a time of constant change and disruption, the focus will switch away from developing a trained and safe workforce to meeting the demand of service need as it did in the 1970s and 1980s. Periodic crises will continue in a cyclical process, moving from one social work problem to another, followed by government reviews that serve no purpose other than to criticise the profession for requiring better trained social workers. It is distinctly possible that a new PQ framework will be developed again, perhaps with its own profession specific regulator. History tells us this is more likely than not.

Society is in an era of deregulation, with a UK government agenda of neo-liberalism as the dominant political paradigm (Harvey, 2005) appearing set to consolidate its position over the coming years (Dominelli, 2010b: 601). In this context regulation is purposely misrepresented as slowing market forces, but what we need is not more regulation but better regulation, or what is now referred to as 'Right Touch Regulation' (CHRE, 2010). The ineffective regulation in health resulted in the Mid-Staffordshire crisis that uncovered hundreds of hospital deaths that could have been prevented (Francis, 2013). The financial and other industries could also repeat the same claim that as a result of poor and weak regulation the private sector has grown at a cost to quality and public safety. The new discourse of effective, open marketisation has masked the true cost of regulatory failure.

In 2012, and for the first time in 50 years of regulating social work education, the profession moved away from its own professionally distinct regulator to a multi-professional, health dominated regulator in the new HCPC. It is difficult to see how HCPC will address the issues raised by the Children's Select Committee and the Social Work Task Force in respect of the need for more robust intervention-ist regulation as HCPC regulate to a minimum standard. A good example of the difference compared to the past is in the specific elements of practice education and how the Department of Health's own input standard (2003b) of 200 days in practice is now removed from regulation and transferred to the College of Social Work under guidance (2012). Although this is acceptable for those programmes wishing to be endorsed by the college, what about those programmes that do not allow the market, rather than quality education, to dominate placement provision? It is changes like this that are allowed to happen without proper analysis and evidence that represent an endemic failure of social work leadership.

Although the regulatory system under the GSCC was not perfect and in many ways weak, it did control funding streams that influenced compliance when standards fell, for example the grant funding for placements. The Children's Select Committee called for a more *active role in quality assurance for either GSCC or Ofsted* (DCSF, 2010b: Annex A, Sec. 7). The chair of the Social Work Task Force in her letter to the Committee welcomed the progress GSCC had achieved and asked for them to be 'authorised and resourced' to develop more robust regulation (Ibid.).

The past 50 years have seen many initiatives come and go at a high cost to the taxpayer. Because of the failure to learn from the past, the cost of abolishing organisations is often more than the cost of setting up new ones, for example see the financial impact assessment published alongside the Health Bill (DoH, 2011). The many organisations that have come and gone, coupled with the investment in new initiatives, leads one to conclude that if we added up the true cost of all the change over the past 10 years we could probably afford an entirely new NHS. One only has to review the regulatory impact assessment in the Health Bill (DoH, 2011) to realise the true cost of change in just one policy area.

Although there is some evidence to support the assertion that social work education has made a difference in building a robust legacy in values and CPD, there is no evidence to say whether regulation really did achieve what it was set up to do in promoting social work and increasing quality because the standards themselves were too low. It is unclear from the self-reporting system of regulation in the GSCC (2002) and now the HCPC (2012) how improvement is achieved. Both the GSCC and now HCPC work to minimum standards. The HCPC is predicated on a strong professional body seeking enhancement beyond the minimum standard. CCETSW was the only body that did both as it regulated against minimum standards and provided an entire continuum of training to promote improvement. The new College of Social Work will hopefully play this role sometime in the future, but what happens now?

Apart from England the other UK countries had greater unity and control because the regulation and sector skills functions were located in one body, whereas in England they were split between three. Moreover, there were three different government departments in England (the Department of Health, the Department of Education and the Department for Business, Innovation and Skills), which did not always work in unison. A good example was the way Department of Children, Schools and Families pushed forward new standards for newly qualified social workers (CWDC, 2008) conflicting with the 'consolidation' phase of PQ (GSCC, 2005), which the Department of Health and the GSCC was promoting as the national CPD policy.

It is the contention here that change comes about not out of evidence or need, but more as a result of political ideology disguised as an altruistic and moral imperative to save the profession, often following a child's death or other such crisis. Governments over the years have constantly meddled and interfered with social work, not to achieve sustainable change but more to gain 'quick wins'. This can best be evidenced when the Labour Party came into office in 1997 and embarked on a major change agenda abolishing CCETSW and setting up the new GSCC. Then, in 2008, the largest reform in social work seen for decades was started, culminating in the Social Work Task Force and based on evidence that the government compiled but which was never published for external scrutiny. The government carried out a 'deep dive' review of social work education which informed the Social Work Task Force of the extent of what it saw as the problem. At the National Social Services Conference, GSCC seminar in October 2009 government officials announced social work education was in a poor state and needed massive reform, but no detail was ever published.

The profession finally accepted the challenge of new government initiatives, as can be seen by the wholesale policy changes being introduced by the Social Work Task Force (DCSF, 2010a). However, once the new government came into office in 2010, the stage of implementation lost momentum as it was over-taken by the new government's own agenda, such as reviewing child protec-tion (Munro, 2011). Government reform should follow evidence rather than drive it. The Coalition Government came into office in 2010 with its own agenda and wasted no time pushing through its de-regulation drive. Consequently, the GSCC and others were abolished without consultation or evidence of need because such action met the political imperative of the time. This is why the Health Bill (DoH, 2011) was published before the full regulatory impact assess-ment and Command Paper for Regulation that dealt with social work regulation (DoH, 2011). Initially, the government gave cost as the reason, but later changed to citing reasons of efficiency, announced at the GSCC conference in London in 2010. Consequently, many of the earlier Task Force reforms of robust regula-tion were lost. The grant funding to education programmes, for example, were transferred to the NHS Business Service Authority instead of the College of Social Work, because in 2012 it was taking too long to establish. Moreover, placing ASYE in regulation was always agreed GSCC policy as announced at the GSCC annual conference in London in November 2010. Once its functions transferred to the HCPC this policy was abandoned, which left a range of post-qualifying initiatives outside regulation. In summary, the transfer of functions was neither planned nor evidence based.

Evidence from history suggests that the profession is not sufficiently established and coherent to self-regulate, which is why independent regulation is so impor-tant. For example, in 2003 very few social workers registered when the Register opened until 'Protection of Title' was made law in April 2005 requiring social workers to be registered. We can learn a great deal from history, but only if we have the will and courage to do so, which sadly few politicians seem to have.

A good example of this is in the current initiatives for fast track to qualification ('Frontline' and 'Step-Up to Social Work'). Both are similar to the Certificate in Social Services initiative developed in the 1970s based on 'learning on the job'. The constant government reviews of social work destabilise the profession rather than improving it. While we are still struggling to implement the full reforms of the Social Work Task Force, yet another new government review is announced and about to take place, looking again at the case for generic qualifying training (DoH, 2013).

Meanwhile, service users continue to rely upon trained, safe and effective prac-titioners to represent their needs in a growing maze of complexity, and now service rationing, while the politicians, professionals and those who speak for ser-vice users consistently fail to acknowledge them in major policy and economic decisions. Meanwhile, social work in England embarks on a new journey and for the first time in 50 years continues in the absence of its own professional regu-lator. The high cost of training is something that the government continues to review. In an age of neo-liberalism there is a risk to the funding of generic social work as the government looks to reduce its investment and possibly transfer services to the private sector. There is no evidence that self-regulation will be any better, in fact there is growing evidence in the social care market that standards are falling, as can be seen in the Winterbourne View abuse case (Brindle, 2011).

Social work education has been weakened by constant political interference, and while organisations such as CCETSW and the GSCC have attempted to give a platform to the many voices of social work, such as service users, they are now lost. While we wait for another 'Seebohm' effect on the profession then let's live in hope that we can take all that is good from the past 50 years, identify what it is and strengthen our resolve to hold on to it rather than 'throw the baby out with the bath water'.

REFLECTIVE QUESTIONS

1. *From your own experience does regulation work – does it give you confidence in the profession?*

2. *How has regulation impacted on you and what benefits or challenges has it provided?*

3. *What are your reflections on how education and training in social work has developed and changed?*

MMENDED
RTHER
EADING

Baldwin, R and Cave, M (1999) *Understanding Regulation: Theory Strategy and Practice.* Oxford: Oxford University Press.

Lafrance, J and Gray, E (2004) Gate-keeping for Professional Social Work Practice. *Social Work Education,* 23(3): 325–40.

Hood, C and Scott, C (1996) Bureaucratic Regulation and New Public Management in the United Kingdom: Mirror Image Developments? *Journal of Law and Society,* 23(3): 321–45.

Hood, C, Rothstein, H and Baldwin, R (2004) *The Government of Risk: Understanding Risk Regulation Regimes.* Oxford: Oxford University Press.

ERENCES

Bates, N, Immins, T, Parker, J, Keen, S, Rutter, L, Brown, K and Zsigo, S (2010) Baptism of Fire: The First Year in the Life of a Newly Qualified Social Worker. *Social Work Education,* 29(2): 152–70.

Brown, K, McClosky, C, Galpin, D, Keen, S and Immins, T (eds) (2008) Evaluating the Impact of Post Qualifying Social Work Education. *Social Work Education,* 27(8): 853–67.

Brindle, D (2011) Regulator to Review Care System after Winterbourne View Abuse Scandal. *The Guardian,* 7 June.

Care Quality Commission (2011) *Review of Compliance Report: Castlebeck Care (Teeside) Ltd. Report into the Care of People living in Winterbourne View,* July.

CCETSW (1972) Press Release – Expansion in Social Work Training, 29 November. London: Central Council for Education and Training in Social Work.

CCETSW (1973a) *Paper 1 – Creating Opportunities for Staff Development*, 2 April. London: Central Council for Education and Training in Social Work.

CCETSW (1973b) Press Release – A New Scheme in Service Training for RSWs, 25 April. London: Central Council for Education and Training in Social Work.

CCETSW (1973c) Press Release – Values in Social Work, 11 April. London: Central Council for Education and Training in Social Work.

CCETSW (1974a) Press Release – CCETSW Recognises Centres for Advanced Studies, 4 February. London: Central Council for Education and Training in Social Work.

CCETSW (1974b) Press Release – Recognition that Law is an Integral Part of Training, 13 August. London: Central Council for Education and Training in Social Work.

CCETSW (1974c) Press Release – Working Party on Training Staff in Day Centres and People Working with Handicapped People Need Better Training, 20 February. London: Central Council for Education and Training in Social Work.

CCETSW (1974d) *CCETSW Guidance: Social Workers in the Juvenile Courts. 5th September 1974*. London: Central Council for Education and Training in Social Work.

CCETSW (1974e) Press Release – Course to Help Social Workers Trained Overseas, 5 February. London: Central Council for Education and Training in Social Work.

CCETSW (1975) *Paper 11 – Social Work Research Study. Student Units in Social Work Education as a Response to Pressures of Growing Resources, by Kathleen Curnock*, 5 November. London: Central Council for Education and Training in Social Work.

CCETSW (1976) *Paper 13 – Values in Social Work Conflict Clarified*, Working Party Report, 16 June. London: Central Council for Education and Training in Social Work.

CCETSW (1977a) Press Release – Short Course for Practice Teachers, 28 August. London: Central Council for Education and Training in Social Work.

CCETSW (1977b) Press Release – Minister for Health Visits Havering Technical College to Talk to CSS Students, 8 November. London: Central Council for Education and Training in Social Work.

CCETSW (1977c) New Guidance – Guidance on Theory and Practice, 21 December. London: Central Council for Education and Training in Social Work.

CCETSW (1977d) *Paper 17.1 – Building on the Base of Qualifying Training*, 5 December. London: Central Council for Education and Training in Social Work.

CEETSW (1978a) *Paper 18 – Learning to be a Probation Officer: Report of a Study Group on Practice Placements in the Probation and After Care Service*. London: Central Council for Education and Training in Social Work.

CCETSW (1978b) Press Release – Secure Unit Staff Offered Training Opportunities, May. London: Central Council for Education and Training in Social Work.

CCETSW (1979a) Press Release – More Students from Multi-Racial Society and Ethnic Minority Groups needed in Social Work, 12 October. London: Central Council for Education and Training in Social Work.

CCETSW (1979b) *Study No 2. Towards a More Systematic Assessment of Competence of Social Work Students*, 8 October. London: Central Council for Education and Training in Social Work.

CCETSW (1980) *Regulation and Guidance for Courses Leading to the Certificate in Social Services*, Paper 9.5. London: Central Council for Education and Training in Social Work.

CCETSW (1981) *Paper 17.1 – Approval of PQ Programmes*, 21 January. London: Central Council for Education and Training in Social Work.

CCETSW (1984) Press Release – More Ethnic Minority Students Needed – 'We are Recruiting More but Not Enough', 21 November. London: Central Council for Education and Training in Social Work.

CCETSW (1985) *Paper 20.5 – Qualifying for Social Work Practice – A Mandate for Three Year Social Work Training*. 18 December.

CCETSW (1986) Press Release – Nursing and Social Work Group to Facilitate Co-operation in Training, 14 January. London: English National Board for Nursing and Midwifery and Health Visiting with Central Council for Education and Training in Social Work.

CCETSW (1987) Press Release – Racism – The Challenge to CCETSW and Social Work Training, 24 June. London: Central Council for Education and Training in Social Work.

CCETSW (1989) *Paper 30 – Assuring Quality in the Diploma in Social Work – 1. Rules and Requirements for the DipSW*. London: Central Council for Education and Training in Social Work.

CCETSW (1991a) *One Small Step Towards Racial Justice*. DipSW Guidance. London: Central Council for Education and Training in Social Work.

CCETSW (1991b) *CCETSW News No. 1 Summer – 'The Training Continuum'*. London: Central Council for Education and Training in Social Work.

CCETSW (1992a) *CCETSW News No. 5 Summer – New Initiative Starts to Show Results*. Central Council for Education and Training in Social Work: London

CCETSW (1992b) *CCETSW News No. 5 – Survey Confirms Placement Crisis*. London: Central Council for Education and Training in Social Work.

CCETSW (1992c) *CCETSW News No. 5 Summer – Views on GSCC*. London: Central Council for Education and Training in Social Work.

CCETSW (1992d) *CCETSW News No. 6 Autumn – Council Concerns over GSCC Plans*. London: Central Council for Education and Training in Social Work.

CCETSW (1994) *CCETS News – Orkney Inquiry Opens Up More PQ Opportunities But a Lack of Resources Limit the Number of Candidates*. London: Central Council for Education and Training in Social Work.

CCETSW (1995a) *CCETSW News, 27 July*. London: Central Council for Education and Training in Social Work: London.

CCETSW (1995b) *CCETSW News No. 16. ... And Lords Gets Backing*, 20 April. London: Central Council for Education and Training in Social Work.

CCETSW (1997a) *Council Report, 27th February 1997*. London: Central Council for Education and Training in Social Work.

CCETSW (1997b) *CCETSW News Issue 25, 1997/98*. London: Central Council for Education and Training in Social Work.

CCETSW (1998) *CCETSW News, Issue 26*. London: Central Council for Education and Training in Social Work.

CHRE (2010) *Right Touch Regulation*. London: Council for Healthcare Regulatory Excellence: London. (Now renamed the Professional Standards Authority.)

Christodoulou, C (1988) CCETSW News on the Black Perspectives Committee. *Journal of Social Work Practice*, 3(3): 106–7.

College of Social Work (2012) *The Professional Capabilities Framework for Social Workers in England*. London: College of Social Work.

CWDC (2008) *Newly Qualified Social Work Pilot Programme 2008–2011. Outcome Statements and Guidance*. Leeds: CWDC.

CWDC (2009) *NQSW: Meeting the Outcome Statements: Record of Achievement: Newly Qualified Social Worker Pilot Programme 2009–2010*. CWDC.

CDWC (2010a) *NQSW Outcome Statements and Guidance*. Leeds: CWDC.

CWDC (2010b) *Step Up to Social Work*. CWDC sponsored by the Department for Children, Schools and Families.

CWDC and Skills for Care (2012) *Assessed and Supported Year in Employment Briefing*. Leeds: CWDC and Skills for Care.

Department for Children, Schools and Families (DCSF) (2009) *Building a Safe, Confident Future: First Report – Training of Children and Family Social Workers – Government Response to Seventh Report*, 9 March. London: HMSO.

Department for Children, Schools and Families (DCSF) (2010a) *Report on the Implementation of the Reform Board. Building a Safe and Confident Future – One Year On*, Social Work Taskforce. London: DCSF.

Department for Children, Schools and Families (DCSF) (2010b) *Children's Select Committee Seventh Report on the Training of Children and Family Social Workers, Session 2008–09*, 9 March. London: DCSF.

Department of Education (DoE) (2012) *Newly Qualified Social Work Programme: Final Evaluation Report (2008–2011)*. Lead author Prof. John Carpenter, University of Bristol. Department of Education, Research Report DFE:RR229.

Department of Health (DoH) (1991) *Sir William Utting Review of Residential Care Services for Children*, 20 August. London: Department of Health, HMSO.

Department of Health (DoH) (2003a) *The Victoria Climbié Inquiry*. Health Committee Sixth Report, 23 January. London: The Stationery Office.

Department of Health (DoH) (2003b) *The Requirements for the Social Work Degree in England. See Practice Placement Minimum Requirement of 200 Days*. Department of Health: London: HMSO.

Department of Health (DoH) (2005) *Shipman – The Final Report. The Sixth Report*, 27 January. London: Department of Health, HMSO.

Department of Health (DoH) (2010a) *'Liberating the NHS', Arms Length Body Review*, 26 July. London: HMSO.

Department of Health (DoH) (2010b) *Building the National Care Service*. White Paper, Department of Health, CM7854, 30 March. London: HMSO.

Department of Health (DoH) (2010c) *Building a Safe and Confident Future: Implementing the Recommendations of the Social Work Taskforce*. CM13945. 25 March.

Department of Health (DoH) (2011) *Health and Social Care Bill 2011: Impact Assessment*, 1A No.6030, January.

Department of Health (DoH) (2013) 'Review of Social Work Announced' under Policy: Making Sure Health and Social Care Work Together. Led by Prof. David Crossdale, Appleby, 24 April.

Dickens, J (2011) Social Work in England at a Watershed – As Always: From the Seebohm Report to the Social Work Task Force. *British Journal of Social Work*, 41(1): 22–39.

Dominelli, L (2010a) *Social Work in a Globalizing World*. Chichester: John Wiley.

Dominelli, L (2010b) Globalisation, Contemporary Challenges and Social Work Practice. *International Social Work*, 53(5): 569–612.

Ferguson, I (2009) 'Another Social Worker is Possible!' Reclaiming the Radical Tradition. In Leskosck, W (ed.) *Theories and Methods of Social Work: Exploring Different Perspectives*, University of Ljubljana, Slovenia: 81–98.

Francis, R (2013) *Mid Staffordshire NHS Foundation Trust Public Inquiry*, Chaired by Robert Francis QC. HC947, 6 February. UK: HMSO.

GSCC (2002) *Accreditation of Universities to Grant Degrees in Social Work*, May. London: General Social Care Council.

GSCC (2003a) Press Release, 25 September. London: General Social Care Council.

GSCC (2003b) Press Release, 3 November. London: General Social Care Council.

GSCC (2003c) 'Have Your Say', General Social Care Council Annual Conference. 3 November at QE11, London.

GSCC (2003d) Press Release, 1 May. London: General Social Care Council.

GSCC (2004) Press Release, 18 November. London: General Social Care Council.

GSCC (2005) *Post-qualifying Framework for Social Work Education and Training*. London: GSCC.

GSCC (2008) *Raising Standards: Social Work Education in England 2006–07*. London: General Social Work Council.

GSCC (2009a) GSCC Reports Comments made by the Chair, Barry Sheerman, MP of Children, Schools and Families Select Committee on Social Work Education in their Giving Evidence, 30 July.

GSCC (2009b) Press Release – CEO of GSCC Argues for New National Curriculum, 18 June. London: General Social Care Council.

GSCC (2009c) *Raising Standards: Social Work Education in England 2007–08*. London: General Social Work Council.

GSCC (2010) *Raising Standards: Social Work Education in England 2008–09*. London: General Social Work Council.

GSCC (2012a) *Learning Report – Service User and Carer Involvement 2001–2012*. London: General Social Care Council.

GSCC (2012b) *Social Work Regulator Publishes Lessons Learnt over its Lifetime*, 20 June. UK Government National Archives.

Harvey, D. (2005) *A Brief History of Neoliberalism*. Oxford: Oxford University Press.

Health and Care Professions Council (HCPC) (2012) *Standards of Training*. London: The Health and Care Professions Council.

Health Professions Council (2012) *Health Professions Standards of Proficiency*, July. London: The Health and Care Professions Council.

ICAEW (2012) *Continuous Professional Development: A Quick Guide.* London: Institute for Chartered Accountants in England and Wales.

Keen, S, Brown, K, Holroyd, J and Rosenorn-Lanng, E (2013) Evaluating the Impact of the IPOP (Improving Personal and Organisational Performance) Programme: An Introductory Leadership and Management Development Module for Social Work Managers. *Social Work & Social Sciences Review*, 16(1), doi: 10.1921/1203160302

Law Commission (2012) *Regulation of Health Care Professionals and Social Care Professionals in England.* Consultation Paper SLCDP 153.NLC 12 (2012). Law Commission for England, Scottish Law Commission and Northern Ireland Commission.

MacAlister, J (2013) *'FrontLine' Programme Development Update*, February. Department of Education.

Martin, D (2010) More Than £1 Billion Cost to Disability Benefit Fraud and Error – and That's Just the Tip of the Iceberg. *Daily Mail*, 24 October.

Moriarty, J (2011) *Literature Review for the Curriculum Development Workstream of the Social Work Reform Board.* Kings College, Social Care Workforce Research Unit: London: 8.

McClenoghan, M (2012) *NHS Reform*, 12 July. The Bureau of Investigative Journalism.

Munro, E (2011) *Munro Review of Child Protection: Final Report – A Child Centred System.* CM 8062. London: Department of Education.

Payne, M (2005) *The Origins of Social Work: Continuity and Change.* Basingstoke: Palgrave Macmillan.

Penketh, L (2000) *Tackling Institutional Racism: Anti-racist Policies and Social Work Education and Training.* Bristol: The Policy Press.

Practice Learning Taskforce (2003) *Practice Learning – Everybody's Business: Summary of Regional Development Projects.* Practice Learning Taskforce/Department of Health.

Pietroni, M (1991) Right or Privilege. *CCETSW News*, No. 1 (summer). London: Central Council for Education and Training in Social Work.

Pinker, R (1995) *Social Workers: Training.* Hansard HL, 19 April, Vol. 863 C05/650.

SCWRU (2008) *Evaluation of the New Social Work Qualification in England.* Social Care Workforce Research Unit, Kings College London.

Smith, J (2002) Speech by Jacqui Smith, Minister of State for Health to the GSCC Conference, 6 November 2002. Published by the Department of Health.

Thompson, N (2005) *Understanding Social Work: Preparing for Practice* (2nd edition). Basingstoke: Palgrave Macmillan.

Thompson, N (2006) *Anti-Discriminatory Practice* (4th edition). Basingstoke: Palgrave Macmillan.

University of Manchester (2010) *Maximum Impact Education: The Impact of Teach First Teachers in Schools Final Report*, 1 October.

University of Warwick (2012) CCETSW Records 1962–1980 held at the Modern Records Centre, University of Warwick, GB 152 MSS.422 (accessed 16 August 2012).

Chapter 13

Professional social work in the future

Mark Doel and Jonathan Parker

It is a Tuesday lunchtime in 1984 and the social work team is in the local pub, decamped there after the morning's regular weekly meeting. Most of the team has a pub curry and two pints of beer, smoke some cigarettes, then they get into their cars and drive off to visit clients in their homes for the afternoon. It might all seem a bit *Life on Mars*[1] but this was the regular experience of one of the editors (Doel) during the 1970s and 1980s. It is a scene that regularly shocks audiences of newly qualifying social workers three decades later, because much of what was taken for granted not very long ago would now be either illegal or the subject of disciplinary action for unprofessional behaviour.

None of the social workers in that 1984 pub considered their actions to be unprofessional, far from it. What, then, do we take for granted in 2014 that newly qualifying social workers three decades hence, in 2044, might look back on and consider unacceptable? It is very difficult indeed to make predictions – like the economy and the weather, the social norms that shape our view of professionalism are notoriously variable. From the journalist who in the 1870s predicted that 'one day every city in the world will have one of these' (a telephone) to the social planners in the 1940s who predicted that demand for the newly created National Health Service would rapidly fall away once it had cleared up the mess left by the old profit-driven system, the forecasts of expert commentators have often been hopelessly short-sighted.

Let us reverse the judgement and ask what the social worker of three decades ago might find unprofessional in today's practices. First, it is likely that the 1984 social workers would be shocked by a survey in 2010 by the then Department for Children, School and Families that showed their successors spent an average of only 26 per cent of their time with service users (when in 1984 it was nearer 75%); the 1984 social work office was deserted during the day apart from a couple of 'duty' (intake) social workers and a receptionist, and any social worker who lingered around the office would be seen as not doing their job properly. The 1984 social worker transported forward in time would probably be surprised by

---

[1]*Life on Mars* is a television drama. The main character is from the present day but wakes up to find himself working in a Manchester police station in 1973; much of the interest stems from the contrast between ideas of professional policing then compared to now.

'eligibility criteria', because a central element of the professional task was for the practitioner to decide, individually or more likely in a social work team, how the universal service of social work was to be delivered. The 1984 social worker would be awed by the 2014 technology, but might conclude that the five minutes with a Dictaphone in the car after a home visit (the norm in 1984) allows for more professional judgement than a tick-box 'assessment framework' and gives more time for face-to-face work with clients, which in 1984 was a benchmark of professionalism.

From these few examples we can already see that the notion of professional social work is subject to a myriad factors: the laws, which in themselves reflect changing social norms; the expectations of and demands on public sector workers; the distribution of economic resources; and the flash fires of regular moral panics fuelled not just by a print and televisual media but now also by a social media that is instantaneous.

Rather than trying to make a prognosis for the future professional climate, it is perhaps more realistic to consider what we would *wish* the future of professional social work to look like (Doel, 2012). In this way we can begin to shape that future. A profession's future might be hard to predict but, rather like the climate and the economy, it is strongly influenced by human activity. One of the problems that social work's professionalism has experienced in recent decades has been the tendency for it to be defined *outside* the profession. So, on one definition of professionalism – autonomy and discretion – we have seen that the social workers of 2014 are de-professionalised in comparison to their predecessors. Having a vision of what the profession of social work could and should look like in the future is one way of taking responsibility for the future back into the profession's own hands.

Relationships

Thirty or more years ago there were fears that 'the professional relationship' had become fetishised in social work, to the point that some considered it to be the *raison d'être* of the work rather than a vehicle for it. Reaction against the reification of relationship and concerns about the abuse of power in client–professional relationships of this nature now seems to have been replaced by the near extinction of the relationship itself. Treating service users holistically (Payne, Chapter 2) and with compassion (Ruch, Chapter 4) is only possible by developing the kind of relationship that, paradoxically perhaps, comes from professionalism. It is not the kind of relationship we have with a neighbour, a friend or a family member, nor the kind we might pay for. An unpaid-for, professional relationship is a unique kind of relationship. If social work becomes a paid-for activity (if only through the intermediary of an insurance company, as is common in the US) the nature of that relationship will change irreparably. So, to preserve the nature of the professional relationship, we hope that the social work of 2044 in the UK will be resourced through central or local taxation, not personal payment.

Social workers' relationships with themselves are important. Through this relationship, social workers develop the personal and professional confidence which enables them to take care of themselves (Thompson, Chapter 5). This is particularly important as working closely with people who are traumatised, anxious, etc. is, itself, traumatising, anxiety-making, etc. Working with indeterminacy and ambiguity requires a strong sense of moral purpose (Shardlow, Chapter 7) and a certainty about why one is a member of this profession and what this means. The terrain might consist of swampy lowlands (Schön, 1995), but that is why we need to have absolute confidence in our footwear and our professional compass.

Collectives

Social work has found the triumph of neo-liberalism particularly traumatic. The current fractured individualism is anathema to a profession largely built on modernist notions of big progress and big government. We see the dissolution of 'the post-war settlement' and the seeming collapse of the notion of collective responsibility in even the tiniest details, such as the increased responsibility placed on the individual for their own continuing professional development (Higham, Chapter 9).

The idea of a profession is, itself, a collective. It is not surprising that 'free'[2] market policies have encouraged the drip-drip destruction of what was known as 'respect for the professions', this destruction was aided by those who saw professional power abused or used in patrician ways. Professions, like unions, provide potential opposition to capital, so they are a target for ridicule and abasement by the organs of capital. However, as Singh and Cowden (Chapter 6) rightly note, there is no going back to the radical social work of the 1970s and 1980s. Our hopes for the profession of 2044 is not that they have come full swing back to some nostalgic Seebohm era, but that they have taken the best from social work's collective tradition and found new ways to express this – in particular, that the 2044 profession of social work is an inclusive one, in strong alliance with service users (Thompson, Chapter 5).

The 'special type of confidence' (White, Chapter 3) that empowers social workers to challenge the 'institutional script' (i.e. their employing agency's agenda) is more likely to arise from collective activity – peer support groups, group supervision, virtual communities of practice, co-working in service user groups and the like. Social work is not a virtuoso profession and, thankfully, it is very unlikely to become one. Social work has collective action in its genes; the profession must make sure these collective traditions become dominant and not recessive.

---

[2]Hardly a free market, considering the level of public subsidy to big business (whether in direct bail-outs to the banks, in indirect subsidies such as those to agri-business, or the support that the public purse buys in terms of the health, education and security of big business's workers and consumers).

Savvy

Some might limit their ambition for social work as a profession in 2044 to one of survival. 'If it's around, that'll be good enough for me!' From the vantage point of 2014, when much that social work holds dear has been marginalised, survival might seem like a triumph. But let us not forget that the same question, 'Can Social Work Survive?', was asked in 1980 in the title of a book by Brewer and Lait (the answer was 'yes' and not many read the book these days), so we should not feel uniquely beleaguered in present times.

Let us, then, have greater ambitions than survival. There are hopes that a professional voice will find expression through the College of Social Work (Higham, Chapter 9). Certainly, to become a strong profession social work will need to become more savvy and, in particular, media savvy. As Jones (Chapter 11) notes, 'there is a story to be told' and he suggests ways in which we can tell it. Social work should resist feeling victimised or uniquely maltreated and should remind itself that the profession that is least trusted by the public is journalism.

The social worker of 1984 could not have foreseen the existence of what we know as social media, much less the way it has come to dominate much of the social space. Quite how the technology will influence the way social work communicates with the world at large is hard to know and we have to remind ourselves that we are still in the 'wild west' of the social media technology, which means that we have not really developed social rules to govern it (think of the early days of mobile phones on trains – now there are quiet coaches). Social media presents an opportunity to bypass the mainstream media, but is there something 'unprofessional' about it – in this opportunity for anonymous commentary? As a supremely individual act, does it add to the fractured singularity or can it best be harnessed for collective action?

The public need to become more savvy about social work, too. We await a popular drama series based around social workers. At least this would provide the public with a fuller range of social work stereotypes rather than just the two (florid or weak) currently circulating.

Accountability and autonomy

Our hope for the future of the social work profession is that it manages to attain the optimum balance between accountability and autonomy. There are multiple accountabilities – to the profession itself, certainly, but also to service users, to employers and to the public at large. The regulation of social work (Ixer, Chapter 12) needs to be provided from both inside and outside the profession. At 'street' level, we would like to see something develop that is similar to the external examining system in higher education; that is, annual scrutiny from peers who are independent and geographically distant from the team that is being examined, and with a remit that includes development (a critical friend) as well as policing. Perhaps expert service users and experienced social workers could provide co-external scrutiny.

Trust is slow-burning and extraordinarily difficult to measure, but it is essential to allow the social work profession the autonomy that will enable it to deliver the work that is required of it. With some laudable exceptions, the current attitudes of government, agencies and the media is utterly stifling; like an overweening parent whose fingers press on every moment of their child's life so that the child can barely act because of fear of reproof, reproach and commentary. Social work will be seen as a semi-profession as long as the actions of social workers are driven by managers, agencies and policy-makers.

Criticality

We expect professionals to bring something different to their encounters compared to someone who is not a professional. What is this difference? It is perhaps best described as a certain *criticality* that one might not necessarily expect from others. Criticality is a kind of self-researching exercise (Fook et al., 2000) in which social workers interrogate their own working hypotheses. This is why continuing professional development and regular supervision are so important, to ensure this process is embedded (Higham, Chapter 9; Bogo, Chapter 10).

Criticality is informed by research knowledge (Smith, Chapter 8) and brings a breadth and depth of understanding that would be absent without the professional's presence. Criticality balances objectivity with subjectivity; objective in seeing situations from many different perspectives and weighing them to arrive at a judgement, and subjective in terms of partisan support for social justice and advocacy with marginalised groups.

A profession should find ways of capturing the knowledge that is generated by its practitioners and in this respect social work has far to go, despite the wealth of practice material that is routinely available. In our roles as external examiners for undergraduate, postgraduate and post-qualifying programmes, we (the co-editors) have access to a slice of this knowledge, presented in systematic fashion in portfolios of practice evidence. Especially at post-qualifying level, the criticality is often advanced, yet the profession has no formalised way to share the knowledge available; even within the same agency it is unlikely that one team has much idea of the knowledge generated by another. This is a loss, particularly as 'portfolio knowledge' is available as usable knowledge in the way that knowledge in scholarly articles often is not. We hope the profession of 2044 is using whatever technologies exist at that time to capture and share this practice knowledge as part of continuing professional development (Higham, Chapter 9), not just for individuals but for the whole profession.

Identity

Ultimately, professionalism is about identity. Do we want social work to be recognised as a profession and, if so, do social workers have the confidence to mould the profession in their own image, the savvy to convince others that it is a profession and the power to realise their vision?

Above all, this new professional identity needs to be an inclusive one. On the one hand this means an appreciation of the particular mix of knowledge, values and skills that come, first, from a formal education in social work and then develop through regular activity in work that requires the social work title and continue to be developed through professional supervision; on the other hand, it means an appreciation of the particular expertise that service users, the people with whom social workers work, bring to each encounter. This combined sensitivity results in a 'tempered passion' that will help the social work profession to organise for change at personal, collective and social levels. In Attlee's (1920) words, now almost a century old, social workers must be social pioneers, social investigators and social agitators. The profession has much work to do.

REFERENCES

Attlee, CR (1920) *The Social Worker.* London: G. Bell and Sons (now a Nabu Public Domain Reprint).

Brewer, C and Lait, J (1980) *Can Social Work Survive?* London: Temple Smith.

Doel, M (2012) *Social Work: The Basics.* London: Routledge.

Fook, J, Ryan, M and Hawkins, L (2000) *Professional Expertise: Practice, Theory and Education for Working in Uncertainty.* London: Whiting & Birch.

Schön, DA (1995) Knowing-in-action: The New Scholarship Requires a New Epistemology. *Change,* November/December: 27–34.

Index